Grocery
Gardening

Published by Cool Springs Press
P.O. Box 2828
Brentwood, TN 37024

Cataloging-in-Publication data available

EAN: 978-1-59186-463-9

First Printing 2009

Printed in the United States of America
10 9 8 7 6 5 4 3 2

Managing Editor: Jean Ann Van Krevelen
Copyeditor: Billie Brownell
Design: Sheri Ferguson, Ferguson Design Studio
Cover: Marc Pewitt

Illustrations of the authors provided by Bill Kersey, Kersey Graphics

All recipes have been contributed by the authors unless otherwise noted.

Photography
Hanan Brailowski: 22, 41, 47, 137, 209, 211
iStockphoto.com: 25, 26, 27, 30, 31, 32, 33, 37, 39, 40, 50, 81, 90, 92, 95, 141, 151, 156, 159, 207, 223, 229, 230, 233, 234, 235, 236, 237, 243
Marsha R Devine: 19
Jupiter Images: 10, 11, 12,13,15, 17, 23, 24, 29, 54, 60, 63, 71, 78, 83, 91, 97, 102, 105, 106, 108, 113, 121, 123, 133, 138, 139, 143, 145, 146, 147, 153, 155, 162, 169, 177, 184, 185, 193, 195, 201, 204, 208, 217, 219, 225, 227, 239
Marcelle Layne: 41, 65, 77, 107
Michael Lieberman: 20
Kat Moes: 65
Teresa O'Connor: 53, 153, 193
Amanda Thomsen: 14, 21, 65
Jean Ann Van Krevelen: 16, 47, 48, 59, 66, 105, 113, 129, 137, 145, 161, 169, 170, 171, 177, 187, 194, 201, 210, 217

JEAN ANN VAN KREVELEN

Grocery Gardening

PLANTING, PREPARING AND PRESERVING FRESH FOOD

WITH AMANDA THOMSEN, ROBIN RIPLEY
AND TERESA O'CONNOR

COOL SPRINGS PRESS

Growing Successful Gardeners™
www.coolspringspress.com
BRENTWOOD, TENNESSEE

Acknowledgements

A big thanks to my coauthors—Amanda Thomsen, Robin Ripley, and Teresa O'Connor—your support has been invaluable! A special thanks goes to my publisher Roger Waynick for his vision of the future of garden writing. Big thanks to Ken Scholes, an amazing author and the best writing buddy a girl could have. A huge thank you to Rosalind Creasy, a pioneer in edible garden writing and a personal hero, and to my champion, Debra Prinzing. Also, thanks to my family— Tracy, Joslynne, and Nathan. Your support is the reason this book has reached fruition. And because they brought me into this world, thanks to Mom and Dad, and the rest of the family.

Most important, I thank all of the gardeners and foodies who contributed of themselves, in one way or another, to this huge undertaking. Your support, inspiration, knowledge, and friendship are invaluable.

This book is dedicated to my grandmother, Bea Van Krevelen, and my mom, Claire Merryman, the two women who helped me see the wonder of gardening.

I spent much of my childhood living with my grandparents. My grandmother wasn't often successful getting me outside to admire her gardening skills, particularly during the hot Oklahoma summers. I knew she loved to "dig in the dirt," but I could not understand why she would choose to be out there, instead of in the air conditioning with me. We had a deep bond, to be sure, but it certainly wasn't because it had anything to do with gardening.

I was grown and living in another state when I learned that my grandmother was terminally ill. I returned home and was fortunate to be with her during her final weeks. She was too ill to do much, so we spent a lot of time watching gardening and cooking shows on television; watching Martha Stewart Living was our morning ritual. When my grandmother passed away, I was deeply distraught. And even though both of my parents were (and are) alive, I suddenly felt like an orphan.

I offered to help with the estate and spent the next few months going through the house, cleaning out closets, painting walls, peeling wallpaper, digging into the attic . . . generally getting the home ready for sale. I welcomed this time spent in her home, not yet ready to move on without her.

Early in the process I realized that the yard would need to be mowed, the beds cleaned up, and the empty pots filled with sunny flowers. I am no real estate expert but even I know that curbside appearance matters. Having absolutely no idea what to do, I called my mom.

Thankfully, my mom had taken the time to learn about gardening from my grandmother. Mom took me on my first spring planting excursion. We went to nurseries and home improvement stores. I still remember our most basic conversation about the difference between an annual and a perennial. We brought our beauties home and started planting. Mom taught me about growing in containers, feeding the roses, keeping the beds watered . . . every time I had a gardening question, her phone started ringing.

Looking back on that time, I now recognize the incredible gift that was given to me by these amazing women. They cared for me as they cared for their gardens, with love and patience, coaxing me along, helping me blossom into the woman I am today. Mom now helps me harvest bushels of raspberries and baskets of blueberries from my berry patch. And when I visit my vegetable garden, I still find my grandmother there. She is the soft breeze, the sweet-smelling earth, and the warm rays of the sun. Each spring, she embraces me with hope and love as I return to work the beds, continuing her gardening legacy.

Table of Contents

Gardening 101   10

Garden planning 10
Soil 12
Fertilizers 13
Seed Starting 15
Mulch 18
Small Space Gardening 19

Organic Disease and Pest Management   23

Cultural Controls 24
Physical Controls 26
Biological Controls 28
Chemical Controls 28
Common Pests 29
Plant Damage and Disease 30

Purchasing Quality Produce   33

What to Ask 34
Where to Shop 34
How Should I Select Produce .37
Most/Least Contaminated
Fruits and Vegetables 38

Edibles   39

Herbs 40
Basil 41
Chives 47
Cilantro/Coriander 53
Dill and Fennel 59
Mint and Oregano 65
Parsley 71
Rosemary 77
Sage and Thyme 83
Fruit 89
Apple 89
Blueberry 97
Brambleberries 105
Grapes 113
Melon 121
Rhubarb 129
Strawberry 137
Vegetables 145
Asparagus 145
Beans 153
Broccoli 161
Carrots 169
Cucumber and Squash 177
Cool Season Greens 185
Lettuces and Salad Greens 193
Peas 201
Peppers 209
Tomato 217

Preserving Your Harvest   225

Canning 226
Freezing 229
Dehydrating 231
Root Cellars 232
Storing Herbs in Oil, Vacuum Sealing 236

Pest and Disease Chart 243
Index 249
About the Authors 254

Introduction

There are several reasons why now is the right time to learn to grow your own food…cost savings, certainty of production methods, supporting your local community. But perhaps most compelling is that most individuals no longer have the knowledge about how to grow, harvest, store, and prepare food for our families and our communities.

There was a time when we knew how to take care of ourselves in this way. We could grow and harvest our own fruits and vegetables, care for our own chickens, and milk our own cows. Even in the past fifty years or so, the family veggie garden was a common part of life.

Looking back on it, I can understand why we were eager to embrace "progress." We had just come through a time when sowing a garden was a necessity due to the hardship of war. Women had assumed a primary role in manufacturing and other parts of the work world, many of them functioning as single mothers. And picking up a bag of potatoes at the store was certainly a lot less work than growing them.

But somewhere in this cultural shift, we've lost our respect for food. We have lost the understanding of what it means to value the earth and the bounty that it provides. We've lost touch with small farmers, now struggling to survive. We've lost the ability to provide for ourselves… and this is a bad time to not know how to provide for ourselves.

The good news is that it takes very little to reclaim our past. Anyone can grow his own food; even if it is in pots on a balcony or in a sunny window, you can grow some portion of the produce you need to sustain your life. Seeds, soil, and pots can be found for little to no cost. Shopping at farmers' markets, grocery stores that prioritize buying from local growers, pick-your-own farms, and food co-ops are some of the ways to have a positive impact on your community.

The bad news is that very few of us have the time to create a farm that provides for all of our needs.

We have high-pressure jobs and over-committed children. We receive information from multiple sources all day long. It is a constant battery of stimuli…all vying for our undivided attention. And after all of that, you may not want to spend hours in the garden. This book is designed to make growing, saving, and preparing at least some of your own food an easy and achievable feat.

We wrote this book with all of this in mind. . . we teach you the basics of gardening, organic pest and disease management, growing, harvesting, market produce selection, and preserving… oh, and lots and lots of recipes!

What may be almost as interesting as what's in this book, is the process we used to write it. The four authors have never actually met in person. We found each other on Twitter, chattering away about our love of gardening and food, often answering questions and suggesting resources. In fact, that is how I bumped into Roger Waynick, president of Cool Springs Press.

He and I had a serious brainstorming session where I approached him with the idea of using collaborative techniques and crowdsourcing to develop the direction and content for this book. Completely excited about the potential in generating new material, fresh perspectives, and faster production times, Roger readily accepted the challenge of publishing such a book.

Between the four authors, we started out with a reach of an estimated 50,000 people. All of us have blogs, Twitter and Facebook accounts, as well as other miscellaneous social media profiles. We reached out to our communities, gathered ideas, went to town, and wrote this book in sixty days. It is full of some of our best wisdom, and yours, too!

This level of community involvement and visibility means that our readers can have interactions with us beyond *Grocery Gardening*. You can meet us, ask questions, talk to other readers, ask them questions…in short, this is a much more personal style of writing and publishing a book. And as far as I am concerned, that is what makes this different than a standard gardening text.

We hope you have fun and learn a bit while reading this book. We would love to hear your feedback and suggestions. Join us at www.grocerygardeningguide.com and sign up to get access to all of our web resources, special events, and grocery gardening deals!

— Jean Ann Van Krevelen

While it's true that growing your own groceries is easier than it sounds, before you ever scrape the surface of the ground with your shovel, you must do a bit of planning. From starting seeds and setting out to soil amendments and mulch, there is quite a lot of good Gardening 101 information here. This is a great section for reference, particularly when you find yourself knee deep in smelly compost.

Where to Plant

Almost all fruits and vegetables need at least six hours of sun to thrive, so pick the sunniest place that has easy access to water. Consistent watering is critical for many vegetables and fruits. Unfortunately, it is easy to get caught up in the excitement of spring planting and start sowing seeds everywhere. But by August, when you are toting a watering can to those tomatoes, you will be wishing you had started your garden closer to the tap.

Once you have determined your site, there are many layout choices—the traditional vegetable garden bed with rows of crops like a tiny farm, raised beds, short, rectangular configurations, the list is endless. You can also grow your food right along with your flowers and other ornamentals, as well as in containers. Just be sure you are using organic practices in those beds as well.

Planning

Though much garden planning happens in the spring, one of my favorite times to map out the garden is in the fall. It is a great time to look back at what grew well, what tasted terrific, where there wasn't enough and where there was far too much.

At the end of the season, you can do some simple things that will make it easier for you to have a more productive garden next year. Record the following kinds of information to help yourself get a head start.

- What did you absolutely *love* this year?
- What was horrible?
- Where was there too much and where was there too little production?
- Where did you plant what? Remember, some veggies shouldn't be replanted in the same spot year after year.

- What did better than expected? Note varieties that like your climate, grew larger than you thought, liked having certain companions, etc.
- What growing tips have you learned?

A simple journal will make your life so much easier next year...and it will help make selecting seed from all of those catalogs more manageable!

What to Grow

The reality is that you have a finite space and endless gardening configurations/planting options. Start by making a wish list of crops you want in the garden. Next, choose the best variety of each crop for your zone by talking with local

growers, researching seed varieties and visiting local nurseries. If you live in the South, you may want to choose seeds that mention being suitable for hot climates. If you live in the North, you may want to look for crops that have a shorter time to maturity.

Make note of how much space it takes to grow each desired crop, how much you're going to grow, and where you're going to grow it. Make sure you factor in trellises for the peas and pole beans and cages for your tomatoes.

There are some additional factors to take into consideration when deciding what to grow:

- Zone (or average temperatures)
- Sun condition needed
- Variety best suited to your region
- Ease of growing
- Soil condition needed
- Pests and disease problems in your area
- General patience versus your desire to grow

Each of these variables affects the likely success of the plant. And, what might be challenging in the Pacific Northwest won't be in warmer climates. Those challenges might not prevent you from growing certain edibles, but do keep in mind that they will require extra care…and extra care equals extra time and energy.

Soil

It takes a bit of time to really build the quality and structure of your soil, but it is one of the foundational elements of gardening. If you don't have healthy soil with good drainage, your poor plants will not have the nutrients they need to produce great vegetables and fruit. In addition to the type and amount of nutrients, the soil texture and pH balance will affect the plant's ability to absorb available nutrition. Investing time and effort into achieving wonderfully rich, loamy soil will always result in a high payoff.

Creating a balance between sand, clay, and organic matter is the first step. If your soil is too sandy, water and nutrients will drain through immediately, leaving your poor plant dying of thirst and starvation. On the other hand, if you have too much clay in your soil, water will drain very slowly, drowning the plant.

The great news is the remedy for both of these problems is compost. Adding compost improves soil structure, adds macro- and micronutrients and boosts microbial activity. And, compost is readily available by the bag or truckload if you don't have your own compost pile.

Raised beds are the easiest way to prepare an area to grow things organically. By building a bed above whatever kind of soil you have, you can fill it with organic materials and give yourself absolute control over your soil texture.

Fertilizers

Although soil amendments like compost also double as fertilizers, there are certain edibles that like extra nourishment. There are many different ways to feed a plant, but before you start, it is important to find out what they prefer. Some plants will like a high-nitrogen fertilizer, while that will cause others to produce a whole bunch of leaves and very little produce.

Plants take in food through their root systems and also through their leaves. Foliar feeding is the practice of spraying a liquid fertilizer on the plant itself. Research has shown that feeding plants this way can increase their production, correct micronutrient deficiencies, and add valuable vitamins to the soil. Many foliar feeders are made from fish and/or seaweed. These fertilizers can be a bit stinky, but are incredibly good for building your soil and growing healthy plants.

Not all plants need supplemental food, and those that do may only need it during certain parts of their growth cycle. Choosing the right fertilizer for the right plant at the right time will result in the best outcome.

Here in the United States we over-fertilize our crops in order to create the highest yields in the shortest amount of time. However, forcing plants to grow in ways that aren't natural to their life cycles can result in floppy, sappy plant growth that is more susceptible to pests and diseases.

When starting seeds, all of the nutrition they need to sprout is in the seed itself. Don't fertilize seedlings until the first true set of leaves appear. At that point, you can apply it sparingly. If you have used compost in your seed starting mix, chances are good that you won't need supplemental nutrition.

These are some excellent organic fertilizers:

- **Compost:** Working it into the soil when starting a bed will boost the nutrition, microorganisms, and overall health of both soil and plants. Once your plants have started growing, you can add compost to the top of the bed for an extra shot of plant food.
- **Fish fertilizer:** This is a foliar food made from fish. It also adds a variety of minerals and vitamins to the soil. Great when used in conjunction with a side dressing of compost. In using a combination of fish fertilizer and compost, you are addressing the nutrient needs through, the leaves and the roots.
- **Manure:** Using manure from animals that eat a vegetative diet is a very common practice. If it is not composted, strong doses can burn your plants, so limit the dose. If you do compost, it removes many of the nutrients, so think of it more like a soil amendment rather than a fertilizer.
- **Packaged organic fertilizers:** Many companies sell pre-packaged organic fertilizers. They can be all-purpose or targeted for specific use. These are great for container gardening and slow release in the vegetable garden.

- **Worm castings:** Earthworms are an organic gardener's best friends. In addition to aerating the soil, these little guys create worm castings. The castings contain nutrients, minerals, and a variety of active, beneficial microorganisms. You can purchase castings or start your own worm farm and harvest their castings. If you are gardening in the ground or in raised beds, you can also purchase earthworm cocoons and add them to the soil to boost your numbers.

Compost

Composting is a cheap and natural way to get the best fertilizer available for your garden. Composting can be as sophisticated as a store-bought plastic tumbling barrel or as low-tech as a heap in a sunny, out-of-the-way location. By adding your lawn clippings, dry leaves, green kitchen waste, and garden waste into a pile and letting Mother Nature do her thing, after a few

Composting Tips

- Add only organic matter to the pile.
- Don't use carnivore manure or meat scraps of any kind.
- Layer carbon-rich materials (dry materials that are often brown or yellow; think straw, and leaves) with nitrogen-rich materials (wet materials that are often green; think grass, vegetable tops, and citrus peels).
- Ensure the pile is moist, not too wet, not too dry, in order to encourage decomposition; also make sure it can drain easily.
- Give your pile a kick-start by adding finished compost or compost booster.
- Don't add too much wood ash, or other substances that will significantly alter the pH of the pile.
- Piles can be in direct sun, part shade, or shade. Keep in mind that a hotter pile processes more quickly.
- Air is an essential part of an aerobic decomposition process. Adding coarse matter to the pile will create pockets of air. Also, giving it a good turn with a pitchfork will help.
- There are a variety of composters that will tumble or otherwise help you process your compost. These can be useful to speed up the process and keep unwanted vermin out of your pile…but they aren't necessary.
- Bury food scraps (no meat or dairy) in the pile so the local wildlife won't have a field day.
- The pile will need some depth to it in order for this intentional composting process to work.

months, the decomposing matter will be the consistency of soil. This can then be used as a soil additive, mulch, or grass fertilizer.

Seed Starting

Seed starting can be both extremely easy and extremely frustrating. There are some seeds that germinate more quickly, some that are a bit more stubborn; some prefer cool temperatures, others like it nice and toasty. The key is in knowing the growing requirements of each kind of seed you are starting. Beyond that, there are some general planting instructions and some tips that will make the process a bit easier.

The three basic requirements for seeds to germinate are light, warmth, and moisture. Seeds come with their own fertilizer packed inside the seed coating. Fertilizing seedlings that don't have their second set of leaves isn't necessary and can encourage tall, spindly growth.

LIGHT

Many seeds need light to germinate, and all need it to grow. Your seed packet will tell you the specific requirements for the seeds inside. Sometimes a very sunny windowsill will suffice. When it doesn't, you will need to use supplemental lighting.

Now, there are very expensive grow lights out there that are so strong they will fry your plants. But you certainly don't need to spend that kind of money to get the light you need. Go to your local hardware store and buy the two-tube shop light. There are full-spectrum bulbs, special grow lights, and plain fluorescent bulbs. Any of these will work; choose the one that best fits your needs, and your pocketbook.

This light needs to be within a couple of inches of your seed containers. You can either use adjustable chain or prop the lights up with bricks or some other non-flammable, sturdy item. As the seedlings sprout, gradually move the light up to accommodate.

Another way to help ensure the seedlings get enough light is to surround the container with reflective material. You can hang this on a nearby wall or use a cardboard surround. Repurpose (clean) used foil, or you can try car windshield reflectors, too.

WARMTH

All seeds need a certain temperature to sprout. Again, this is something that can vary significantly. You can supply this heat by keeping the whole area warm enough to sprout the seeds.

Or, you can save on your energy bill and use a seedling warming mat. Seeds need a higher temperature to sprout than they do to continue growing. By using a mat, you target the heat to the location where it will do the most good. Once seeds are sprouted, they can be moved to a cooler location.

MOISTURE

Seedlings can't survive without water, nor will they survive in a swamp. When they are first started, use a mister to keep them moist. As they mature, you can switch to a gentle watering can. Another way to keep moisture in is to enclose your container in a plastic bag, creating a tiny greenhouse. Don't use this in conjunction with a seedling mat, and don't allow it to touch the plant light.

Containers

Another thing to consider when starting your own seeds are the containers you will use. This is a great opportunity to recycle and reuse.

Here are some ideas:

- Gallon milk jugs, cut to size
- Plastic containers from salad mixes
- Egg cartons
- Yogurt, sour cream, or cream cheese containers
- Old buckets
- Sturdy cardboard boxes
- Old shampoo containers, cut to size

The list goes on and on…just remember to wash and sanitize anything that might have had non-food contents. And while many books will tell you to use a bleach solution as a rinse following the wash, a more environmentally friendly option is to use plain white vinegar, then rinse well.

Starting Medium/Soil

There are special seed starting mixes you can purchase at the store. Some of these are great, some not so great…all are more expensive than making your own. Combine a blend of well-aged compost and sand or compost and Perlite. Whatever combination you use, make sure it is a mix that drains well and is very soft. You don't want your little seedlings to be trapped under a crust or heavy bit of compost.

Ventilation

Seedlings need air flow to prevent fungal diseases. Damping off is one of the most often found diseases in the greenhouse environment and is caused by very common fungi. Many growers only use sterilized soil and pots and plant in a quick-draining medium.

However, the risk at home is a bit different than in a commercial greenhouse. If something happens to a nursery owner's seedlings, the whole operation could go down. For you, it might cost

Transplanting Outside or "Planting Out"

When the ground has warmed sufficiently and it is time to transplant your little seedlings outside, they must go through a process of hardening off. Since they have been in such a sheltered environment, they won't be able to withstand the drastic cultural changes of a direct move outside. Start by moving the seedlings outdoors for an hour a day. When you have done this for a week, it is time to move the little guys to the ground.

If the weather is a bit iffy, or you have a late freeze, you can use milk jugs with the bottom removed to cover the top of the plant. You will want to leave the lid off if daytime temperatures warm up, and make sure to secure it by pushing it down into the soil a couple of inches. Another way to protect your plants is to use row covers.

There are three important things to remember when planting these guys in the ground.

- For most veggies you will want to plant at the same level as when they were in the pot.
- Don't let the beds dry out; they won't withstand drought at this stage.
- Provide protection from bugs until they become established. Mature plants can handle the environment much better than seedlings can.

you the price of a seed packet. Practicing good sanitation with containers, keeping the surrounding areas clean, making sure your potting mix drains well, and immediately removing diseased flats will help reduce the risk significantly.

After seeds have sprouted, it is a good idea to keep a fan blowing on a low setting for ten or so hours a day. This reduces mildew and fungal problems and helps the plants grow stronger for the move outside.

Kinds of Mulch

ORGANIC:

- **Compost**—Many people suggest using compost as mulch. However, all plants, including weeds, love compost. All of the weed seeds around the yard blow in and sprout, making this not such a great choice for mulch.
- **Hay** (preferably weed and seed free)—Great all-purpose mulch that decomposes well.
- **Paper**—There are new mulches made from recycled paper, and recycled newspapers are also a great mulch. This method is great for blocking out weeds. Start by laying out a thick layer of newspaper, wet it down, then top with a couple of inches of straw (great for pathways).
- **Shredded or chipped bark**—This is best used for ornamental plantings.
- **Sawdust**—The breakdown of sawdust can initially leech nitrogen from the soil, making it best used for paths and non-plant areas.
- **Chopped leaves**—A covering of chopped, dried leaves is an excellent way to put your garden to bed in the fall.
- **Grass clippings**—These are best composted first to reduce the likelihood of spreading weed seeds.
- **Pine needles**—These are also great for walkways and for acid-loving plants, but not in the vegetable garden, as they alter the pH of the soil.

INORGANIC:

- **Black plastic**—Good for warming the ground early in the spring. Also used for killing weed seeds and soil-borne disease when used in the heat of summer. If you are using this with live plants, you must be sure to poke holes to allow water to get through. And add a layer of straw mulch in the heat of summer so your plants don't get too hot.
- **Gravel**—This mulch is best used in a spot where you won't be cultivating much. And if you have a problem with a neighborhood cat using your edibles bed as a cat box, a layer of sharp gravel can help keep them from digging in your soil.
- **Landscape fabric**—This can be used with varying degrees of success. A lot depends on what type of fabric you are using. Landscape fabric allows some light and water to permeate, but is fairly successful in suppressing weeds. However, if it is left in place for an extended period of time, the root systems of nearby plants will enmesh themselves in the fabric…this makes for difficult removal and potential damage to the plants.

Mulch

Mulch is a gardener's best friend. It is the key to keeping even moisture, warming plants in winter, and cooling roots in summer. If you are using organic mulch, the decomposition of the materials will feed the soil and earthworms. But one of its greatest charms is its ability to suppress weeds.

There are several kinds of mulches to choose from, and a few things you need to know to make sure you don't mulch your plants to death. The most important thing is not to push it right up against the stems and crown of the plant. The second most important is to pull it away from the plants if you have a particularly wet spring. Otherwise, both of these conditions can lead to rot.

Small-Space Gardening

One of the biggest challenges city-dwellers face is lack of space. Small yards, patio homes, and apartments are the biggest offenders. But with a little creativity and ingenuity, you can be growing at least some of your own produce in no time.

FRONTYARD BEDS

There is a big movement to reduce lawns and create more space for edibles. Whether that means a bed dedicated to vegetables, or kale worked into an ornamental border, people are looking for ways to build more functionality into their yard space. Removing sod can be physically exhausting and time intensive. Why not try building a couple of raised beds right on top of the existing turf?

VEGETABLES IN FLOWER BORDERS

Adding vegetables to your flower borders is a great way to grow your own food. And, some veggie varieties are absolutely gorgeous! Just remember to practice organic methods in these beds as well.

CONTAINER GARDENING

Almost anything can be grown in a container. Add them to your patios, balconies, driveways… you can find a size that will fit in almost any space. Remember a couple of things though:
1) You can use many things as a container, just make sure it is big enough for a full-grown plant and that it didn't/doesn't contain any chemicals that are harmful…wash, recycle, and reuse!

2) Containers dry out more quickly than in-ground plantings; in the heat of summer you may have to water twice a day.

3) If they are on concrete, the reflective heat will make the surrounding environment much hotter than if they were planted in the ground.

4) They need to be fertilized and amended each planting cycle.

5) You can build raised beds on unused areas of your patio/driveway, etc. Just make sure they are at least 24 inches deep and have a tight mesh or landscape fabric stapled to the bottom. You don't want your dirt streaming down the driveway.

6) Hanging baskets are a great way to increase your space. Some veggie varieties thrive when grown this way…and it doesn't get much easier to harvest.

VERTICAL GARDENING

Remember that you are not limited to horizontal growing. The use of trellises, growing vines up fences, and using teepees will all increase your space significantly.

ESPALIER

This is a technique that was originally used for fruit trees, though you could use it for a variety of things, including vining fruit. Essentially, the trees are pruned to grow along wires attached to a wall or fence of some sort. In order to do this successfully, the tree has to be young and vigilantly pruned.

WINDOW BOXES

Don't forget you can hang window boxes to expand your growing space. Because you are replanting in a contained space, you will need to amend your soil well each time you plant.

GROWING INDOORS

You can also plant and grow your veggies indoors. If you do not have an exceptionally warm, sunny spot, you may need to use supplemental heat and light. This can be done with seedling mats and regular fluorescent bulbs or special bulbs designed for plant growth (see the Seed Starting section for more information).

COMPANION PLANTING

Companion planting is a great way to increase your yield. Inter-planting corn with vining crops like beans doubles the use of your space. The corn serves as a living trellis and the nitrogen-fixing beans provide a natural fertilizer. You can also grow early harvest vegetables along the edges of the bed. They will be grown and gone before the later summer plants take over. For more information on companion planting as a pest deterrent, see the Pests and Disease section.

YARDSHARING

The concept of yardsharing is very simple, yet so few people try it. It is literally collaborating with a neighbor (or two) and creating a shared yard space…a mini community garden that is maintained by neighbors.

There are so many benefits to yardsharing; here are just a few:

- more land
- shared costs
- shared labor
- time saving
- increase in yields
- building community
- shared gardening wisdom
- pairing able bodies with those that have challenges

SUCCESSION PLANTING

This is one of the easiest ways to prolong your harvest. Instead of sowing all of your seeds at once, sow them over the course of several days or weeks. This means yummy fresh produce for longer periods of time. When a segment has finished producing, you can replant with a new kind of veggie. Because you are planting in an intensive way, you will need to amend your soil well each time you plant.

ORGANIC PEST & DISEASE MANAGEMENT

When it comes to using organic methods to deal with pests and diseases, good growing practices go a long way toward staving off problems. This is not to say that the proper use of some organic pesticides and disease treatments won't be necessary. Sometimes, despite your best efforts, the cabbage worms or aphids will reach critical mass and an extreme intervention is necessary. The key is in knowing which formulations are safe and which are not. There are some organic treatments that are as deadly as the harshest inorganic chemicals. A general rule of thumb is to start with the least invasive method and step upward if needed.

Building a Strong Ecosystem

For organic gardeners and farmers, the best defense is a strong offense. By creating optimal growing conditions and choosing disease resistant varieties, the need to "defend" or respond to a threat is limited until there is clearly a danger. That means a lower use of chemicals and overall healthier plants.

Cultural Controls

Proactively building a strong ecosystem with healthy soil, mulch, and fertilizer is the foundation for ensuring your plants are healthy enough to fight off small disease and pest problems. When that isn't possible, it is time to move on to the first stage of intervention. Cultural controls are the least invasive with the smallest amount of chemical impact. But, keep this one important thing in mind when determining what, if any, action should be taken: *Part of your garden planning should include the understanding that some percentage of your food will be eaten by vermin. This means that you should expect your plants to look as they would naturally. And blemish-free is not a natural state. Embrace the perfection of imperfect produce…and be willing to share your food with other members of your ecosystem.*

Start by thinking about the soil. In addition to feeding the soil with compost, nutrients, and other beneficial components, crop rotation is another great way to keep it healthy. Using a garden planner, whether it is web-based or pencil and paper, is helpful in making sure plants (and their relatives) are not planted in the same spot year after year.

Crop rotation does two things. One, it reduces the chances of any overwintering pests or diseases getting a head start on next year's vegetables. And two, it creates the opportunity for creatively planting various crops to benefit the soil. For example, you might plant a nitrogen-fixing crop like peas, then follow with a plant that pulls nitrogen from the soil, like tomatoes.

The use of cover crops is another organic practice that has multiple benefits. In addition to boosting your soil's nutrient content, cover crops build organic matter, preserve soil structure, and prevent erosion.

One of the most important things you can do for your soil is to make sure there are enough

earthworms frolicking beneath the surface. These guys simultaneously aerate the soil and create the best fertilizer around.

Plant selection can be crucial to the success of your crops. Choose varieties with resistance to diseases that are present in your area. And if you don't know what is present in your area, contact your local extension office. They are a great resource!

hands, can spread bacteria and spores like there's no tomorrow. Clean your tools, gloves, and hands regularly.

Planting schedules can be altered to take advantage of times when pests are least likely to be on the attack. Bugs have lifecycles and are more of a problem at certain times of the year. If your crop can be grown in more than one season, choose the one that has the least bugs.

Inter-cropping or polycultural practices have long been recommended as a way to reduce pests and increase yields. You may have heard it identified as companion planting. And though there are a ton of books written about what plants do what for each other, many of the conclusions are not research based.

That's not to say there is no benefit to diversified planting. Instead of planting five rows of tomatoes, plant a row of tomatoes, a row of squash, a row of carrots…this prevents insects from moving from one dinner to the next, and on through your entire crop.

Inoculants are most often thought of as legume boosters. Dusting peas, lentils, and beans with rhizobia species ensures that the plants have the necessary components to fix nitrogen in the

Plant care is critical in avoiding diseases and pests. Planting the wrong plant in the wrong spot under the wrong conditions will lead to a waste of resources, poor yield, and lots of yelling on the part of the gardener.

Improving circulation is a great way to reduce mildew and fungi. Make sure plants have room to grow and are staked in a way that allows for airflow. Don't be afraid to prune growth to create openings for the sun and summer breezes.

Clean your garden tools and gloves. *You* can be a disease carrier, too. Make sure that you don't use gardening tools on a diseased plant, and then move on to a healthy one. Gloves, and even your

soil. Without their beneficial buddies, the plants would starve.

Adding mycorrhizal fungi to the soil helps boost the ability of the root system to absorb nutrients. If you turn your soil, particularly with a tiller, it can negatively impact mycorrhizal colonization. Adding a bit in the spring will help ensure healthy plants and higher yields.

Physical Controls

Physical controls can be very effective in eliminating or reducing pests and diseases. This is a more assertive stand, but still avoids chemicals. As the name implies, these require more work than squirting a bottle. Of course, there is the added benefit of saving the environment...

Controlling Bugs

Believe it or not, the pick and stomp method of bug removal can be really effective, particularly with caterpillars, slugs, and larger beetles. If you are vigilant about checking the plants, you can eliminate an entire generation of pests and reduce the impact on the harvest.

Traps are also used in dealing with bugs. Slugs, earwigs, moths, and many others can be trapped with varying degrees of success. The beer-in-a-saucer trap has brought many slugs to their final resting place. Sticky traps in trees and on posts have captured creepy crawlies and flying insects of all types.

Using trap crops is another way to divert harmful insects from the crop you want to harvest. By inter-planting the main crop with another that is more tantalizing, the bugs are re-directed to a less important plant. A caution about trap crops:

they can do too good of a job of attracting pests and evolve into a nursery. If you notice the numbers of pests are multiplying at a rapid rate, pull the crops and toss them far from the original site.

Row covers and netting are physical barriers to keep the bad guys away, particularly when new crops are getting established. It is important to know whether your crop needs pollinators in order to produce. If it does, you will need to remove the row covers once flowers start to form.

Bands and collars can also be used as a physical deterrent for pests. For example, adding a little collar to the base of your seedling can stop cutworms. Both sticky and non-sticky bands can be useful in preventing soil-dwelling pests from making the move. This method is often used with fruit trees.

Dust and gravel barriers are also good deterrents for soft-bodied insects. Diatomaceous earth is a dehydrating dust that generally kills insects that roll around in it. Sharp gravel (and in some cases, sharp sand) is a good textural barrier for slugs and snails... and cats.

Controlling Disease

A little bit of research will go a long way toward finding the right plants for your area. Different regions foster different diseases. Talk with your local county extension office to find out what is most prevalent, then search for varieties with a built-in resistance.

The first step in reducing any type of disease is to prune and/or remove diseased plants. At the first sign of trouble, remove the damaged portion of the plant, or the whole plant, and dispose of it far away from the original site. Pick up any litter on the ground around the diseased plant. If you had plants that were diseased at the end of the last growing season, be sure to remove any remaining litter before planting in that location. Next season, do not grow plants of the same family or plants that are susceptible to that disease in that spot.

Control insects, like aphids, that spread disease. Some bugs bring a double whammy. They eat the plant and they carry spores and bacteria that facilitate the spreading of diseases. By keeping their numbers down, you automatically reduce your risk.

Soil solarization is a commonly used method that can help reduce disease and pests in the ground. Dig a trench several inches deep around an unused bed. Cover with a thin layer of clear plastic. Secure by pushing the ends of the plastic into the trench, then cover with soil. This method uses the heat of the sun to kill weed seeds and harmful organisms in the soil, so it should be done in summer to be maximally effective. Leave plastic in place for one-two months, dependent upon temperatures and region. Gardeners in the North will probably need two months; in the South, one month.

Biological Controls

Biological controls consist of the use of beneficial insects, microbes, nematodes, fungi, and bacteria to control pests and disease. And despite any concerns you might have about *adding* bugs and bacteria to your ecosystem, it is one of the best ways to give your garden the support it needs to fend off problems without chemical intervention.

Beneficial insects are probably the most fun controls an organic gardener uses. Each year, people purchase ladybugs, praying mantis eggs, lacewings, minute pirate bugs, and predatory wasps and release them into the garden. These predators help to keep populations of damaging bugs under control. But unlike an insecticide, which indiscriminately kills all insects, beneficial insects generally only kill the bad guys.

Bacterial insecticides combat all kinds of problems. Bt (bacillus thuringus) is a great way to deal with cutworms and other soft-bodied insects. They key is to make sure you are using the right beneficial bacteria for your problem and applying it on a regular basis.

Beneficial nematodes help rid the garden of their cousins, the evil nematodes, as well as voracious grubs. Both bacterial insecticides and

beneficial nematodes need certain conditions to be effective. Remember, these are living organisms and need to be treated as such. Follow application and storage directions to ensure the greatest level of effectiveness.

Chemical Controls

If cultural, physical, and biological controls are not successful, there are chemical controls you can use to address the problem. Ideally, you want to use the lowest level first, advancing to stronger products if needed. When using insecticides, you kill the good, the bad, and the ugly. And inadvertently killing off beneficial insects can lead to an increase of populations of whatever bugs they were controlling.

Remember, the goal is to try and restore balance to the ecosystem, not blast all living creatures out of the garden. If you have a healthy system, it has its own ways of dealing with pests and diseases…and you should support it in that effort. By starting with the least invasive chemical, you give the system a chance to respond in its own way.

You will get the greatest benefit of pest and disease management by integrating your control methods. A combination of a strong ecosystem, an attentive gardener, and judicious use of organic chemical controls can keep your garden healthy and happy!

A short list of organic chemical controls includes:

- Insecticidal soaps
- Oils (spray and dormant)
- Neem
- Pyrethrum
- Spinosad

Common Pests

This is a short list of common pests with recommendations for treatment. There are many good resources that are already in existence that can guide you in identifying your plant problems, some of these are online and are interactive. Check the Pest and Disease Charts at the end of the book for more information.

- **Pests:** Worms, Moths, and Butterflies: Cabbage loopers, Corn earworms, Tomato hornworm, Parsleyworms, Cutworms, Cabbage worms, Armyworms, Corn borers, Squash vine borer

This is a collection of worms or caterpillars, most of which evolve into moths or butterflies. The larvae eat the leaves of plants and can eradicate seedlings in no time. Of these, the cutworm can be the most destructive, cutting seedlings off at ground level.

Effective controls for this group include row covers, plant collars, pick and stomp, beneficial insects and nematodes, inter-planting, diatomaceous earth, trap crops, crop rotation, and bacillus thuringus.

- **Sucking insects:** Aphids, Whiteflies, Harlequin bug, Squash bug, Spider mites, Scale, Tarnished plant bug, Thrips

These insects feed on the sap in the plant. They use their sharp mouths (some of which look like beaks) to pierce the skin and suck out the plant's juices. These insects, particularly aphids, can also transmit disease from one plant to the next. You may notice the plant damage before the bugs themselves. Plants can look withered and yellow. Leaves become distorted and drop off of the plant.

Effective controls for this group include: pick and stomp (for larger bugs), row covers, beneficial insects, Neem oil, insecticidal soap, and inter-planting. A strong shot of water will knock off most aphids.

- **Flies:** Carrot rust flies, Leafminer

Flies that cause damage to crops do so as larvae. The larvae can either attack the roots or the leaves. You may not even realize there is a problem until you attempt to harvest. Tops of the plants can continue to look healthy while the root system is destroyed.

Effective controls include crop rotation, sticky traps, and growing during seasons when the pest isn't as active. Physical barriers can be effective, such as row covers or a ground barrier that prevents adults from laying eggs.

Common Plant Damage and Diseases

There are two types of common plant damage and disease—those caused by cultural conditions and those caused by microorganisms. Knowing which is which is really helpful in preventing it from spreading and in treating it properly.

When you have a plant that is damaged or diseased, there are some general steps to take in order to address the problem.

- Evaluate the plant thoroughly to identify what caused the problem. Insects and environmental causes can have very similar symptoms.
- Anytime you are working with diseased plants, be sure to wash hands, tools, and gloves before touching another plant. Many diseases spread through contact.
- Increase circulation to the area by pruning the plant and nearby plants to allow for increased airflow.
- Remove any infected parts of the plant, well below the diseased area, if possible.
- Remove any fruit or vegetable that is infected.
- Clean up any fallen leaves, vegetables, or fruits that are on the ground near the plants.
- If a plant looks very unhealthy, remove it right away.

With the exception of heat stress and wilting related to lack of water, a scary looking plant is likely to have a much bigger problem. Don't let what starts as a problem with one plant end as a problem with your whole crop.

- **Plant Damage Caused by Environmental and Cultural Factors:** Boron Deficiency, Iron Deficiency, Zinc Deficiency, Root Rot

Plants require certain conditions for health. Available nutrients, frequency of watering, temperature of the soil, and the air surrounding the plant all affect its ability to grow. And many infectious diseases are able to get a foothold because a plant is stressed and weakened. Root rot, for example, starts with poor drainage, which weakens the plant and creates an environment conducive to bacteria and fungi.

Some signs of non-infectious diseases include yellowing of leaves, dropping of leaves, stunted growth, black spots on fruits, and progressively smaller leaves. There are many websites that will help you diagnose your problem through a series of questions and pictures. You can also take a soil sample to your local county extension office and have the soil tested. Much of this kind of plant damage can be avoided or lessened by promoting a healthy ecosystem.

- **Plant Damage Caused by Microorganisms:** There are three major categories of microorganisms that cause plant disease. It is not always necessary to know exactly which disease is affecting your plant in order to treat it. Often, knowing which of the three categories it belongs to is sufficient.

- **Bacteria:** Bacterial blight, Bacterial wilt, Fireblight

Bacterial damage can have many symptoms: rotting stems and roots, black or brown spots on stems or leaves, and lesions. There is no safe and effective organic treatment that can reverse that kind of damage. Remove plant(s) and debris and dispose. Do not add them to your compost pile.

To avoid the problem the following year, practice crop rotation and plant disease-resistant varieties. Amend soil in problem area with compost. Check soil for drainage rate and amend with sand or other coarse materials if drainage is a problem. Try planting in raised beds, and watering at the root only.

- **Fungi:** Anthracnose, Powdery mildew, Gray mold, Rust, Damping off, Fusarium Wilt, Verticillium wilt

Fungal disease symptoms can include white patches on leaves, discolored and yellowing leaves, dead portions of leaves or plants, wilting, and seedling collapse. There is no safe and effective organic treatment that can reverse fungal damage, but there are products that can prevent it from spreading.

Start by removing infected areas and disposing away from plants. Do not add them to your compost pile. Alter watering practices

to reduce the amount of water that actually touches the plant's leaves and stems. Don't water after dark, as plants will likely stay wet all night long. Prune and stake plants for maximum air exposure.

To avoid the problem in the following year, practice crop rotation and plant disease resistant varieties.

- **Treatment Options:** Baking soda spray, Milk spray, Sulfur, Neem oil, Serenade

- **Viruses:** Tobacco mosaic virus, Bean common mosaic, Potato virus diseases

Viruses can affect plant growth, cause distortion of leaves, and cause strange patterns of color. Unfortunately, the only effective treatment is the removal of all plants and plant debris affected by the disease. Remove plant(s) and debris and dispose. Do not add them to your compost pile.

To avoid the problem in the following year, practice crop rotation and plant disease-resistant varieties. Never dispose of or leave tobacco products of any kind in the garden. They can harbor a virus that can be passed on to certain types of plants.

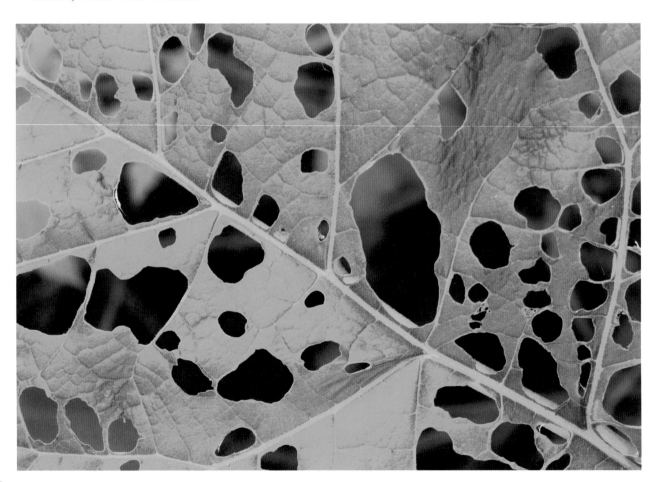

THE SECRET TO PURCHASING QUALITY PRODUCE

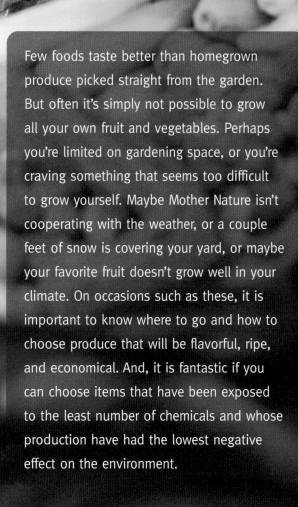

Few foods taste better than homegrown produce picked straight from the garden. But often it's simply not possible to grow all your own fruit and vegetables. Perhaps you're limited on gardening space, or you're craving something that seems too difficult to grow yourself. Maybe Mother Nature isn't cooperating with the weather, or a couple feet of snow is covering your yard, or maybe your favorite fruit doesn't grow well in your climate. On occasions such as these, it is important to know where to go and how to choose produce that will be flavorful, ripe, and economical. And, it is fantastic if you can choose items that have been exposed to the least number of chemicals and whose production have had the lowest negative effect on the environment.

What Questions Should I Ask?

When you shop, take a moment to consider what you're buying. Ask yourself these questions:

- **How fresh is the produce?** Most fruit and vegetables grown in the United States travel about 1,500 miles before they are sold, according to the Natural Resources Defense Council. This requires long-distance transportation, which drains precious natural resources and contributes to greenhouse gases.

- **Is the produce in season?** Eating seasonally allows you to purchase fresh foods grown locally, which taste the best and provide the greatest health benefits. Studies show nutrient levels are at their highest around the time produce is harvested.

- **Where did it grow?** For the most nutritious and best-tasting produce, buy from local growers whenever possible. Locally grown foods are usually sold within 24 hours of being harvested while food shipped in from far distances can be 3 to 10 days older than locally grown produce, according to FamilyFarmed.org. Buying local keeps those dollars in your community, and supports your regional economy.

- **How was it grown?** Produce quality begins on the farm, and depends on many factors including soil type, fertilization, and irrigation practices. Unless the produce is labeled differently, assume it was grown conventionally. Organic or pesticide-free produce is typically marked.

- **What variety is it?** Many modern varieties of fruit and vegetables were bred for shipping over long distances, not necessarily for their flavor. This is particularly true of tomatoes, which can vary considerably by taste depending on the variety and whether they ripened on the vine.

"Shall I not have intelligence with the Earth? Am I not a partly leaves and vegetable mould myself?"

—*Henry David Thoreau*

Where Should I Shop?

The good news is there are plenty of retail choices for purchasing fresh vegetables and fruit year-round. Each type offers advantages and disadvantages.

- **Supermarkets and Specialty Grocery Stores:** If you must have an out-of-season fruit or vegetable, the grocery store is probably your best bet. These retail outlets typically have the largest variety of produce available for sale. Their selections, however, often skew toward fruit and vegetable varieties that can withstand long-distance travel rather than the more unusual and tastier heirlooms. Many vegetables and fruits—particularly when they're offered out of season—are shipped from across the country or overseas to reach your store. Fortunately, a growing number of specialty grocery stores sell locally grown, pesticide-free vegetables and fruit. These stores are also more likely to sell heirlooms and rare varieties than a large chain retailer.

- **Food Co-op:** Another option is to buy produce from a food cooperative. These worker- or customer-owned businesses offer high-quality fruit and vegetables, often from local growers. You'll find co-ops are typically very committed to providing consumer education and product quality, but they don't always have the largest selection, depending on their size.

- **Buying Direct from Farmers:** When it comes to fresh seasonal produce, it's hard to beat buying direct from the farmers who grew the food. You'll not only find a wide variety of delicious fruit, vegetables, and herbs—typically picked that day—but you'll also help support your community and keep that small family farm in business. Here are ways to buy produce directly from farmers:

- **Farmers' Markets:** Looking for orange tomatoes, purple carrots, or striped beets? Check your local farmers' market first. Many towns and cities offer farmers' markets, which allow a group of farmers to sell their seasonal produce to the public. You'll find these markets often have a wide variety of produce, as well as live entertainment. Their selection, however, tends to be limited to what these farmers are growing at the moment. If you're looking for out-of-season produce, you're better off shopping at your local grocery store.

- **Farm Stands:** Whether it's a roadside stand near a farm or the back of a truck, farm stands provide healthy local produce at a reasonable price. Open during the warm-season months, farm stands sell what the farm is growing at the time.

- **U-Pick Farms:** Want to pick your own produce? U-pick farms sell strawberries, watermelons, pumpkins, and other seasonal produce directly to the public during the growing season. Their selection tends to be reasonably priced, but is limited to a few crops.

- **Community-Supported Agriculture (CSA):** You can also take it to the next step and buy a membership in a CSA. This is a great way to receive fresh, healthy produce regularly, and develop a relationship with the farmer who grew it. Members make financial commitments to the farm in the form of weekly, monthly, or advanced payments. In exchange, members receive a basket or box of fresh produce and

DID YOU KNOW?

Family farms are disappearing. According to the Environmental Protection Agency (EPA), three thousand acres of productive U.S. farmland are lost to development each day. Over the last seventy years, nearly five million family farms went out of business. And only 6 percent of the remaining farmers are younger than 35, according to the United States Department of Agriculture (USDA). If these trends continue, the family farm as we know it will no longer exist.

other products, often weekly. The produce selection is based on what the farmer is growing at the time. Many farms allow you to tour the property on certain days.

Find local farmers' markets, CSAs, and more at www.localharvest.org.

TERESA O'CONNOR

It's a Saturday tradition for us to shop our local farmers' market during the warmer months. We plan our menu around what's available locally and seasonally. Those fresh fruits and vegetables inspire some of our simplest and most delicious meals.

Support Local Farmers
- Purchase your produce directly from local growers, and farmers earn as much as 90 cents on the dollar, according to the Eat Local Challenge.
- Purchase your produce in traditional retail markets, and farmers receive about 20 cents on the dollar, reports the USDA.

How Can I Save Money?
Here are simple ways to get the most produce for your money:
- Buy produce in season from farm stands, farmers' markets, and U-Pick farms. You may have to be flexible on your purchases, but you'll find the prices are more reasonable.

- Right before closing up shop for the day, farmers often drop their prices to get rid of any remaining produce. You may find some excellent deals on freshly picked items.

- Buy larger quantities of in-season produce and freeze the extra. Check out our chapter on preserving for ideas on how to keep your produce as tasty as possible, for as long as possible.

- Save money and buy conventionally grown produce that is the least likely to be contaminated with pesticides. Then invest in pesticide-free, organic produce that is more likely to be contaminated. How can you know? Keep reading.

When Should I Buy Organic?
Understanding how fruits and vegetables are grown can help you determine whether to buy conventionally grown or organic, pesticide-free produce. To help consumers make the right purchasing decisions, the Environmental Working Group (EWG) ranks pesticide contamination levels for forty seven popular fruits and vegetables. EWG bases their ratings on an analysis of 87,000 tests of pesticides used on these foods. These tests were conducted by the USDA and Food and Drug Administration from 2000 to 2007. All produce in the studies had been rinsed or peeled first.

TIP: Learn more about produce not on these lists and EWG research at www.foodnews.org.

How Should I Select Fresh Produce?

Produce	What to Look For	Storage*
Apple	Firm with no decay; avoid shriveled or soft apples	R
Asparagus	Uniform color on most of the spear; closed, compacted tips; avoid decayed, moldy, or bruised spears	R
Avocado	Slightly soft when ripe; harder fruit must ripen; most cultivars stay green; Hass avocados change from green to black peel when ripe	C/R
Banana	Firm fruit with bright peel color; avoid bruised or discolored bananas	C
Bean, dry	Clean, firm whole beans of uniform size and color; avoid withered, wrinkled, or blistered beans	P
Bean, snap	Brightly colored, firm beans; avoid limp, shriveled, or discolored beans	R
Berries	Firm fruit with good color; avoid rotten or bruised berries	R
Broccoli	Dark green, compact heads; avoid tough stems, yellow or open florets, and decayed broccoli	R
Brussels Sprouts	Bright-green color; tight fitting outer leaves; avoid wilted or blemished sprouts	R
Cabbage	Heavy, firm heads with good color; avoid brown, decayed, or wilted leaves	R
Cantaloupe	Consistently thick peel; pleasant aroma	C/R
Carrot	Plump, firm carrots without cracks	R
Cauliflower	Clean, compact curds; avoid heads with separated or discolored bud clusters	R
Celery	Crisp, green stalks; avoid discolored or wilted celery	R
Cherry	Glossy, large, plump, hard, and dark-colored for variety; fresh and green stems; avoid soft, flabby, bruised, or cut cherries	R
Corn	Bright-green husks; fresh, plump kernels; check for worm injury or decay at silk end of corn	R (best eaten day bought)
Cucumber	Firm skin with no sign of discoloration or bruises	R
Eggplant	Firm, smooth-skinned with no soft or brown spots; flesh will give slightly and bounce back when ripe; if indention stays, it's overripe	R

*Storage Symbols
R = refrigerator
C/R = ripen on counter, then store in refrigerator
C = counter
P = pantry

Produce	Description	Storage
Grape	Firm, brightly colored berries; avoid soft or shriveled grapes	R
Grapefruit	Heavy, firm fruit with smooth skin; avoid discolored or shriveled grapefruit	C
Honeydew	Heavy, firm fruit with smooth skin; pleasant aroma	C/R
Lettuce	Crisp, brightly colored leaves; avoid decayed or water-soaked heads	R
Mango	Brightly colored; soft fruit means it's ripe; avoid those with pitted skin or gray or black spots	C
Mushroom	Good coloring for type; avoid discolored, soft, or decayed mushrooms	R
Onion	Firm and dry; avoid sprouted, bruised, or decayed onions	P
Orange	Heavy, firm fruit; avoid decayed or bruised oranges	C
Papaya	Unblemished skins with vibrant colors; heavy fruit should give a little when pressed; avoid papayas with dark spots, excessively hard or soft fruit	C
Peach & Nectarine	Plump and juicy; avoid fruit with bruises, shriveled spots, or decay	C/R
Pear	Unblemished skin on slightly green, unripe pears; avoid old, soft, bruised, or cut pears; fruit ripens better off the tree	C/R
Peas	Firm, velvety, and smooth pods; avoid peas with puffy or decayed pods	R
Peppers	Smooth, firm skin; avoid ones with soft spots or bruises	R
Pineapple	Dark-green crown leaves; heavy, firm fruit with no decay or defects	C
Potato	Firm smooth skin; avoid ones with bruises, sprouts, or green areas	P
Spinach & Swiss Chard	Crisp leaves with fresh fragrance and no signs of discoloration or decay	R
Squash, Summer	Glossy, firm skin; avoid discolored squash; smaller sizes taste best	R
Squash, Winter	Firm, heavy squash without cuts or moldy or sunken spots	C
Sweet Potato	Bright, uniformly colored with no cuts, worm holes, or defects	C
Tomato	Firm with good color for type; avoid bruised or decayed fruit	C
Watermelon	Firm, relatively smooth surface; avoid those with soft spots	C

*Storage Symbols
R = refrigerator
C/R = ripen on counter, then store in refrigerator
C = counter
P = pantry

Fruit and Vegetables Most & Least Contaminated by Pesticides

Dirty Dozen (Most)
1. Peaches
2. Apples
3. Nectarines
4. Strawberries
5. Cherries
6. Grapes
7. Pears
8. Bell Peppers
9. Celery
10. Kale
11. Lettuce
12. Carrots

Clean Fifteen (Least)
1. Onions
2. Sweet Corn
3. Asparagus
4. Sweet Peas
5. Cabbage
6. Eggplant
7. Broccoli
8. Tomatoes
9. Sweet Potatoes
10. Avocados
11. Pineapples
12. Mangoes
13. Kiwi
14. Papaya
15. Watermelon

EDIBLES

There are so many herbs, fruits, and vegetables in the world that you can spend your life gardening without repeating growing any of them. But the fact remains that there are some that always top the list of all-time gardening hits—like tomatoes, cucumbers, peppers, strawberries, and melons.

If your tastes are very specific or you want to explore many different varieties of a single vegetable or fruit, there's no reason you can't grow a whole tomato garden…or a whole pepper garden…or a whole melon garden. The only judge of what is right for your garden is you.

If you're feeding just yourself, plant what you like to eat. If you are feeding a family, have a meeting to narrow everyone's wishes to a manageable list. If you plan to feed your neighbors, plant zucchini!

The herbs, fruits, and vegetables selected for this book were chosen because they are the ones most often grown and eaten by home gardeners. They are also the ones that will give you the best chances of gardening success.

The beginning gardener can easily grow nearly all the vegetables in this book by following the simple, basic steps for good gardening in the Gardening 101 chapter. If you're not accustomed to using fresh herbs when cooking, now is the time to start experimenting. Most herbs are easy to grow, drought tolerant, and relatively pest- and disease-free. Even a few herbs sprinkled around your yard can yield huge returns in flavor for cooking as well as a head-rush of success for growing some of your own food.

Among the fruits, strawberries, blueberries, and melons are the easiest to grow in the home garden. Fruit plants that need a longer time to grow to maturity, such as grapes and apples, can be a bit more challenging because of their pruning requirements and the number of pests and diseases you may need to combat.

We recommend you start small and work your way toward a more ambitious garden as your skills and confidence grow. The rewards are tremendous—*groceries!*

herbs:// Basil

planting and growing | varieties | produce selection and harvest | preserving

Basil is an easy herb to grow as long as it has warmth, sun, and well-drained soil. A little regular watering and a shot of organic fertilizer once in a while and you are set. Basil needs to be pruned or "pinched back" in order to continue healthy growth. By harvesting this herb regularly, you will prevent it from blooming and losing vigor.

Basil can be started from seed or bought as a plant from your local garden center or nursery. By starting from seed, you save money as well as having access to greater variety. Sow about $1/8$ inch deep in a seed-starting mix. Basil needs soil temperatures of 75 to 85 degrees in order to germinate. Use a seedling mat to help bring the soil up to the correct temperature. Start them about eight weeks before your local frost-free date. This head start ensures they will be strong and productive early in the season.

Basil is very sensitive to cool temperatures and it is the first thing the frost zaps in fall (in cooler climates). You'll have great success bringing it in by placing it in a sunny windowsill and keeping the soil just barely moist.

planting and growing | **varieties** | produce selection and harvest | preserving

There are so many amazing and different kinds of basil. There are great standards and fantastic variations.

Standard Basil 'Genovese', 'Napoletano', 'Sweet Basil', 'Lettuce Leaf Basil'

Thai Basil 'Siam Queen', 'Thai Holy Basil', 'Thai Magic'

Purple Basil 'Dark Opal', 'Red Rubin', 'Purple Ruffles', 'African Blue Basil'

Sweet and Citrus Basils 'Cinnamon Basil', 'Lemon Basil', 'Lime Basil', 'Spicy Clove', 'Licorice Basil'

AMANDA THOMSEN

Mammoth Basil can have leaves the size of your hand and larger. It can make a scrumdiddly-umptious substitute for a wrap and it's carb-free.

| planting and growing | varieties | **produce selection and harvest** | preserving |

Basil does not store well once it's cut, which makes it somewhat challenging to buy it fresh. However, basil can be found at the grocery store in small plastic containers. You can also buy it at farmers' markets or produce stands, but if it isn't kept cool enough it wilts rather quickly. Look for basil that has vibrantly colored leaves that are healthy in appearance.

DID YOU KNOW?

You can easily start a basil plant from the stems of the ones sold in the grocery store box, or any cutting for that matter. Just make a clean cut at the bottom of the stem and let it sit in a small glass of water until it roots; it usually happens within a few days.

In the home garden, basil can be harvested and eaten right away. If you started it from seed, start using it as soon as there are 6 to 8 well-formed leaves on the plant. If you purchased a plant, you could start eating it on the way home from the market!

| planting and growing | varieties | produce selection and harvest | **preserving** |

Although fresh basil can't be beat, it can be dried, but it becomes a lot less potent and its flavor changes drastically. Luckily, there is a great and easy way to always have fresh-tasting basil at your fingertips. Just toss your clean and dry harvested leaves into a blender with just enough olive oil to loosen the mixture. Then throw it into a freezer bag and pop it in the freezer. When you need basil for a recipe, just break off a piece and add; it will taste like you just harvested it. If you decide to dry basil, just cut the branches and hang them upside down (or on a flat rack) in a warm, dry place. It should dehydrate in a couple of days. Once dried, store basil in an airtight container and use within six months.

pest and disease

Mealybugs	*Spitbugs*	*Root rot*
Slugs/Snails	*Fusarium wilt*	

Got a bug bite? Rub a fresh basil leaf on insect bites to reduce itching and inflammation.

Basil Sorbet

Try African Blue Basil (leaves and flowers) or Cinnamon Basil for something different.

$\frac{1}{2}$ **cup sugar**
$\frac{1}{2}$ **cup water**
25 fresh basil leaves (or more), coarsely chopped

- Dissolve the sugar in the water and bring to a boil. Reduce the heat and simmer for 5 minutes. Remove the sugar water from the heat and cool.
- Pour the cooled mixture into a blender or food processor. Add the basil and blend well. Pour the mixture into a shallow pan, cover, and freeze until firm.
- Transfer the frozen basil mixture to a blender or food processor and blend well. Return to shallow pan, cover, and freeze until ready to serve.
- Serve with a sprig of basil or basil flowers.

Basil Sorbet

Lazy Margherita Pizza

The key to this pizza is not just the ingredients themselves. It is also using a pizza stone. Be sure to preheat the oven and the pizza stone to 450°.

CRUST

1 packet fast-acting yeast

Pinch sugar

1 cup hot water

3 to 4 cups flour

- In a large mixing bowl, combine the yeast, sugar, and water; let it sit until the yeast is frothy. Slowly add the flour, mixing with a dough hook until a clean ball is formed. You can also mix this dough by hand. Cover with a kitchen towel and let the dough rise in a warm, but not hot, location for one hour. After the dough has risen 1 hour, cut it in half. Roll out half the dough on a floured surface roughly to the size of your pizza stone; fold in half. The dough should be thin, but not too thin to pick up and move to the stone.

TOPPINGS

2 ripe garden tomatoes, sliced

Salt

2 Tbsp. olive oil

2 to 3 fresh bocconcini (mini-mozzarella balls), cut into 3 pieces each

Fresh-grated Parmesan cheese

10 basil leaves (Genovese, Napoletano, or Sweet Basil), cut into thin strips

- Prepare the tomatoes by placing the slices on a large plate and salting them. Drain any liquid after one hour. This reduces the likelihood of a soggy pizza.
- Preheat the oven to 450° F. with the pizza stone in the oven. Carefully unfold the pizza dough over the hot pizza stone and spread it out. Brush the olive oil on top of the pizza dough, and top with the mozzarella and prepared tomatoes. Bake 8-14 minutes until the mozzarella is bubbly. Remove from the oven and sprinkle the Parmesan and basil on top.

Lazy Margherita Pizza

Thai Basil Fried Rice

5 Tbsp. peanut oil

2 Tbsp. garlic, minced

2 fresh red chilies, seeded and finely chopped

2 cups mixed red, green, and yellow peppers, finely chopped

$\frac{1}{2}$ cup onion, finely chopped

Salt and fresh-ground black pepper to taste

4 cups prepared Jasmine rice

1 Tbsp. sugar

2 tsp. white pepper

4 Tbsp. fish sauce or light soy sauce, plus more to taste

Up to 2 cups Siam Queen basil leaves, hand torn

Sriracha chili sauce to taste

- Heat a wok or large frying pan over high heat until the surface is almost smoking. Add the oil and coat the surface evenly.
- Set the wok aside, off the heat, and add the garlic and chilies; stir about 10 seconds. Add the peppers and onion and move the wok back to the high heat. Add two pinches each of salt and black pepper and toss about 30 seconds.
- Add the rice, stirring to ensure the grains are separated.
- Stir the rice and the vegetables well until the rice is coated with the oil. Add the sugar, white pepper, and fish or soy sauce. Stir the mixture for another minute. Adjust salt to taste by adding more fish sauce, if desired.
- Turn off the heat and add basil leaves and stir to mix well.
- Add sriracha chili sauce to taste.

Not Just Another Pesto

Not Just Another Pesto

2 cups basil

2 oz. honey roasted cashews

2 oz. honey roasted almonds

1 small shallot, diced

$\frac{1}{4}$ cup grated Parmesan cheese

1 tsp. rice wine vinegar

$\frac{1}{4}$ to $\frac{1}{2}$ cup extra virgin olive oil

- Combine the basil, cashews, almonds, shallot, Parmesan cheese, and vinegar in a food processor. Pulse to break up the mixture.
- Slowly pour in the olive oil as the food processor is running. Add enough olive oil to loosen the mixture well, but don't let it get too soupy.

information:// Nutrition

Basil has long won the hearts of cultures around the world. In Haiti, basil was linked to a pagan love goddess Erzulie, and considered a powerful protector. In some Greek Orthodox churches, basil is used to prepare the holy water.

Believe it or not, basil was considered dangerous to eat by many for centuries. The Greek physician Dioscorides recommended against eating basil in the first century A.D., as did the herbalist Nicholas Culpeper nearly six hundred years later.

Fortunately, we've learned not only is basil safe to eat, it's healthy, too. Just two tablespoons of this leafy green herb provide more than a quarter of your daily needs for vitamin K, as well as some vitamin A and C . . . and all for 1 calorie! Basil contains essential oils rich in phenolic compounds, as well as flavonoids and other polyphenols with important health benefits. Research shows these natural compounds may have antioxidant, anti-inflammatory, and anti-cancer properties.

Although all basils contain antioxidants, the purple varieties appear to have more than the green cultivars, according to Rutgers University research. Among those tested, 'Dark Opal' basil scored the highest, with an antioxidant activity level similar to red and black raspberries.

herbs:// Chives

planting and growing | varieties | produce selection and harvest | preserving

Perennial and tough-as-nails, chives are the easiest of herbs to grow. A member of the Allium family, they form small bulbs underground like their relative the onion. Chives are not picky about soils or fertilizers and they are tough enough to grow and overwinter in a container; just make sure they get six hours of sun a day.

Chives can be purchased as plants and shared by division. They are available at any garden store. Chives need to be divided every three years or so, which makes them a great plant to snag from a friend, neighbor, or relative; just be sure to have 6 to 8 bulbs in the transplanting clump. Chives can also be started from seed, but they are very slow to germinate and must be started in darkness. Since chives germinate best when kept fairly warm (65 to 70°), sow them in starter pots and place on a seedling mat to facilitate growth. Don't forget to keep them moist.

After seedlings are a month old, they are ready to be set out. Harden off by setting outside an hour the first day, then increasing an hour a day for 7 days. Transplant 4 to 6 weeks before your area's last frost date. It will take a few months for a new plant to become vigorous enough for

you to use, but once it reaches that point, you will never be chive free.

planting and growing | varieties | produce selection and harvest | preserving

Since we are talking about the onion family, there are a million close relatives, but not many are truly classified as chives. There is the true chive plant, *Allium schoenoprasum*, and a cultivar called 'Forescate'. These two varieties taste the same, but 'Forescate' has bigger, more beautiful flowers and is considered an ornamental as well as an edible. There is also a kind called garlic chives, which are very easy to grow and have a slightly more garlicky taste.

AMANDA THOMSEN

We used garlic chive flowers in the bouquets and boutonnieres for our wedding. Near the end of the night someone said, "Why is it every time I hug you, I smell onions?" to my new husband. Oops!

| planting and growing | varieties | **produce selection and harvest** | preserving |

Chives can be continually harvested from early spring until late in fall, and year-round in warmer climates. They are easily found in grocery stores and farmers' markets. Look for the chives that are not wilted and show no signs of yellowing or drying. If you're going to store fresh chives, keep them cool and dry and they should last up to a week.

DID YOU KNOW?

Chive flowers are great to eat; just use them in salads, flaked apart into individual florets. Don't pop the whole thing in your mouth, though! It's a little overwhelming . . .

| planting and growing | varieties | produce selection and harvest | **preserving** |

When dried, chives lose quite a lot of flavor, so why not try freezing them in an ice cube tray? Just wash, dry, and chop, packing tightly into an ice cube tray with just enough water to hold it all together. When you need chives, you can just pop out a cube and experience fresh-cut flavor.

You can also bring chives in for the winter. Divide the chives and transplant a portion into two separate, household-friendly containers. Bring the first in just as cold weather arrives. Leave the second container in a protected location and allow the chives to die back. When your first pot of chives starts to look lifeless, bring in the dormant chives. They will start growing again, and you will have chives all winter long!

| pests and diseases |

Chives have no real pests or disease problems.

(Shared by Marcelle Layne) Chive Dip

A simple and quick-to-make recipe, great for serving with chips, spicy potato wedges, and vegetable sticks for the healthier ones among us.

½ cup plain yogurt

½ cup cream cheese

3 Tbsp. chives, finely chopped, divided

¼ tsp. dried chili flakes

¼ tsp. smoked paprika

¼ tsp. salt, or to taste

¼ tsp. white pepper, or to taste

¼ tsp. garlic powder, or to taste

1 tsp. olive oil

1 Tbsp. chive flowers, if desired

- In a small bowl, combine the yogurt with the cream cheese.
- Add 2½ Tbsp. of the chives with the chili flakes, smoked paprika, salt, white pepper, and garlic powder to the yogurt mix and stir well.
- Refrigerate at least 1 hour.
- Just before serving, drizzle the olive oil on top of the dip. Garnish with the remaining ½ Tbsp. (1½ tsp.) of the chives and the chive flowers, if desired.
- Serve with chips and raw vegetable sticks.

(Almost) Mashed Potato Salad

6 to 8 medium to large red potatoes, cubed

½ cup Greek yogurt

½ cup sour cream

½ medium red onion, diced

4 slices bacon, cooked and crumbled

1 big bunch chives, chopped

³/₄ cup shredded cheddar cheese

Sea salt and fresh-ground black pepper

- Boil the potatoes until they're tender when pierced with a knife. Do not overcook or they will become too soft. Drain and return them to the pot; do not place over direct heat. Allow the residual heat of the cooking pot to remove any excess water in the potatoes. Let potatoes cool completely.
- Add the yogurt, sour cream, onion, bacon, chives, cheddar cheese, salt, and pepper; stir to combine.
- Let stand in the refrigerator for 1 hour, or longer, to let the flavors blend.

Roasted Sweet Corn and Chive Scones

This is a great dish for using leftover roasted corn. You can substitute frozen corn that has been thawed and drained.

2³/₄ cups whole wheat flour

4 tsp. baking powder

¹/₂ tsp. baking soda

1 tsp. sea salt

¹/₂ cup very cold butter, finely cubed

1 handful of chives, chopped

³/₄ cup roasted sweet corn kernels

1 cup buttermilk, divided, plus more if needed

2 Tbsp. melted butter

- Preheat the oven to 400°. In a food processor, combine the flour, baking powder, baking soda, and sea salt; pulse a couple of times. Add the butter; pulse 5 to 8 times or until the mixture is crumbly and has an appearance like dried oats.

- Transfer the flour mixture to a large bowl and add the chives, corn, and ¾ cup of the buttermilk. Stir. If the mixture is too crumbly, add the remaining ¼ cup of the buttermilk, and more buttermilk if needed. The mixture should stick together and have some elasticity, but should not be soupy.

- Turn out onto a floured surface and knead a couple of times to pull the dough together. Roll out to a thickness of ½ inch and use a knife to cut the dough into squares. Cut the squares on a diagonal to make triangles; place the triangle pieces on an ungreased baking sheet. Brush the tops of scones with the melted butter. Bake 15 to 20 minutes, depending upon the size of the scones. Remove when the tops are brown and a toothpick inserted into a scone comes out clean.

Roasted Sweet Corn and Chive Scones

Chive Oil

Chive Oil

A great addition to roasted vegetables and other savory dishes. Use it as a finishing oil just before serving.

1 bunch chives (the more chives you use, the stronger the flavor)
½ cup extra virgin olive oil
Pinch of salt

- Combine all the ingredients in a food processor or blender and process until smooth.
- Store in a refrigerator and use within a week.

 information:// Nutrition

Chives share many health benefits with onion, garlic, and other members of the Allium family. Members of this family have been featured in folk remedies for a wide array of ailments throughout the world. In ancient Egypt, onions and garlic were fed to the workers building the great pyramids. Evidence of the highly revered onion was even found in the tomb of King Tut. Later, alliums became crucial ingredients in the medieval kitchen, where they were valued for their culinary and medicinal values. Today, we're learning just how accurate these earlier cultures were about amazing alliums.

These vegetables have an odor due to different smelly sulfur compounds, which are believed to help protect the digestive, respiratory, and circulatory systems; it is said that the stronger the smell, the greater the health benefit! With their milder taste, chives have fewer sulfur compounds than their relatives. But they still offer similar properties to a lesser degree.

Alliums are well documented to have anticlotting, antiviral, and decongestant properties. Studies have shown a high intake of alliums, such as chives, may reduce your risk of several types of cancer, including stomach and prostate cancer. Chives have strong antibacterial properties that inhibited 38 strains of salmonella, the most common bacterial food-borne illness, in research conducted by North Carolina AT&T State University. While the amount tested was too high to be very appetizing, it's still a good idea to eat this tasty herb regularly.

herbs:// **Cilantro & Coriander**

planting and growing | varieties | produce selection and harvest | preserving

This one herb has two names. The younger, leafier growth is called "cilantro." As it grows and "bolts" (or matures), it becomes more ferny, then flowers and goes to seed. The seed is known as "coriander." The roots of this plant are also edible and used to flavor many Thai dishes. Those are a whole lot of options from just one herb!

If growing cilantro is your goal, harvest the leaves often; pinching will help prevent early bolting. However, bolting is inevitable (as it's brought on by hot weather) and the solution is a combination of consistent pruning, succession planting, and afternoon shade. To ensure a continuous harvest, plant a few cilantro seeds every two weeks or so. This way you will always have young, fresh cilantro leaves and you can let your older plants bolt and flower.

Cilantro is easy to start from seed. Soak seed in water overnight and then direct sow outside. This is an herb that tolerates light frost, so it can be started a week or two prior to the frost-free date in your area. In warm climates, it can be a fall or even winter crop. Cilantro grows very fast and doesn't like being transplanted; so don't bother starting them indoors. If you choose to let your coriander go to seed, you will notice how truly easy it is to grow cilantro. It will be popping up all over!

planting and growing | **varieties** | produce selection and harvest | preserving

There aren't many varieties of cilantro, and if you choose to buy a plant rather than start from seed, your choices will be quite limited. Most often you will find 'Long Standing', which is the standard cilantro variety. 'Santo' has a nice big leaf and is a little slower to bolt. 'Delfino' is the talk of the town since it's much slower to bolt, but some might find the needle-thin leaves difficult to use in recipes.

planting and growing | varieties | **produce selection and harvest** | preserving

Cilantro is available year-round at produce stands and grocery stores, sold in small bundles. Make sure that the bunch you choose has no brown or slimy leaves. When you get it home, unbundle it and cut off the bottoms of the stalks. Stand them in a clean drinking glass filled with clean water, cover with a clear plastic bag, and store in the refrigerator. By changing the water frequently and removing any leaves or stalks that are turning brown, you can keep cilantro about ten days. If you choose to leave it in a bag in your crisper drawer, expect it to last just a few days. Coriander is readily available on the spice aisle in a grocery store.

Cilantro leaves can be harvested once the plant is about 4 inches tall and there are enough large leaves for the recipe you're making. Coriander seeds can be harvested by collecting the seedheads as they begin to turn brown. Hang them upside-down covered by a paper bag to catch the seeds. Store the seeds in a jar or plastic storage bag.

AMANDA THOMSEN

If you're buying cilantro, do yourself a favor and buy limes, too. They go together better than peanut butter and jelly!

DID YOU KNOW?

Coriander is old—more than 5,000 years old. You'll find this noble spice referenced in Sanskrit texts, Egyptian papyri, and the Bible. In the Middle Ages, coriander was considered a popular ingredient in love potions.

planting and growing | varieties | produce selection and harvest | **preserving**

Cilantro is best stored for use after the season by simply freezing the leaves. Lay them flat on a sheet pan and put them in the freezer. Store in a resealable container.

pests and diseases

Aphids; Thrips; Powdery mildew

Rock Star Salsa

5 large ripe tomatoes, chopped

1 large yellow onion, chopped

2 cups chopped cilantro

1–3 jalapeños, seeded and finely chopped

2 cloves garlic, finely chopped

8–10 limes, juice only

2–3 tsp. kosher salt

- In a very large bowl, mix the tomatoes, onion, cilantro, jalapeños, garlic, lime juice, and salt. Refrigerate overnight. Enjoy the salsa with tortilla chips for a taste fiesta!

Ramen at the Ritz

One package ramen noodles, your choice of flavor

1 lime, juice only

5–10 cilantro leaves

5–10 basil leaves

1 piece lemongrass

1 green onion, sliced (white and light-green part only)

$\frac{1}{4}$-inch piece of fresh ginger, peeled and grated

2 Tbsp. peanuts, crushed

Dash of soy sauce

Dash of Sriracha sauce

- Prepare the ramen noodles according to the package directions.
- Add the lime juice, cilantro, basil, lemongrass, green onion, ginger, peanuts, soy sauce, and Sriracha sauce. Mix well. Enjoy!

Rock Star Salsa

Ramen at the Ritz

Cucumber Tomato Salad

4 cucumbers

2 ripe tomatoes

2 yellow onions, peeled

1 jalapeño (can leave the seeds in for extra heat)

10 limes, juice only

2 cups white vinegar

3 Tbsp. kosher salt

1 large bunch cilantro, chopped

- Slice the cucumbers, tomatoes, onions, and jalapeño by feeding them through the slicing blade of your food processor, or cut into thin slices. In a large bowl, combine the sliced vegetables with the lime juice, vinegar, and salt. Add the cilantro. Let it "pickle" overnight in the refrigerator.

Coriander Pork Chops with Hot Stuff Sauce

4 pork chops

6 Tbsp. ground coriander

10 limes, juice only

2 tsp. salt

2 tsp. pepper

- Combine the pork chops, coriander, lime juice, salt, and pepper inside a zip-top plastic bag. Marinate overnight in the refrigerator. Grill the pork chops and serve with Hot Stuff Sauce.

Hot Stuff Sauce

- Take all leftover hot peppers from your garden and remove their skins by roasting over your stovetop (a gas one is great). Remove the stems and seeds and blend the roasted peppers with olive oil until it reaches a sauce consistency. Add a pinch of salt. Use with great caution.

Red Quinoa Salad with Cilantro

This is one of those salads that gets better with age.

1 cup prepared red quinoa, cooked according to package directions, chilled

1 medium cucumber, seeded and diced

2 large tomatoes, seeded and diced

1 medium yellow onion, diced

1 green pepper, seeded and diced

½ cup chopped cilantro

½ cup fresh-squeezed lemon juice

½ cup olive oil

1 tsp. salt

1 tsp. ground cumin

- In a large bowl, mix the prepared quinoa, cucumber, tomatoes, onion, green pepper, and cilantro.
- In a separate small bowl, whisk the lemon juice, olive oil, salt, and cumin. Pour the lemon-olive oil mixture over the quinoa-vegetable mixture, and toss well.
- Refrigerate for several hours and toss again before serving.

Cilantro Pesto

Cilantro Pesto (Shared by Jennifer Hammer)

2 Tbsp. coarsely chopped walnuts

2 medium garlic cloves

1½ cups loosely packed cilantro leaves

½ cup loosely packed Italian flat leaf parsley

½ tsp. kosher salt

¼ tsp. fresh-ground black pepper

½ cup olive oil

- Combine the walnuts and garlic in a food processor and pulse until coarsely chopped. Add the cilantro, parsley, salt, and black pepper. Process until finely chopped. With the processor running, slowly drizzle in the olive oil through the feed tube to create a smooth purée.

 information:// Nutrition

One of the world's oldest spices, coriander seeds have been acclaimed for their healing properties by cultures around the globe. The seeds are chewed or infused into a tea as a digestive tonic and mild sedative. When made into an essential oil, coriander is often used for sore muscles.

The ancient Romans combined coriander seeds with cumin and vinegar to concoct a meat preservative. Today, we're learning that both the seeds and leaves are packed with a potent antibacterial agent. In fact, coriander has a chemical called dodecenal, which is twice as effective as the commonly used antibiotic gentamiacin at killing salmonella, according to researchers at University of California, Berkeley.

That's not all! The plant is rich in healthy phytonutrients, which demonstrate anti-diabetic properties in animal tests by helping diabetic mice to secrete insulin and lower blood sugar. Coriander helped reduce cholesterol in animal tests as well.

Do you prefer the leaves to the seeds? Just nine sprigs (20g) of cilantro provide 27 percent of daily vitamin A needs, as well as vitamin C, complex B vitamins, iron, and other nutrients, all for 5 calories!

herbs:// Dill & Fennel

planting and growing | varieties | produce selection and harvest | preserving

Dill and fennel are quite similar in appearance, both tall and ferny with large umbrellas of yellow flowers, but they taste very different. Both are very easy to grow and are big producers. Dill is grown for its leaves and seeds; fennel, for its bulb, leaves, and seeds.

Both dill and fennel are very easily started from seed, but plants can be found in garden centers. They both grow quickly, getting very tall—some reach six feet in height. Neither cares for being transplanted. Dill and fennel don't care much about soil quality nor do they even need much water. They do, however, need plenty of sun or they will get floppy. These guys are big reseeders and you may have a forest of plants before you know it. Make sure you either harvest the seeds or deadhead most of the seedheads. Leaving just a few to self-sow, however, is quite economical.

planting and growing | varieties | produce selection and harvest | preserving

Both dill and fennel come in a couple of varieties. Make sure you make the right choice for your garden.

Dill: Dill comes in two varieties, those that are grown primarily for seeds and those that are grown primarily for leaves. They also vary in size significantly.

Grown for Seed: 'Mammoth' dill is prolific and stunning at over 6 feet tall. 'Bouquet' dill is prettier, shorter, and has a silvery hue.

Grown for Leaves: 'Hercules' and 'SuperDukat' are large, spreading plants. 'Fernleaf' only reaches about 18 inches tall and is a little slower to flower.

Fennel: Fennel comes in both bulbing and non-bulbing varieties. Both are great for leaves and seeds. The base, or "bulb," of bulbing fennel can also be eaten.

Bulbing: 'Florence', 'Zefa Fino', 'Perfection'

Non-Bulbing: 'Dulce' or sweet fennel, 'Purpureum' or bronze fennel is highly ornamental as well as having tasty leaves and seeds.

planting and growing | varieties | **produce selection and harvest** | preserving

Fennel bulbs are available most of the year in grocery stores and at produce stands; look for white, firm bulbs. Dill and fennel leaves are sometimes available in small plastic boxes at a grocery store. Dried dill leaves and seeds and fennel seeds are readily available at grocery stores and have their own fantastic flavors.

If you are growing these herbs for the leaves, you can begin harvesting very early. These tender, young "micro greens" are especially good in salads. Fennel bulbs can be unearthed with a fork when they are about three inches in diameter. Act quickly when harvesting the bulb; once a flower stalk goes up, the bulb may become bitter.

AMANDA THOMSEN

As much as I like to eat dill and fennel, swallowtail butterfly pupae dine solely on these plants. If you see black-and-yellow striped caterpillars on your dill or fennel, you know that butterflies are on the way! Plant extra so that both you and the caterpillars can enjoy the feast!

planting and growing | varieties | produce selection and harvest | **preserving**

Dill foliage can be easily and quickly dried by hanging (or placing flat on a screen) in a warm, dry place. Fennel foliage does not retain its flavor when dried. Seedheads from both can be removed at the end of a growing season and hung upside-down with a paper bag over them to catch the seeds.

Dill and fennel work well in recipes even when frozen. Just wash, dry thoroughly, store in a plastic bag, and throw in the freezer.

pests and diseases

Butterfly larvae

DID YOU KNOW?

Dill and fennel make beautiful, back-of-the-border, showy ornamental plants. In addition to being tasty, fennel was hung over doors in medieval times to ward off evil spirits.

Tuna Pasta Salad with Dill and Capers

Dressing

1 Tbsp. Dijon mustard

3 Tbsp. olive oil

1 tsp. white wine vinegar

1 lemon, zest only

1 bunch dill fronds, chopped

¼ tsp. celery salt

Pinch of sea salt and fresh-ground black pepper

Salad

1 8-oz. can tuna, drained

1 cup small pasta shells, cooked

½ small red onion, diced

2 Tbsp. capers

- In a medium bowl, whisk the Dijon mustard, olive oil, vinegar, lemon zest, dill, celery salt, salt, and pepper until well combined. Add the tuna, pasta, onion, and capers. Stir lightly to combine. Refrigerate to chill, or serve immediately.

(Shared by Tamara Jo Rankila) # Lemon-Dill Tartar Sauce

1 cup light mayonnaise

Dash of hot pepper sauce

Handful of dill, chopped

Handful of parsley, chopped

1 lemon, zest and juice only

1 tsp. sea salt

½ tsp. lemon pepper

1 Tbsp. pickle relish

- Mix the mayonnaise, hot pepper sauce, dill, parsley, lemon juice and zest, sea salt, lemon pepper, and relish. Cover and refrigerate at least 3 hours for the flavors to meld.

Chicken & Fennel Salad Sandwiches

1 tsp. salt

½ tsp. fresh-ground black pepper

¾ cup plain nonfat yogurt or mayonnaise

1 Tbsp. Dijon mustard

2 Tbsp. chopped fresh chives

1 Tbsp. chopped fresh tarragon

1 cup finely diced fennel bulb

1 pound chicken, cooked, sliced into ½-inch pieces

Sliced bread of your choice

Micro greens, in season

- In a small bowl, combine the salt, pepper, yogurt, Dijon mustard, chives, and tarragon. Add the fennel. Add the chicken to the dressing, and mix well. Serve as sandwiches with the micro greens (if available).

Braised Fennel

4 fennel bulbs, washed and quartered, tough outer leaves discarded

3½ Tbsp. butter

1½ cups vegetable or chicken stock

Salt and fresh-ground black pepper to taste

1½ cups grated Gruyère cheese

3½ Tbsp. butter, melted

- Preheat the oven to 400º. Lay the fennel, cut side down, in a large casserole dish. Dot with the butter; add the stock, salt, and pepper. Bake 45 minutes until the fennel is tender yet firm. Drain the butter and juices from the casserole dish. Place the fennel back in the casserole dish, cut side up. Sprinkle with the Gruyère cheese and the melted butter. Bake 10 minutes. Switch to broiler heat and broil until golden brown.

(Shared by Donalyn Ketchum) Herbed Cucumber Salad

¼ cup apple cider vinegar

1 Tbsp. sugar

1 tsp. kosher salt

10 to 15 grinds of 5-peppercorn blend

1 garlic clove, mashed

⅓ cup extra virgin olive oil

2 Tbsp. chopped fresh herbs (a mix of whatever you have on hand such as oregano, thyme, fennel, dill, basil, rosemary, and parsley)

4 medium cucumbers or 2 large English cucumbers, sliced in ⅛-inch slices

½ small mild onion, sliced very thinly

- In a medium bowl, whisk the vinegar, sugar, salt, and the peppercorn grinds until the sugar and salt are dissolved. Whisk in the garlic and olive oil. Add the mixed herbs (if dried herbs are all you have, use them but cut the amount roughly in half, as some dried herbs have a stronger flavor).

- In a large dish, layer the cucumbers and onion; pour the cider-herb dressing over them. Cover and marinate in the refrigerator for at least a couple hours before serving. This will keep several days refrigerated and will taste even better the next day.

Fennel-Flavored Hollandaise Sauce

Fennel-Flavored Hollandaise Sauce

This sauce is great on salmon, veggies, or spinach-filled crepes.

½ cup unsalted butter
3 egg yolks
1 handful fennel fronds, chopped
½ lemon, zest only
Sprinkle of salt

- Melt the butter in a microwaveable container for 40 seconds; do not overheat. Drop the egg yolks into a food processor and slowly add the melted butter and process. Do this slowly so you don't make scrambled eggs. Once the egg yolks and butter are blended, add the fennel fronds, lemon zest, and salt and pulse a few times. If you don't feel like hauling out the food processor, this can also be accomplished with a whisk and a bowl.

information:// Nutrition

Dill and fennel have important health benefits. A cup of fresh dill sprigs contains 12 percent of your daily vitamin C needs and 14 percent of vitamin A needs. A cup of raw fennel bulb provides 17 percent of vitamin C needs, as well as folate and potassium.

Dill was beloved by ancient Egyptians and Greeks for a wide array of medicinal uses. In the Middle Ages, the aromatic herb was believed to protect against witchcraft. Over the centuries, dill seeds have been used for everything from relieving colic in babies to stimulating nursing mothers' milk flow. Seventeenth-century herbalist Nicholas Culpeper recommended the herb for stomach troubles.

Today, we're learning dill contains monoterpenes substances with anti-cancer activity. The herb also contains polyacetylenes with anti-bacterial and anti-inflammatory properties. An Iranian study discovered dill seed extract might help prevent ulcers.

Fennel is one of our oldest cultivated plants—and many early cultures believed the seed was an effective slimming agent. Ancient Roman women ate fennel to watch their weight. The Greek name 'marathon' is derived from a verb meaning, "to grow thin." And William Coles wrote in 1650, "the seeds, leaves, and root of our Garden Fennel are much used in drinks and broths for those that are grown fat..."

herbs:// Mint & Oregano

planting
and
growing | varieties | produce
selection
and harvest | preserving

Mint and oregano are closely related to each other and have similar "take no prisoners" growing habits. Neither is overly fussy about soil type or fertilizer; they thrive simply on full sun to part shade and regular watering. They are both so aggressive that they are best suited to being corralled in containers. Most of their spreading is via roots and runners, but both can seed extensively, so when you see flowers, pinch them off.

Both can easily be started from seeds or bought from local garden centers as plants. Start seeds early; they can tolerate outdoor temperatures once it gets about 50°. Both can be started from cuttings, as well. These two are happy to grow inside in sunny windowsills in winter and are easier to tend as houseplants than many other herbs.

Mint and oregano can cross-pollinate with other mints and oreganos, which is another good reason to make sure they don't make it to flower! However, if you want to harvest seeds you will need to isolate the herbs from each other and leave a certain number of flowers growing. By doing so, you will have seeds that stay true to their cultivar.

planting and
growing | varieties | produce
selection
and harvest | preserving

There are many, many kinds of mints and each has its own distinctive flavor. Grow different varieties in a few containers for fun!
Standard Mints: 'Spearmint', 'Peppermint', 'Kentucky Colonel Mint'
Flavored Mints: 'Chocolate', 'Pineapple', 'Apple', 'Ginger', 'Lavender', 'Lemon', 'Orange'

There are not as many options for oregano. You may want to start with Greek oregano, which provides the strong, pungent flavor that you're familiar with in Italian and Greek cooking. For a milder flavor and a prettier plant, try 'Aureum', also called golden oregano.

planting and growing	varieties	**produce selection and harvest**	preserving

Mint and oregano are so easy to grow that harvested bunches are seldom seen in farmers' markets. You'll be more likely to see plants for sale instead. At the grocery store, you can find small containers of fresh mint and oregano, usually in the refrigerated section in the produce area. Look for leaves that aren't brown or wilted.

planting and growing	varieties	produce selection and harvest	**preserving**

Very few recipes call for fresh mint or oregano because dried have more punch than fresh. Both herbs are very easy to dry on a screen or tied together and hung upside-down in a warm, dry location.

pests and diseases

Mint: Verticillium wilt, Rust, Aphids, Loopers, Leafrollers, Slugs & Snails

Oregano: Root rot, Fungal disease, Spider mites, Aphids, Leaf miners

AMANDA THOMSEN

If you ask a gardening friend for a division of their mint plant, they will give you some. I promise. Tell them I sent you.

DID YOU KNOW?

Mint was a favorite herb of earlier cultures. In 1568, the English herbalist John Gerard wrote that the aroma of mint "rejoiceth the heart of man." This aromatic herb was strewn upon dirt floors, sickrooms, and storage areas to freshen the air and repel mice—two really important benefits in those less sanitary times. During the American Revolutionary War, mint tea became a popular drink because it wasn't taxed by the English.

Oregano was said to be a gift from the Greek goddess of beauty and love, Aphrodite. And the herb has remained popular to this day. Incidentally, Cuban oregano and Mexican oregano aren't true oreganos and grow very differently than true oregano.

Fresh Mint Chocolate Chip Ice Cream

2 cups heavy cream

1 cup whole milk

2 cups packed mint leaves, washed and dried (try orange mint or chocolate mint for a twist)

2 large eggs

¾ cup sugar

3 oz. fine-quality semisweet chocolate, chopped

- In a food processor, combine the cream, milk, and mint and process until the mint is finely chopped. In a medium saucepan, add the cream-mint mixture and bring to a simmer. Remove from the heat and cool, about 15 minutes. (This is to enhance the mint flavor.) Beat in the eggs and sugar and cook over medium heat, stirring constantly, until slightly thickened. When the temperature reaches 170°F on a food thermometer, remove from the heat.

- Pour the cream-mint custard through a sieve into a bowl to remove the mint bits. Cover and chill the custard until it's very cold. Freeze it in an ice-cream maker according to the manufacturer's directions. When it's frozen, transfer the ice cream to an airtight container with deep sides and mix in the chocolate. Freeze until firm.

Slow and Low Pot Roast

This is a great recipe for a slow cooker. Do the prep work the night before and start the cooker when you leave for work the next morning. It tastes best when it's been cooked on the lowest setting for the longest time possible.

2–3 pounds bottom round or rump roast
Salt and fresh-ground black pepper to taste
Olive oil
1 yellow onion, sliced
2 carrots, sliced
2 ribs celery, sliced

4 Tbsp. tomato paste
2 tsp. dried oregano
1 Tbsp. dried basil
1 tsp. dried rosemary
1 Tbsp. fennel seeds
5 cloves garlic, peeled and sliced
1/2 cup red wine
3 cups beef stock

- Salt and pepper all sides of the roast. Heat a large pan over medium heat; when it's hot, add the olive oil to coat the bottom. Place the roast in the hot pan, searing all sides. When all sizes are browned, transfer the meat to the slow cooker. If there is any fat remaining in the pan, drain all but 1 tablespoon. Reduce the heat to medium and add the onion, carrots, and celery. Sauté 5 minutes. Add the tomato paste, oregano, basil, rosemary, fennel seeds, and garlic and sauté for 5 minutes. Add the red wine to deglaze the pan and, using a spatula or wooden spoon, scrape any remaining bits off the bottom.

- If you are preparing the recipe in advance, let the ingredients cool. Place the cooled ingredients in a slow cooker, cover, and store in the refrigerator overnight. If you are preparing the recipe to serve immediately, pour the vegetable mixture over the roast and start the slow cooker.

- Add enough beef stock so that the stock fills between one-third to one-half of the way inside the slow cooker. Set the slow cooker timer and dinner will be ready when you get home from work!

New Potatoes and Green Beans
(Shared by Donalyn Ketchum) in Herb Garlic Béchamel

3 pounds small, waxy new potatoes, cut into bite-sized pieces

2 tsp. kosher salt

1½ pounds fresh green beans, ends and strings removed, cut into 2-inch pieces

Béchamel Sauce

3 Tbsp. butter

2 medium garlic cloves, minced

3 Tbsp. all-purpose flour

1½ cups whole milk

½ cup half and half

¼ cup dry white wine

¼ tsp. kosher salt

Few grinds of fresh black pepper

2 Tbsp. fresh basil, chopped

1 tsp. dried oregano

2 tsp. fresh thyme leaves, stripped from the stems

- Place the potatoes in a 3-quart saucepan with the salt, and fill the pan half full with water. Bring the potatoes to a boil; simmer 10 minutes. Add the green beans. Cook another 5 minutes or until the potatoes are done, but not mushy. Drain and pour into a large serving bowl.

- Melt the butter in a medium sauté pan; add the garlic and cook, stirring, about 2 minutes. Stir in the flour and cook another 2 minutes. Combine the milk and half and half and whisk ¼ cup into the flour mixture, mixing thoroughly. Bring the milk-garlic mixture to a simmer. Repeat, adding ¼ cup of the milk mixture at a time and bringing to a simmer, until all the milk mixture is incorporated. Add the wine, salt, pepper, basil, oregano, and thyme. Bring the mixture to a simmer and cook a couple of minutes, stirring constantly. Pour the sauce over the vegetables to serve.

Blender Tabouleh

Blender Tabouleh

1 cup bulgur wheat
½ cup fresh mint, chopped
½ cup fresh parsley, chopped
½ cup extra-virgin olive oil
⅓ cup fresh lemon juice
Pinch of salt
⅔ cup chopped green onions (white and light-green parts only)
1 medium cucumber, seeded and quartered
1 large tomato, seeded and quartered

- Soak the bulgur in cold water for 2 hours (or as directed on the package). Drain well, squeezing out any water. Add the mint, parsley, olive oil, lemon juice, and salt in a food processor; process until roughly chopped. Add the green onion, cucumber, and tomato; process with a few pulses to coarsely chop. In a large bowl, combine the bulgur and the mint-vegetable mixture, and toss well. Cover and chill prior to serving.

 information:// **Nutrition**

Mint's medicinal benefits have been acclaimed since ancient times. In the first century A.D., Pliny encouraged students to wrap mint sprigs around their heads to benefit their minds and delight their souls. The English herbalist Nicholas Culpeper wrote in the seventeenth century, "Mint is an herb that is useful in all disorders of the stomach, as weakness, squeamishness, loss of appetite, pain and vomiting."

More recently, studies have shown peppermint oil can relieve indigestion. But that's not all. A phytonutrient in peppermint called monoterpene has been shown to inhibit the growth of pancreatic, mammary, and liver tumors in animal studies. Plus, the herb contains vitamins C and A, as well as manganese.

The ancient Greeks called oregano *panakes*, meaning "all heal." More recently, studies have shown that oregano is antiseptic, anti-inflammatory, and antiviral. This herb contains a number of compounds that may reduce blood pressure, and it is packed with antioxidants. In fact, oregano had the highest antioxidant activity of any herb examined in a USDA study. Just one tablespoon of fresh oregano contains the same antioxidant activity as one medium-sized apple.

herbs:// **Parsley**

| planting and growing | varieties | produce selection and harvest | preserving |

Parsley isn't as easy to grow as, say, mint or dill, but it's well worth trying because of its flavor, health benefits, and its beauty. Parsley enjoys a moist, well-drained soil and lots of sun. It's considered a biennial but it isn't quite as vigorous its second year. Many people treat parsley as an annual, reserving a plant or two for the following year for seed production.

Parsley can be a bit difficult to germinate and can take quite a while to show the first signs of life. It is not unusual for the first seedlings to take 3 to 4 weeks to start showing. If you are impatient, there are a number of things that can be done to boost the rate and speed of germination. Try pouring boiling water over the seeds and letting them stand overnight in a bowl prior to planting. Or place seeds in a damp paper towel and let them sit in a warm windowsill until they sprout. Parsley can be transplanted as seedlings or direct sown, and it is quite tolerant of cool temperatures.

Though parsley makes a great container plant, it is only a so-so houseplant. For fresh parsley all winter, harvest and freeze this herb for future use.

| planting and growing | varieties | produce selection and harvest | preserving |

There are three types of parsley: **curled, Italian, or Hamburg**. Curled parsley is the curly-leaved variety that has been garnishing plates for years. Italian, or flat leaf, parsley is a very common ingredient in recipes. It has a stronger flavor and adds a burst of fresh flavor when added just before serving a dish. Hamburg parsley is grown for its leaves and roots. It forms a singular root, much like a carrot, and tastes somewhat like a parsnip. The leaves of the plant taste like parsley.

AMANDA THOMSEN

For some reason, parsley is an herb that has a lot of mystical, evil stories about it. It has been associated with death, witches, and the devil. So, of course, I had to grow it . . .

planting and growing	varieties	**produce selection and harvest**	preserving

Both curled and flat leaf parsley are readily available at grocery stores and produce stands in bundles. Choose those that show no brown or slimy spots and look as if they were just cut from the plant.

Harvesting at home is easy; just cut leaves and stems when needed. Be sure to leave enough on the plant for photosynthesis.

DID YOU KNOW?

Parsley is one of a few plants that support the larvae of the Swallowtail butterfly. Parsley is a member of the Umbelliferae family, which also includes Queen Anne's lace and carrots, two other Swallowtail favorites.

planting and growing	varieties	produce selection and harvest	**preserving**

Parsley is an herb that requires having fresh and dried on hand. It can be dried by hanging a bundle upside-down or by drying flat on a screen in a warm, dry place. It can then be crumbled and stored in a jar or zip-top baggie.

Parsley can be stored fresh by putting cleaned, chopped parsley into ice cube tray compartments. Cover with water and freeze. The ice cubes can be popped out of the tray and stored in a zip-top storage bag and used where fresh parsley is required.

TERESA O'CONNER

The best time to add parsley to your recipe is right before serving. We toss a handful of Italian parsley on everything from tabouleh to soups.

pests and diseases
Butterfly larvae

Turkey Noodle Soup

Soups are great for using leftovers of any kind. When you use the leaves of a big bunch of parsley, throw the stems in a baggie in the freezer, and pull them out later to flavor stock.

2 pounds roast turkey (on the bone)

2 large yellow onions, 1 chopped and 1 sliced

1 head garlic, cloves removed, one-half chopped, one-half smashed

8 carrots, 4 chopped, 4 sliced

6 ribs celery, 3 chopped, 3 sliced

6 bay leaves

1 Tbsp. dried thyme

1 Tbsp. dried rosemary

1 Tbsp. dried oregano

1 big bunch fresh parsley

1 big bunch fresh basil

3 leeks, cleaned and sliced (white and light-green parts only)

Olive oil and butter

$\frac{1}{2}$ tsp. dried chipotle pepper flakes

4 oz. bow-tie pasta

Salt and fresh-ground black pepper to taste

Parmigiano-Reggiano cheese

- Place the turkey in a large stockpot and cover with water. Add the chopped onion, smashed garlic, chopped carrots, and chopped celery. Add the bay leaves, thyme, rosemary, oregano, parsley, and basil. Bring the stockpot ingredients to a boil over high heat; reduce the heat to a low boil. Cook for 1 hour, making sure it doesn't boil over.

- Strain the contents and return the stock to the stockpot. Remove the turkey, de-bone, and set aside. Bring the stock back to a boil; lower the heat to a low boil and reduce the stock to half of its original volume. Add the sliced onion and leeks to a pan coated with the olive oil and a bit of butter. Cook over low heat until the onion caramelizes (becomes brown). Once the turkey stock is reduced by one-half, add chopped garlic, the sliced carrots, sliced celery, and chipotle pepper flakes. Simmer until the carrots are tender. Add the pasta and cook according to the package directions. Add the turkey during the last few minutes to reheat. Salt and pepper to taste. Serve with curls of Parmigiano-Reggiano cheese on top.

Turkey Noodle Soup

Chicken Kiev *(vertical tab)*

Chicken Kiev

This dish starts with the making of a compound butter and ends with a delicious, moist, crumb-coated medallion of chicken.

Compound Butter

½ cup fresh flat leaf parsley, chopped

¼ cup fresh chives, chopped

½ cup butter, softened

- Add the parsley and chives to a food processor and process until it forms a paste. Place the butter in a small bowl and add the herbs. Stir to combine well.

4 skinless, boneless chicken breasts, pounded to ⅛-inch thickness

Salt and fresh-ground black pepper to taste

2 eggs

2 cups Panko breadcrumbs

Vegetable oil for frying

- Salt and pepper both sides of the chicken. Place one piece of chicken on a piece of plastic wrap. Add 1 to 2 tablespoons of the compound butter along one side of the chicken, fold in the ends, and roll the chicken very tightly. Secure by wrapping tightly with plastic wrap. Repeat with the remaining 3 chicken breasts. Chill in the refrigerator overnight.

- Prepare two plates or shallow bowls for breading. In one, whisk the eggs and 1 tablespoon water. In the second, add the breadcrumbs. Dip each chicken breast into the egg mix, then the breadcrumbs, coating well. Wrap and refrigerate for 30 minutes, or until the crumbs are dry.

- In a 4-quart saucepan, heat 3 inches of vegetable oil to 300°. Slowly add 2 chicken breasts (to avoid spattering); fry for 15 minutes. When the chicken breasts are firm to the touch, remove them from the oil. Make sure you don't accidentally pierce the chicken. Let them drain on paper towels for a couple of minutes prior to serving.

Pork Churrasco and Chimichurri

Churrasco (pronounced shoo-hash-koo) is an Argentinian term for grilled meat. Chimichurri is a flavorful condiment served alongside many Argentinian meals.

Marinade

1 pound pork tenderloin

3 limes, zest and juice

3 Tbsp. fresh thyme leaves, chopped

4 cloves garlic, smashed

1 small yellow onion, coarsely chopped

Olive oil

Kosher salt and fresh-ground black pepper to taste

- Combine the tenderloin, lime zest, thyme, garlic, onion, olive oil (enough to coat all the ingredients), and salt and pepper to taste in a large zip-top plastic bag. Refrigerate for 1 hour (or longer). Add the lime juice at the last hour of marinating. (If you are only marinating for 1 hour, then add the lime juice with the other ingredients.) Prepare your grill according to the type you have. Grill the tenderloin.

Chimichurri

1 big handful parsley leaves, chopped
2 Tbsp. fresh oregano leaves, chopped
4 cloves garlic, chopped
1 tsp. medium hot paprika
2 Tbsp. red wine vinegar
$\frac{1}{3}$ to $\frac{1}{2}$ cup olive oil
Kosher salt and fresh-ground black pepper to taste

- In a medium bowl, combine the parsley, oregano, garlic, paprika, vinegar, olive
  oil, and salt and pepper to taste. Let stand for 15 minutes to let the flavors infuse.
  Drizzle over the pork tenderloin to serve.

 information:// Nutrition

More than a simple garnish, parsley deserves a prominent place on your plate. This mighty herb won the respect of the ancient Greeks, who used parsley for a variety of medicinal uses. In ancient Rome, parsley was eaten at banquets and made into garlands to counteract strong odors and discourage hangovers.

Even today, parsley leaves are infused into a digestive tonic. The leaves are often eaten raw for healthy skin and fresh breath, as well as tossed into facial steams to soften dry skin.

Incidentally, parsley has more nutrients than many vegetables. One cup of raw parsley has 101 percent of your daily vitamin A requirements and 133 percent of the vitamin C requirements.

Parsley also contains folate, iron, and other important vitamins and minerals.

A multivitamin in an herb, parsley has powerful flavonoids and volatile oil components as well. One of these volatile oils, myristicin, has been shown in animal tests to inhibit tumor formation, particularly in the lungs. Parsley is a natural diuretic, which has long been used by German and Chinese herbalists to control high blood pressure.

herbs:// Rosemary

planting and growing | varieties | produce selection and harvest | preserving

Depending on where you live, rosemary can be a fussy annual or a massive evergreen. Native to the Mediterranean, rosemary thrives on heat, full sun, and a well-drained soil. This is one plant that does not like to be moved, so if you live in an area where it overwinters, make sure the place you plant it is the place you want it to stay.

Rosemary can be grown in containers, but it is somewhat of a challenge. The roots need good drainage, so using a planting mix that has a good amount of sand, gravel, or perlite will bolster your chances. It will need consistent moisture—not too much and not too little. As the herb grows larger, it is important to "pot up" to the next size, giving the roots room to expand.

This is another herb that is not too fond of indoor growing. Although it often fails as a houseplant, you can try putting it in a very sunny but cool place (around 60°) for the winter.

Growing rosemary from seed can be problematic, with the result often being poor germination or sickly seedlings. It's much easier to buy a plant from a garden center or farmers' market. If you feel particularly adventurous, grow it from cuttings. Snip the top three inches from one of the branches. Remove the leaves from the lower inch and dip the stem in hormone rooting powder. Place in a moistened growing mix that has really great drainage. Mist fairly regularly, keeping in mind that this is a plant that neither likes too much nor too little water. Once the cuttings have rooted (within 2 to 3 weeks), transplant to a container.

planting and growing | **varieties** | produce selection and harvest | preserving

Rosemary comes in a variety of forms from giant shrubs to cascading plants. It is easy to find one that fits well in your garden.
Upright, Shrub: 'Blue Spire', 'Tuscan Blue', 'Dutch Mill'
Upright, Herb Bed: 'Collingwood Ingram' (aka 'Wood' or 'Majorca'), 'Golden Rain' (yellow variegation), 'Majorca', 'Pink Flowered'
Trailing: 'Mrs. Howard's Creeping', 'Prostrate (aka 'Recumbant')
Cold Hardy: 'Mrs. Reed's Dark Blue' and 'Gorizia' (to 15°), 'Dutch Mill' (to -5°)

AMANDA THOMSEN

Because rosemary is so temperamental as a houseplant, I have always called it "the plant of death." As it slowly dies, it drops needles all over your floor, which makes for a great air freshener when it's vacuumed!

| planting and growing | varieties | **produce selection and harvest** | preserving |

Rosemary is a very pungent herb and little is needed to have a big impact. Both farmers' markets and grocery stores sell fresh rosemary. Look for deep-green needles with silvery undersides and no browning or other discoloration. It is also available as a dried herb in grocery stores. Since its flavor is so strong, buying this herb dried may even be preferable to some people. Look for it in the spice aisle.

If you're growing rosemary, you can harvest bits and pieces as you like since you only need small pieces at a time. Try using the long, straight, woody branches as shish kebab skewers.

pests and diseases

Mealy bugs; Powdery mildew

| planting and growing | varieties | produce selection and harvest | **preserving** |

Since rosemary enjoys a good pruning, you can kill two birds with one stone by shaping your plant and drying the cuttings for a long winter's use of the herb. If the clippings are small, dry them on a screen in a warm, dry place. If they are longer pieces, you can hang them upside-down to dry.

If you want the flavor of fresh rosemary all year, wash your harvest and dry very well. Put your bounty into zip-top storage bags and freeze. These can keep for over a year.

DID YOU KNOW?

Cuttings from your rosemary plant are a great addition to the grill. If you are using a charcoal grill, just cut a few sprigs and place them directly on the fire. For a gas grill, create a foil pouch, and add some rosemary and a bit of water. Close the pouch and cut slits in the top. Place the packet on the grill grate and let the smoking begin!

Rosemary Refried Black Beans

Traditionally, refried beans are made with pinto beans, but many types taste yummy made this way, including black beans.

8 oz. dry black beans, soaked overnight (or 8 oz. canned beans,
  rinsed and drained)

2 bay leaves

1 twig rosemary

1 Tbsp. garlic powder*

Pinch of hot chili pepper flakes

Salt and fresh-ground black pepper to taste

$\frac{1}{2}$ to 1 cup chicken stock or water

Olive oil (or, if you are feeling daring, 1 Tbsp. bacon grease)

1 large yellow onion, chopped

Cotija cheese

- If you used dried beans, drain the soaking water. Place the beans in a medium saucepan. Add the bay leaves, rosemary, garlic powder, chili flakes, salt, and pepper; add the chicken stock or water. Cook over low heat for 30 minutes, letting the flavors infuse and the beans soften.

- Coat the bottom of a sauté pan with the olive oil (and/or bacon grease if you're using it). Add the onion. Cook the onions over medium heat until they have caramelized (become brown and soft). Remove the bay leaves and rosemary and add the beans to the sauté pan. Add more oil to the sauté pan if needed to prevent the beans from sticking. Cook 10 minutes, stirring occasionally. Use a potato masher or immersion blender to mash the beans. Stir again and check the consistency; it should be similar to thick oatmeal. Serve topped with the Cotija cheese, a wonderfully flavorful Mexican cheese.

(*Using garlic powder will ensure that you don't burn any garlic when cooking the beans.)

Rosemary Bread

(Shared by Jessica Hibbard Elenstar. This is adapted from a recipe by Junie Ely,
a family friend from Dimock, PA.)

1 ¼ cup skim milk
¼ cup olive oil
¼ cup honey
1 package (¼ oz.) rapid-rise dry yeast
1 tsp. salt
2 Tbsp. fresh rosemary, chopped
1 cup whole wheat flour
3 cups unbleached all-purpose flour

- Mix the milk, olive oil, and honey in a small saucepan over medium-low heat on the stovetop. Let the milk-honey mixture get fairly hot, but avoid curdling the milk. Remove from the heat and cool until it's no longer hot, just warm.

- In a medium mixing bowl, combine the yeast, salt, rosemary, whole wheat flour, and 2 cups of the all-purpose flour.

- Add the milk-honey liquid to the mixing bowl and beat until the dry ingredients are combined. Add the remaining 1 cup of all-purpose flour slowly (this can be done with a mixer and dough hook).

- Lightly coat a baking sheet with olive oil. Oil the top of the dough, place it on the baking sheet, and cover with plastic wrap and a towel. Let the dough rise until doubled in size.

- Punch down the dough, and divide in half. Make 3 ropes from each half and braid them into 2 loaves. Lightly coat a second baking sheet with olive oil. Cover both loaves with plastic wrap and a towel and let them rise until doubled in size, about 1 hour.

■ Preheat the oven to 375°. Remove the plastic wrap and towels. Bake each loaf 15 to 20 minutes. The bread is done when it turns golden brown on top and sounds hollow when tapped.

■ If you keep this bread in a sealed container or bag it will stay fresh for a few days. The honey acts as a natural preservative, so it doesn't become stale as quickly as home-baked bread made with sugar.

Rosemary-Infused Vinegar

Rosemary-Infused Vinegar

1 quart-sized sterilized container and lid
4–5 sprigs rosemary, well washed and dry
4 cups vinegar (any type), boiled

- Crush the rosemary a bit and place in the sterilized container. Add the hot vinegar within one-half inch of the top. Loosely add a lid to the container and allow the vinegar to cool. Refrigerate 1 to 2 weeks before using to allow for the flavor to develop.

 information:// **Nutrition**

Don't forget rosemary the next time you cook. This herb has many health benefits worth remembering, and has been used for culinary and medicinal purposes since the earliest times.

For centuries, rosemary was considered a brain tonic and a symbol for remembrance. Ancient Greeks wore sprigs in their hair to refresh their memory. Rosemary sprigs were tossed on gravesites in memory of the deceased. Now, science is learning that rosemary contains antioxidants and other compounds that may help prevent Alzheimer's disease.

That's not all. Rosemary contains more than 24 antioxidants that may prevent heart disease and various types of cancers.

Several studies have shown rosemary also has powerful phenolics, flavonoids, and rosmarinic acid. These antioxidants demonstrated anti-carcinogenic and anti-inflammatory properties in animal tests, and may reduce the risk of breast and skin cancers.

With all these health benefits, it's little wonder that Shakespeare wrote, "There's rosemary, that's for remembrance: pray you love, remember."

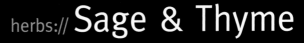

herbs:// **Sage & Thyme**

| planting and growing | varieties | produce selection and harvest | preserving |

Sage and thyme are tough, perennial herbs that like it hot and dry. They do best with well-drained soil, full sun, and infrequent watering. Both are a little tricky and time consuming to start from seed and make good candidates for starting them as cuttings/divisions from a neighbor or purchasing transplants from the local garden center. Take cuttings from either plant in spring. Snip off 3 inches of new, soft growth. Place the cuttings in damp sand and wait for root development. It should take about two weeks. Divisions are also best in early spring. Dig and gently divide into 2 to 4 clumps, replanting immediately. Though these plants love warm, dry climates, it is important to water well until they are established.

In many climates, these herbs are perennials that don't die back completely over winter. If they aren't perennial in your area, freezing is a good way to preserve that fresh taste. Sage and thyme are really great when dried. Both retain their flavor, though it changes noticeably. If you have both fresh and dried on hand, you double your flavor options!

| planting and growing | varieties | produce selection and harvest | preserving |

Thyme comes in lots of varieties, many of which are easily found at your local nurseries and farmers' markets. Keep in mind that the creeping varieties of thyme that are sold as groundcovers smell wonderful, but have little taste.
Standard: 'English' or 'Common', 'Turkish', 'Provencal'
Scents/Flavors: 'Lemon', 'Oregano', 'Tangerine', 'Lavender', 'Orange Balsam'
Sage has fewer varieties, but most are equally easy to find.
Standard: 'Garden Sage', 'Tri-Color', 'Berggarten', 'Dwarf Garden Sage'
Scents/Flavors: 'Greek', 'Grape', 'Pineapple'

planting and growing | varieties | **produce selection and harvest** | preserving

Fresh sage and thyme can be found at the grocery store and at farmers' markets. Make sure the leaves look fresh, not withered, and that there are no brown edges or spots. Keep refrigerated for freshness.

These two herbs can also be found in dried form on the spice aisle. Generally, purchasing them on dried form makes them more affordable and prolongs their shelf life.

In the home garden, sage and thyme can be harvested once the plants are about 4 inches tall. Bring them inside, and if not using immediately, store in a baggie with a damp paper towel.

AMANDA THOMSEN

I love to put a huge bundle of fresh sage inside my Thanksgiving turkey. The leaves perfume the meat and add lots of flavor. I think my turkey enjoys it, too.

pests and diseases

Thyme: Botrytis; Root rot; Aphids; Spider mites
Sage: Aphids

DID YOU KNOW?

Clary sage reaches up to three feet in height and is often grown for its ornamental value. People are said to either love or hate its strong, pungent aroma. Words that have been used to describe the scent include "sweaty," "spicey," and "hay-like."

planting and growing | varieties | produce selection and harvest | **preserving**

Sage is easy to dry. Clip off a "bouquet" and hang it upside-down. You can also place sage in a single layer on a screen to dry. Be sure it is kept in a warm, dry space to prevent mold.

Thyme can be dried in a similar manner. Clip several long branches and secure them with a rubber band, then hang upside-down to dry. Thyme leaves can also be removed from the twigs and spread in a single layer to dry.

Freeze sage and thyme by washing your harvest and making sure it's thoroughly dry. Then toss into zip-top freezer bags and freeze. Use them as fresh whenever you like!

Squash Sausage Soup

(Shared by Donalyn Ketchum)

Olive oil

1 pound spicy Italian sausage

12 oz. button mushrooms, thickly sliced

1 large onion, coarsely chopped

3 ribs celery, coarsely chopped

¾ cup dry white wine

5 cups chicken stock

5 cups cooked, pureéd winter squash (can use frozen winter squash)

2 large cloves garlic, finely chopped

5 4-inch sprigs fresh thyme

4 4-inch sprigs fresh oregano

4 Tbsp. fresh parsley, chopped

6 oz. reduced fat cream cheese, at room temperature

1 cup half and half or light cream

Salt and fresh-ground black pepper to taste

Additional thyme leaves for garnish

- Add 2 tablespoons of the olive oil to a heavy stockpot and heat to just under the smoking point. Add the Italian sausage and brown well. Remove the sausage and set aside.
- In the same stockpot, brown the mushrooms, about 5 minutes. Remove and set aside. Add olive oil (if needed) to the stockpot with the onion and celery. Reduce the heat to medium and sauté until the onion and celery become translucent. Deglaze the pan with the wine and cook a couple of minutes to reduce the wine a bit. Add the stock and cover. Lower the heat and simmer 20 minutes.
- Stir in the squash. Slice the sausage and add with the mushrooms. Add the garlic, thyme, and oregano. Allow the mixture to come back to a simmer.
- Place the cream cheese in a small bowl and add small amounts of the warm soup, stirring it completely until it is very smooth. Stir the warmed cream cheese into the soup and add the half and half. Bring the soup back to serving temperature but do not allow it to boil (or it might curdle). Salt and pepper to taste. Top each serving with a sprinkle of thyme leaves.

Pesto, Meatballs and Pasta, 2.0

Meatballs

1 pound ground pork

1–1 ½ cups Panko breadcrumbs

⅓ cup shredded Parmesan cheese

1 egg

1 Tbsp. fennel seeds

1 Tbsp. fresh basil, chopped

1 tsp. dried sage

1 tsp. fresh thyme, chopped

1 tsp. fresh rosemary, chopped

Red pepper flakes to taste

¼ cup white wine or chicken stock, plus more for deglazing

Salt and fresh-ground black pepper to taste

Olive oil

- In a medium bowl, combine the pork, breadcrumbs, Parmesan cheese, egg, fennel seeds, basil, sage, thyme, rosemary, red pepper, wine, and salt and pepper to taste. Squish together with your hands until just combined. Divide and roll into balls about the size of a golf ball.

- Coat the bottom of a heavy, enamel-coated cast-iron pan with olive oil; make sure the pan is hot before adding the meatballs. Brown the meatballs and cook until center is no longer pink. Remove once they are browned and drain on paper towels. Deglaze the pan (scraping up any bits in the bottom of the pan) with a small amount of wine or stock.

Pesto

2 cups fresh basil
1 tsp. fresh thyme, chopped
1 cup shredded Parmesan cheese
$\frac{1}{2}$ cup pistachios, toasted chopped
4 garlic cloves
$\frac{1}{3}$-$\frac{1}{2}$ cup extra virgin olive oil

- Add the basil, thyme, Parmesan cheese, pistachios, and garlic to a food processor; pulse to create a paste. Continue processing while adding the olive oil through the feed tube until the desired consistency is reached.

Pasta

- Prepare your favorite pasta according to the package directions. Drain well.

- Return the meatballs to the pan with the deglazing liquid; add the pesto and the pasta. Stir to combine. Serve immediately.

Tempura Sage Leaves

Tempura is so much easier to make than it seems it should be!

Batter

1 egg

1 cup flour

1 cup very cold water

- In a medium bowl, mix the egg, flour, and water.

1 cup sage leaves, stems removed

Vegetable oil for frying

- Dip the sage into the tempura batter and fry in a medium sauté pan containing 1 inch of the oil on medium-high. Fry 2 minutes. Drain and eat right away!

information:// Nutrition

Show your wisdom by eating sage regularly. Sage's official name, *Salvia officinalis*, derives from the Latin word *salvare*, which means "to heal and save." In earlier times, folks concerned about their health heeded this advice: "He that would live for aye must eat sage in May." Even today, a "sage" is considered a wise person.

Sage helps in the digestion of rich fatty meats and stuffing, which is why the herb is such a natural at Thanksgiving dinners. It is also used by herbalists to combat diarrhea and soothe coughs and colds. Traditionally, sage leaves were added to hair rinses to darken the color.

It's little wonder the herb is so respected, as it has a number of volatile oils, flavonoids, and phenolic acids with important health benefits.

These antioxidants may help inflammatory conditions like rheumatoid arthritis. Sage may also boost brainpower; one study found it a strong memory enhancer. A Swiss study found dried sage may even reverse bone loss.

Make time for thyme, too. The herb's powerful antiseptic and preservative qualities led the ancient Egyptians to use it for embalming. Even today, this herb is used by some to protect important papers from mold.

Just 2 tablespoons of fresh thyme provides 75 percent of daily vitamin C needs. The herb also contains vitamin A, iron, calcium, and other nutrients.

fruit:// **Apple**

| planting and growing | varieties | produce selection and harvest | preparation methods |

Tree fruits have a reputation for being difficult to maintain, particularly if you are using organic methods. They certainly aren't the only edibles that need a healthy amount of attention, but the sheer size of a full-size apple tree makes proper care seem daunting. Unfortunately, this has resulted in many home gardeners avoiding tree fruits completely.

The good news is that dwarf varieties are on the market. Apple hybrids have been scaled down and some can even be grown in containers. Columnar varieties produce one main trunk and no branches, making harvest a breeze. Because growing apples can be a complex task, this chapter will specifically deal with mini-dwarf selections.

Mini-dwarf is a designation that can mean a multitude of sizes, so make sure it is a good fit for your yard. It is also helpful to purchase a self-pollinating variety. Apples also need a certain amount of "chill hours," or time spent at 45 degrees or less. Choose a type that fits your climate.

Apples need full sun and well-drained soil. In addition, they are heavy feeders, so plan to add compost each year, as well as a slow-release organic fertilizer. If you are growing it in a container, use at least a 15-gallon pot. Regardless of where the apple tree is planted, if it is a dwarf it will need to be permanently staked. The roots of the small varieties are shallow and often can't serve as an adequate anchor.

Remove the blooms from new trees for the first three years to direct energy toward growth. Prune to a shape that allows air and light to easily penetrate. Always eliminate suckers or growth that occurs along the bottom 12 to 18 inches of the tree and any vertical sprouts on branches.

| planting and growing | varieties | produce selection and harvest | preparation methods |

Make sure you choose a variety that fits your region, as well as the allotted site space. Also, look for varieties that are resistant to disease and come from a reputable grower.

Mini-Dwarf: 'Akane' (scab and mildew resistant), 'Enterprise' (fire blight, scab, cedar apple rust, and mildew resistant)

Columnar: 'Golden Sentinel', 'Scarlet Sentinel' (both have good disease resistance)

planting and growing

varieties

produce selection and harvest

preparation methods

When purchasing apples, look for firm fruits with good color. Check for bruising and either avoid them or buy several and use for applesauce. Apples in the store are already ripe, but will continue to ripen once you bring them home. Overripe apples are grainy and soft—again, good candidates for applesauce.

Depending upon variety, apples can be harvested from July to October. By choosing two that ripen at different times, you can extend your harvest. Also, consider choosing at least one type that produces apples that are good for storage. After harvest, some varieties will hold all the way to the following spring.

There are a couple of ways to tell if apples are ripe enough to harvest. Color offers a clue as do changes in size and the number of days from bloom. As the apples mature, pick one and slice it open. The seeds should be brown and the flesh white. A taste should reveal crisp, sweet (or tart for some apples) flavor. If it is bitter or starchy, the apple isn't fully developed. They will ripen off the tree, but they must already be well on their way to maturity.

pests and diseases

Fire blight; Apple scab; Black rot; Cedar apple rust; Powdery mildew; Apple maggots; Codling moths; Plum curculio; Aphids; Scale; Tarnished plant bugs

JEAN ANN VAN KREVELEN

There are few plants that drive me to consider using non-organic pesticides but tree fruits are at the top of that list. The creepy crawly apple maggots are enough to send any sane person right over the edge. If you aren't committed to pest and disease management, it is better to buy apples from your local farmers' markets or groceries. Even the mini-dwarfs will need a pest- and disease-management plan.

preserving

Canning; Freezing; Dehydrating;
Vacuum packing

| planting and growing | varieties | produce selection and harvest | preparation methods |

Apples can be used in a number of ways, most traditionally as a sweet ingredient.

- **Jams/Compotes:** As with most fruits, apples lend themselves to the creation of fantastic preserves. In addition to yummy compotes, apples can be made into apple butter. This tasty spread has the flavor of apples and the texture of butter.
- **Dried:** Apples can easily be dried and added to cereals, baked goods, and snack mixes.
- **Fresh:** They can be added fresh to any number of recipes. Try adding them to chicken or tuna salad for extra crunch.
- **Pies/Fillings:** The apple plays a significant role in America's favorite desserts. It is the star in pies, pastries, and cakes. Its sweet, crisp nature makes apples a cinch to pair with other fruits in a variety of recipes.
- **Sauces:** Homemade applesauce is so easy to make. If you have an abundance of apples, this is one way to use them quickly. This is also a great candidate for home preserving. When fall harvest hits, making big batches of applesauce for canning is a fast method of storing all of that apple-y goodness!
- **Juice:** Apple juice and apple cider are two of the most common and well-loved juices in the United States. Making homemade juice requires a juicer or a press, and cider requires fermentation. Nonetheless, apples still make a great smoothie component; just coarsely chop an apple and add it to your favorite berry smoothie to boost the fiber and nutritional content.
- **Baked:** Baked apples are hands down the easiest dessert to make. They are terrific for ushering in the cool nights of fall.

DID YOU KNOW?

Many people dislike overripe apples due to the mealy or grainy texture. If you find yourself with a handful of such apples, peel and core them. Slice them and pop them into a dehydrator. They taste fantastic and feel just like any other dried apple...great for snacking!

Blue Cheese Baked Apples

Blue Cheese Baked Apples

$\frac{1}{2}$ cup chopped, toasted pecans

$\frac{1}{4}$ cup dried currants

$\frac{1}{4}$ cup dried cranberries

4 large baking apples (such as Courtland, Pippin, Braeburn, Gravenstein), well-washed and cored (take care not to pierce the bottoms of the apples)

$\frac{1}{4}$ – $\frac{1}{2}$ cup cubed or crumbled blue cheese (such as Roquefort, Stilton, or Cambozola)

1 cup boiling water

- Preheat the oven to 375°. Combine the pecans, currants, and cranberries in a small bowl; mix well. Fill the apple cavities with the pecan-fruit mixture. Top with a cube or spoonful of the blue cheese.

- Place the stuffed apples in a small baking dish and add the boiling water to the pan. Bake 20 minutes, until the apples are softened but not falling apart.

Apple, Fennel, and Goat Cheese Dressing

3 cups cubed whole grain bread
2 cups cubed sourdough bread
Olive oil
1 fennel bulb, thinly sliced
1 medium onion, chopped
3 ribs celery, chopped
3 cloves garlic, minced
1 Tbsp. dried sage
½ tsp. dried thyme or 3 sprigs
  fresh thyme
3 bay leaves

2 Tbsp. fennel seeds
Salt and fresh-ground black pepper
  to taste
1 large, crisp, tart apple (such as
  Granny Smith), chopped
1 handful fresh flat leaf parsley,
  chopped
½ to 1 cup chicken or turkey stock
4 Tbsp. unsalted butter, melted
4 oz. goat cheese, crumbled
2 Tbsp. fresh chives, chopped

■ Preheat the oven to 375º. Place the whole grain and sourdough bread cubes on baking sheets, drizzle well with the olive oil, and sprinkle with salt. Toss to coat. Bake 8 minutes; remove from the oven and give the bread a toss. Bake 5 more minutes or until the bread cubes are crispy and look like croutons. Remove the bread cubes from the oven. Reduce the oven temperature to 350º.

■ Place a large sauté pan over medium heat. When the pan is hot, add olive oil to coat the bottom. Add the fennel, onion, celery, garlic, sage, thyme, bay leaves, fennel seeds, and salt and pepper. Sauté until the vegetables start to soften. Add the apple and sauté 2 to 3 minutes. Remove from the heat.

■ In a large bowl, combine the toasted bread cubes, fennel-apple mixture (remove bay leaves and thyme sprigs if fresh thyme was used), and the parsley. Add ½ cup of the stock and the butter. Season again with salt and pepper. Add stock until the dressing is well moistened, but not soupy. Adjust seasoning to taste. Pour the dressing into a large baking pan and dot with the goat cheese. Bake at 350º for 20 to 30 minutes or until the cheese is melted and dressing has a crusty, brown top. Garnish with the chives.

Applejack Chicken

Olive oil

3 slices maple flavored bacon, cut into ½-inch sections

1 large yellow onion, diced

3 carrots, chopped

2 Tbsp. fennel seeds

2 cups apple juice

4 bay leaves

1 whole chicken, giblets removed, washed and patted dry

1 baking apple (such as Golden Delicious), several thin slices; remainder coarsely chopped

Salt and fresh-ground black pepper to taste

toothpicks

- Preheat the oven to 400°. Place a Dutch oven on the stove over medium-high heat; add a drizzle of olive oil. Add the bacon and cook until crisp. Remove the bacon pieces and drain on paper towels. Add the onion, carrots, and fennel seeds. Sauté for a few minutes. Add the apple juice and bay leaves. Let the mixture simmer while you are preparing the chicken.

- Separate the skin of the chicken breast from the meat by gently sliding your hand between the two. Try not to break the skin. Position a few of the apple slices and the bacon under the skin. Once that is complete, pull the skin closed, anchoring with a toothpick or two. Put the remaining apple pieces in the cavity of the chicken.

- Stir the vegetable mixture in the Dutch oven and place the chicken on top. Add enough water to bring the fluid level up to the middle of the drumsticks. Bring to a boil on the stovetop. Then cover and bake for 45 minutes.

- After 45 minutes, remove the cover and baste the chicken with its juices. Bake an additional 45 minutes uncovered, basting every 15 minutes. The cooking time will vary depending upon the size of the chicken. Test internal temperature using a meat thermometer; the meat in the thickest part of the thigh should register 165° to 170° to indicate doneness and the chicken juices should run clear.

- When the chicken is done, remove it from the Dutch oven and place on a serving platter. Place the Dutch oven on the stove over medium-high heat to reduce the cooking liquid for a sauce; strain. If you like, you can pour the reduction liquid into a gravy separator, which will help remove excess fat. Serve the chicken with the applejack reduction sauce drizzled over the top.

Applejack Chicken

Easy Applesauce Bundt Cake

1¼ cups whole wheat flour
1¼ cups unbleached all-purpose
 flour
½ tsp. baking powder
1½ tsp. baking soda
1 tsp. salt
1 tsp. ground cinnamon
1 tsp. ground ginger

½ tsp. ground cloves
½ cup butter
1 cup brown sugar
1 Tbsp. unsulfured molasses
1 egg
½ cup apple juice
16 oz. applesauce

- Preheat the oven to 350º. Grease and flour a 12-cup bundt pan (or substitute a 13 x 9-inch pan; baking time will vary). In a small bowl, combine the whole wheat flour, all-purpose flour, baking powder, soda, salt, cinnamon, ginger, and cloves. Whisk to remove any lumps.

- In a large mixing bowl, combine the butter and brown sugar and beat until thoroughly combined. Add the molasses and egg and mix well. Pour in the dry ingredients, apple juice, and applesauce. Beat until just combined.

- Bake 55 to 65 minutes or until a knife inserted comes out clean. Drizzle the Citrus Glaze over the cake while the cake is still warm.

Citrus Glaze
2 cups powdered sugar
1 orange, zest and juice

- In a small bowl, combine the powdered sugar and the orange juice and zest. Mix well.

Almost Applesauce

Almost Applesauce

4 apples, peeled, cored, and sliced
2 Tbsp. butter
2 Tbsp. spiced rum
1/3 cup brown sugar
1/2-inch piece of ginger, peeled
   and grated

1 tsp. ground cinnamon
1/4 tsp. freshly grated nutmeg
1/4 tsp. ground cloves
1/2 tsp. salt

- Sauté the apples in the butter for 2 to 3 minutes. Add the spiced rum, brown sugar, ginger, cinnamon, nutmeg, cloves, and salt. Mix well. Serve the apples while they still retain their shape, but are fairly soft. If you overcook the apples, just pour them into a blender or food processor for instant applesauce. (Hint: Leaving the peels on red-skinned apples that will be blended for applesauce makes pink applesauce!)

 information:// Nutrition

"An apple a day keeps the doctor away" is an old saying that's actually true.

Apples may not have the highest nutrient levels, especially when compared with other produce, but these high-fiber fruits have traces of almost every nutrient. The real health value of apples, however, is the high levels of phytochemicals that function as disease-fighting antioxidants.

Apples have the second highest levels of antioxidants among the most commonly eaten fruits. The antioxidant activity of one serving of apples is equivalent to about 1500 mg. of vitamin C—considerably more than your daily needs.

These antioxidants may prevent some cancers. Phytochemicals in apple peels inhibited colon cancer cell reproduction in one study by 43 percent. Mayo Clinic research discovered quercetin—another antioxidant in apples— inhibited the growth of prostate cancer cells. Several studies have associated apples with reducing lung cancer risk.

That's not all. Eating apples may also help prevent cardiovascular disease, asthma, and diabetes.

planting and growing | varieties | produce selection and harvest | preparation methods

Blueberries are one of the easiest fruit crops to grow as long as their two primary requirements are met. First and most important, they must have acidic soil. Some gardeners will take a soil sample to their local county extension office to have it analyzed, and will then apply the recommended soil conditioners. However, most soil is not likely to be as acidic as blueberries prefer. Try mulching with a blend of compost and naturally acidic materials such as shredded oak leaves and pine needles to reduce the pH of your soil.

Second, blueberries need good drainage. Though they like a decent amount of water, they do not like to have their feet wet all the time. If your soil is full of clay, add materials such as compost and sand to improve aeration and drainage.

Their growing requirements are relatively few. Ensure the shrubs are well watered the first year and during fruit set in following years. Plant and prune to ensure blueberries are in full sun. They will tolerate some shade but will be most productive in full sun. Feed them with an organic fertilizer formulated for acid-loving plants at the time of bud formation and again in midsummer.

Previous wisdom has recommended to remove blooms from newly planted shrubs for the first three years, in order to give the plant time and energy to establish a healthy root system. However, many farmers report that early harvest has no negative effect at all.

planting and growing | **varieties** | produce selection and harvest | preparation methods

There are three types of blueberries: low bush, high bush, and rabbit eye. Low bush varieties grow low to the ground, some low enough to be groundcovers. High bush blueberries can grow to 7 to 8 feet tall, with a spread of 3 to 4 feet. Prune high bush varieties after fruiting to keep the berries at a reasonable height for harvest. Rabbit eye blueberry is a variety that is particularly suited to climates with warm summers and few chill hours.

Low Bush: 'Top Hat' is particularly good for containers and 'Brunswick' doubles as a groundcover

High Bush: 'Patriot', 'Bluecrop', and 'Nelson'

Rabbit Eye: 'Sharpblue', 'Jubilee', and 'South Moon'

pests and diseases

Botrytis; Stem canker; Blueberry maggot; Cherry fruitworm; Mummy berry

| planting and growing | varieties | **produce selection and harvest** | preparation methods |

If you are purchasing blues at the farmers' markets or grocery stores, look for deep-blue berries that have a silvery coating. This coating is a protective barrier for the fruit and, once removed, the berry starts to lose freshness. Also, give the container a little jiggle to make sure the berries move around easily. They should not be mushy or sticky.

Beyond that, there is only one way to know if they are ripe, and that is by taste. Many farmers' markets and some grocery stores will let you taste the berries prior to purchase; so give them a try before you buy!

Harvesting blueberries at home is very simple. The fruits are ready to harvest about a week after

DID YOU KNOW?

Blueberries are one of very few fruits native to North America, which continues to be the largest producer of them in the world. Native Americans harvested the berries and used them in teas, as seasonings, and as a preservative.

JEAN ANN VAN KREVELEN

After hearing horror stories about the challenges of growing fruit at home, many gardeners have avoided it all together. If you are one of those gardeners, give blueberries a try. They are super simple to grow and, once established, they will provide years and years of fruity goodness!

they turn blue. The ripe berries will easily fall off the stem when picking. To be sure they are ready, snag one off the shrub and pop it in your mouth. If it is really tart, it's not quite ready. Wait until the berry has had time to sweeten before you start harvesting in earnest.

| planting and growing | varieties | produce selection and harvest | **preparation methods** |

Blueberries can be used in a number of ways, in both savory and sweet dishes. Here are a few of my favorites:

- **Jams/Jellies/Compotes:** As with most fruits, blueberries lend themselves to the creation of fantastic preserves. These are very easy to make and taste great on any number of foods, such as toast, ice cream, Belgian waffles . . . even as a layer in a trifle.

preserving

Canning; Freezing; Dehydrating;
Vacuum packing

- **Dried:** Blueberries can easily be dried and added to cereals, baked goods, and snack mixes. Dried berries can also be ground and used as a rub for poultry, pork, and fish.
- **Fresh:** They can be added to any number of fresh food recipes. In addition to salads of all kinds, they are terrific in smoothies, milkshakes, or even eaten right off the bush!
- **Sauces:** Since these berries are both sweet and tart, they lend themselves to fantastic sauces for poultry, pork, and fish. Used as the foundation for a basting sauce, blueberries are fantastic on all kinds of grilled foods.
- **Juice:** Blueberry juice is incredibly nutritious and tasty. If you prefer a smooth texture, whir the berries in a blender, then strain. The juice also makes a great backdrop for a variety of mixed drinks that utilize light colored alcohol, such as vodka, rum, and gin. And, don't forget to add a splash to homemade salad dressings to perk up standard vinaigrettes.
- **Flavoring for Grains:** A handful of dried blueberries is an amazing flavor agent for couscous, quinoa, rice, or bulgur. Fresh berries can also be added at the last minute as a flavor boost in grain dishes.

Blueberry Ginger Muffins

6 Tbsp. unsalted butter, melted
1 cup packed light brown sugar, plus extra for topping
1/2 cup milk
1 large egg
1 1/2 tsp. baking powder

1 tsp. ground cinnamon
1/2 tsp. salt
1 1/2 cups all-purpose flour
1/4 cup chopped crystallized ginger
1 1/2 cups blueberries

- Preheat the oven to 350° and prepare a muffin tin with paper liners or nonstick spray.

- Mix the butter, brown sugar, milk, and egg until well blended. Add the baking powder, cinnamon, and salt; mix well. Gently fold in the flour until just combined. Very gently fold in the ginger and blueberries. Divide the batter among the prepared muffin cups. Top each muffin with 1/4 teaspoon of brown sugar. Bake 25 minutes or until a knife or tester inserted comes out clean. (This recipe makes 9 large or 12 smaller muffins.)

Blueberry Ginger Muffins

Blueberry Chicken Salad

3 chicken breasts, skin on

Olive oil for coating, plus 1 Tbsp.

Good-quality sea salt and fresh-ground black pepper to taste

4 oz. Greek-style yogurt (can substitute plain yogurt)

2 Tbsp. white wine vinegar

1 tsp. finely chopped fresh lavender leaves (can substitute herbes de Provence)

1 small apple, peeled and chopped

$\frac{1}{2}$ red onion, finely diced

1 cup fresh blueberries, washed and dried

$\frac{1}{4}$ cup roasted chopped almonds

Lettuce for serving

- Preheat the oven to 400°. Coat the skin on the chicken breasts with the olive oil, salt, and pepper and roast for 30 minutes, or until no pink remains. Cool. In a small bowl, whisk the 1 Tbsp. of the olive oil, yogurt, vinegar, lavender, 1 tsp. of the salt, and 1 tsp. of the black pepper. Add the apple and stir to prevent browning. Add the onion, blueberries, and almonds; mix well. Remove the skin from the chicken breasts and discard (or freeze for use in making stock). Separate the chicken from the bone and cut into 1-inch pieces. Add the chicken to the yogurt-blueberry mixture; stir gently to combine. Serve on a bed of crisp lettuce.

Blueberry-Basted Grilled Pork

1 cup fresh or frozen blueberries
2 dried bay leaves
1 tsp. sugar (adjust according to sweetness of berries)
1 tsp. thyme
¼ cup of water
1 tsp. sea salt
1 tsp. fresh-ground black pepper
Olive oil
4–6 bone-in, 1-inch-thick pork chops

- Prepare the grill according to the type you have, bringing to medium-high heat. Make the basting sauce by combining the blueberries, bay leaves, sugar, thyme, ¼ cup water, salt, and pepper in a medium saucepan over medium-low heat. Bring to a simmer; allow to reduce by one-half; set aside one-half of the sauce.

- Prepare the pork chops for grilling by drizzling with olive oil, salt, and pepper. Sear both sides for 2 minutes over a very hot grill, moving the chops to indirect heat to finish cooking. About 5 minutes prior to the end of cooking, baste the chops with the blueberry sauce and turn the chops over. Repeat on both sides at least once. Serve the remaining sauce as a condiment.

Note: There has been great debate about the internal temperature needed to ensure pork is free from parasites. Due to current farming practices, cases of trichinosis from pork are rare. Some recommend cooking pork to an internal temperature of 145°, and some government agencies recommend 170°. However, cooking pork to that high of a temperature results in very dry meat. Try to find a balance between the two so that you feel comfortable with the level of safety and the tastiness of the dish.

Blueberry Mascarpone Pancakes

Blueberry Mascarpone Pancakes

1 ½ cups all-purpose flour

1 tsp. baking powder

1 ½ tsp. baking soda

2 Tbsp. sugar

Pinch of sea salt

1 egg

2 Tbsp. vegetable oil

1 lemon, zest and juice

½ to 1 cup milk

¾ cup blueberries, washed and dried

Maple syrup

- In a large mixing bowl, combine the flour, baking powder, soda, sugar, and salt. Whisk to eliminate any lumps. In a small mixing bowl, whisk the egg, oil, lemon zest and juice, and ½ cup of the milk. Add the liquid ingredients to the dry ingredients; stir until just combined. If the mixture seems a little dry, add more milk, a bit at a time. Add the blueberries; stir lightly to combine. Cook the pancakes on a griddle set to medium-high heat, flipping when bubbles appear in the center of the pancake. Serve with real maple syrup.

Blueberry Ice Cream

This recipe is a hybrid ice cream-frozen custard that is comprised of just two components: blueberry compote and a vanilla custard base. When frozen together it makes a magnificent dessert!

Blueberry Compote

1 cup blueberries
1/2 cup sugar (can vary depending upon the sweetness of the berries)
Pinch of salt

- In a small saucepan over medium-low heat, combine the blueberries, sugar, and salt. Stir frequently to prevent burning, until the blueberries start to release their juices as they break down. Reduce the heat to simmer until the compote is reduced by half. Stir occasionally.

Vanilla Custard Base

3 cups half and half
1/2 cup sugar
1/2 tsp. sea salt
2 eggs, whisked
1/2 tsp. vanilla paste or extract

- In a medium saucepan over low heat, combine the half and half, sugar, and salt. Taking care not to scorch the half and half, watch for bubbles to form on the sides of the pan. When bubbles form, slowly drizzle the hot liquid into the eggs while simultaneously whisking. Slowly add the egg mixture back to the saucepan while whisking. Cook 3 minutes to thicken. Do not let the mixture come to a boil at any time. Remove from the heat and add the vanilla and prepared blueberry compote.

- Pour into a storage container and refrigerate at least 2 hours; the colder the better. Add the blueberry custard base to your prepared ice cream maker, until it is half full. Churn 30 to 45 minutes, until it forms ice cream. Save any unused ice cream mix in the refrigerator for up to 48 hours for a second batch.

Blueberries and Barley

Blueberries and Barley

Blueberries and barley is more than a fun alliteration, they are a magic combination. Though the pair could easily be used to create a yummy breakfast treat, this recipe makes a great side dish for chicken, fish, or pork.

8 oz. packaged barley

2 cups chicken or vegetable stock

1/2 cup dried blueberries

1/2 cup shredded Parmesan cheese

1 Tbsp. butter

1/2 lime, zest only

Sea salt and fresh-ground black pepper

- Cook the barley according to the package directions, substituting stock for water. Once the barley is cooked, add the blueberries, Parmesan cheese, butter, and lime zest. Add a healthy dose of a high-quality sea salt and black pepper to taste. Stir and serve.

- It really doesn't get much easier than this, and the barley stores well, too. You can serve it as a side dish for multiple dinners.

Variation: This recipe is easily adapted for breakfast. Make the barley (with water) according to the package directions. Add 1 to 2 tablespoons sugar, 1 teaspoon ground cinnamon, and a splash of milk.

 information:// Nutrition

Blueberries are a sweet, healthy fruit. One cup of fresh blueberries will give you about one-quarter of the daily requirements for vitamin C and manganese, as well as 36 percent of vitamin K needs. Plus, there are traces of nearly every other nutrient, for only 84 calories.

When it comes to antioxidants and other immune-boosting compounds, blueberries are off the chart. In fact, they have the highest antioxidant performance level of any fruit. Wild blueberries showed the greatest anticancer activity of several different fruits in a University of Illinois study.

Blueberries are also packed with a powerful compound called pterostilbene, which may inhibit breast cancer, diabetes, and heart disease.

Eating blueberries also boosts your brainpower. A Tufts University study found that blueberries actually help neurons in your brain communicate with one another better. As a result, blueberries may help keep your memory sharp and improve motor coordination as you age.

fruit:// Brambleberries

planting and growing

varieties

produce selection and harvest

preparation methods

Brambleberries, like raspberries and blackberries, are relatively easy to grow. Plants have canes that grow in a variety of habits (erect, semi-trailing, and trailing) and some have thorns. Brambleberries can tolerate some shade, particularly in warmer climates.

Regular water, well-drained soils, and a slightly acidic soil pH are the best conditions for fruit production. In addition to a good dose of supplemental compost each year, use an organic fertilizer that is formulated for acid-loving plants.

Raspberries like cooler temperatures, making most varieties more suitable for northern gardens. Summer-bearing varieties ripen as one large crop, usually around July. Everbearing varieties fruit in June/July, then again in the fall. There are red, black, yellow, and purple raspberries, all with slightly different flavors.

Raspberries are perennial plants, with canes that are biennial. There are two types of canes: primocanes (first year) and floricanes (second year).

Canes bear fruit in their second year and then die. In order to keep plants healthy and productive, it is necessary to prune them by removing the floricanes after fruit production and pruning the primocanes to 2 to 3 strong canes per clump.

Blackberries can tolerate quite a bit more heat and are a good option for southern gardens. They are very vigorous and can easily develop into a large bramble if they're not pruned and managed. Like raspberries, they also have first- and second-year canes that need to be pruned as described. It is beneficial to prune the primocanes back to about 3 feet in midsummer. This encourages branching and increased production of fruit in the following year.

Providing a trellising system helps with harvest, pruning, and disease management. A simple structure of posts and wire will suffice. Drive posts at either end of a line of berry plants. String a heavy-gauge wire from post to post, on both the left and right sides of the posts. This gives canes support from both sides with minimal work for the gardener.

planting and growing | **varieties** | produce selection and harvest | preparation methods

Red, yellow, and purple raspberries all grow best in northern climates. When deciding which to plant, consider whether it is everbearing or summer bearing and the flavor and sweetness of the berry. Black raspberries and blackberries are better at tolerating heat.

Red raspberries: 'Amity' everbearing; 'Meeker', summer bearing; 'Latham', summer bearing

Yellow raspberries: 'Fall Gold', everbearing; 'Golden Harvest', everbearing

Purple raspberries: 'Brandywine', summer bearing; 'Royalty', summer bearing

Black raspberries: 'Black Hawk', summer bearing; 'Jewel', summer bearing

Blackberries: 'Apache Thornless', summer bearing; 'Loch Ness' late summer/fall bearing; 'Triple Crown Thornless', summer bearing

JEAN ANN VAN KREVELEN

For the past two seasons, my raspberries looked beautiful, but had almost no taste. It completely stressed me out to spend all of that time harvesting with the resulting "no flavor" fruit. After much trial and error, I discovered that my berries were sweetest after about 4 to 5 days when there had been no rain and warm, sunny days. Fantastico!

planting and growing | varieties | **produce selection and harvest** | preparation methods

If choosing berries at the farmers' market, ask to taste before buying. This will ensure you pick the most flavorful, freshest berries. At the grocery store, berries are sold in packages to protect them from the damage associated with handling. Unless you are buying from a store that is dedicated to fresh produce, buying berries that are flash frozen will often result in a better tasting fruit.

When bringing fresh berries home, either eat within the next 24 to 48 hours or freeze immediately. Berries do not have a long storage life.

Harvest for brambleberries is all about timing. The berries should be ripe and sweet, but not so ripe that they fall apart or are mushy when they're picked. If a berry yields to a gentle tug, it is generally ripe and ready for harvest. Handle the berries very carefully as they can be easily injured.

planting and growing | varieties | produce selection and harvest | **preparation methods**

- **Jams/Jellies/Compotes:** As with most fruits, brambleberries lend themselves to the creation of fantastic preserves. These are very easy to make and taste great on any number of foods like breads, pancakes, ice cream, and custards.
- **Fresh:** Blackberries and raspberries are at their best when fresh. The flavor captures the essence of summer. Add them to yogurt, salads, and cereals and be sure to eat a few while picking!

DID YOU KNOW?

It is easy to tell blackberries and black raspberries apart. When you remove a blackberry, you harvest the whole fruit. When a raspberry is harvested, the core remains on the cane. This leaves a hole in the center of the fruit, and that hole is the signal that you are about to eat a raspberry.

preserving

Canning; Freezing; Dehydrating; Vacuum packing

- **Baking:** Brambleberries are found in all kinds of baked goods. However, it is important to remember that different berries have different sizes and amounts of seeds. This knowledge determines whether you add the berries whole, or first make a sauce or compote that is strained before serving.
- **Sauces:** Brambleberries vary in their balance of sweet and tart. However, all taste fantastic in savory sauces. Try raspberries with lighter meats such as poultry, pork, and fish. Blackberries have a strong enough flavor that they can be paired with any meat, including beef and wild game.
- **Juice:** The juice of these berries, when served as a stand-alone drink, can be a bit too strong for some palates. Mix with other juices or add tonic water for a berry fizz. Brambleberries also make wonderful additions to cocktails. Stay with light colored alcohols such as vodka, rum, and gin. It also makes a great component for sangria or as a partner with Prosecco.
- **Flavoring for Grains:** A handful of raspberries or blackberries is an amazing flavor agent for couscous, quinoa, rice, or bulgur. Add at the last minute as a flavor boost in grain dishes.

Berry Crumble

Berry Crumble

4 cups brambleberries (any kind or a mixture), washed and drained
$\frac{1}{2}$ cup sugar (adjust for sweetness of berries)
Pinch of salt and fresh-ground black pepper
2 Tbsp. cornstarch
$\frac{1}{2}$ cup whole wheat flour (can substitute all-purpose)
$\frac{1}{2}$ cup crushed graham crackers
$\frac{1}{2}$ cup rolled oats
$\frac{1}{2}$ cup dark brown sugar
8 Tbsp. cold butter, cut into pieces

■ Preheat the oven to 350º. Place the berries in a large baking dish. Sprinkle the sugar, salt, black pepper, and cornstarch evenly over the berries. In a food processor, add the flour, graham cracker crumbs, oats, brown sugar, another pinch of salt, and the butter. Pulse until the butter is incorporated and the mixture is crumbly (not a dough). Do not overmix. Spoon the streusel on top of the berries. Bake 30 minutes, or until the top is browned and the berry mixture is bubbly.

Berry Delight

This is an easy summertime recipe that combines fresh, seasonal berries and an easy, flavorful lemon cake.

Topping

2 cups fresh brambleberries, washed and drained

$^1/_2$ cup sugar

Pinch of salt

■ In a medium bowl, combine the berries, the sugar (adjusting for the sweetness of the berries), and salt. Lightly mash some of the berries with a fork to speed maceration (release of the juices). Refrigerate until the cake is ready.

Cake

$^1/_2$ cup butter

1 cup sugar

2 eggs

$^1/_2$ tsp. vanilla

1 tsp. baking powder

1 lemon, zest and juice

$1^1/_2$ cups all-purpose flour

Prepared whipped cream

■ Preheat the oven to 350º. Grease an 8-inch square cake pan. In a medium mixing bowl, cream the butter and sugar thoroughly. Add the eggs, one at a time, beating after each addition. Add the vanilla, baking powder, and lemon juice and zest. Mix to combine. Add the flour; mix until just combined. Pour into the prepared pan and bake for 25 minutes or until a toothpick inserted in the center comes out clean. Let the cake cool. Serve by topping a slice of cake with a generous amount of the berries. Add a dollop of whipped cream to finish the dish.

Bramble Refrigerator Jam

Bramble Refrigerator Jam (Shared by Lisa Bell)

Avoid the hassle of actual canning . . . go ahead, you know you want to. Uncooked berries remain deliciously sweet-tart and flavorful and this super-easy refrigerator jam packs the goodness of ripe summer berries into every bite. As an added bonus, with this type of refrigerator jam you can control the amount of sugar, which is not only good for you, it's just plain good eating!

3 pounds (12 cups, between 5 to 6 pints) brambleberries (raspberries, blackberries, loganberries, tayberries, or any mix you find pleasing)

4½ cups sugar, divided

2 (1.75 ounces each) packages pectin for low sugar recipes

1½ cups warm water

- Press half of the brambleberries through a fine mesh sieve or food mill to remove seeds. Combine the berry purée with remaining whole brambleberries. In large bowl, crush the remaining berries lightly to release juices; add 3 cups of the sugar. In small saucepan dissolve the pectin in the warm water; add the remaining 1½ cups of sugar. Bring to a boil over medium heat, stirring constantly. Remove from the heat. Pour the pectin mixture over the berries, stirring to combine. Refrigerate at least 8 hours until set.

- Store the jam in a large container or spoon into small plastic storage containers that seal tightly. Jam will keep in a refrigerator for up to 4 weeks. Individual containers of jam can be stored frozen up to 1 year.

(Shared by Marcelle Layne) Raspberry Ripple Ice Cream

This is my favorite ice cream flavor. I hope you will like it! For a really decadent dessert, drizzle the ice cream all over with a rich chocolate sauce and top with chopped, roasted hazelnuts.

2½ cups heavy cream

1¼ cups whole milk

1 vanilla bean, split

6 large egg yolks

¼ cup sugar

1½ to 2 cups fresh raspberries

Confectioner's sugar to taste

Fresh raspberries and mint sprigs,
   for garnish

- In a heavy saucepan, heat the cream and milk with the vanilla bean until just below boiling. Remove from the heat to cool slightly. In a large bowl beat the egg yolks and sugar until thick, creamy, and very pale yellow in color. Remove the vanilla pod from the cream mixture. Whisk the egg mixture while pouring over the cream mixture to form a smooth custard.

- Return the custard to the pan and heat on very low heat for 10 minutes, stirring constantly. The mixture should lightly coat the back of a wooden spoon. Remove the custard from heat and allow it to cool. Strain the custard through a sieve into a clean bowl; refrigerate 30 to 40 minutes. Using an ice cream maker, freeze the custard until it is very thick and holds its shape.

- Put the raspberries in a blender and process until they form a sauce. Press the raspberry mixture through a sieve to remove the seeds. If the sauce tastes tart, add confectioner's sugar to taste. Use extra sweet raspberries, if possible, to eliminate the need for the confectioner's sugar.

- Using a spoon (or knife), swirl the raspberry sauce through the custard to make a ripple effect. Cover and freeze until firm. Remove the ice cream from the freezer 10 minutes before serving to soften. Serve with fresh raspberries and sprigs of fresh mint.

Raspberry Ripple Ice Cream

Blackberry Apple Compote

The blackberries are added to this dish without cooking in order to preserve their shape. But you can certainly add them to the apple mixture, resulting in a lovely color of compote.

3 Tbsp. butter

5 apples, peeled, cored, and chopped

1-inch piece ginger, peeled and coarsely chopped

2 Tbsp. honey

4 Tbsp. spiced rum

1 vanilla bean

1 tsp. ground cinnamon

$\frac{1}{2}$ tsp. ground cloves

$\frac{1}{8}$ tsp. ground cardamom

Grating of fresh nutmeg

Pinch of salt

Apple juice, if needed for cooking liquid

1 pint blackberries, washed and drained

1 Tbsp. sugar

- In a medium saucepan over medium heat, melt the butter. Add the apples, ginger, honey, rum, vanilla bean, cinnamon, cloves, cardamom, nutmeg, and salt. Let the mixture simmer until the apples are soft, but still hold their shape, 10 to 15 minutes. If the apples don't release enough juices to keep the mixture moist, add a bit of apple juice as it reduces.

- Serve with ice cream or whipped cream..

information:// Nutrition

It seems almost too good to be true, but brambleberries, like raspberries and blackberries, are healthy for you. Rich in vitamin C, a cup of raw raspberries provides 54 percent of your daily needs while a cup of blackberries contains 50 percent. Both are excellent sources of manganese, and have folate, potassium, and other nutrients, as well.

Blackberries and raspberries are among the highest-fiber fruits available. Eating a fiber-rich diet can help you lose weight, reduce cholesterol, and prevent heart disease.

Berries are high in powerful antioxidants with anticancer properties. Raspberries and blackberries contain ellagic acid, shown to inhibit cancer tumor growth in laboratory tests. Ellagic acid is also believed to have antiviral and antibacterial properties.

Blackberries and especially raspberries contain compounds called anthocyanins, which give berries their deep color. These anthocyanins provide valuable pain relief and may have more powerful anti-inflammatory effects than aspirin, according to Michigan State University research.

fruit:// Grapes

planting and growing | varieties | produce selection and harvest | preparation methods

Grapes are a relatively easy and low-care fruit to grow. There are a couple of critical components to ensuring a tasty crop. When choosing a variety, decide if you will be using the grape for wine or for snacking. Then select the best type for your region. If you are purchasing plants from local garden stores or nurseries, they will have the right stock on hand for your climate and zone.

Grapes are planted in very early spring and often as bare-root selections. Most are hardy from zones 4 to 8; some are better adapted for the South and extend to zone 9. They prefer moist but well-drained soil, and full sun. Mulch their base with a good dose of compost.

It is best to have a trellis in place prior to planting, as it is a critical component for growing grapes. Some gardeners create a post-and-wire trellising system; others use existing structures such as a fence line. In either case, you will want

a top support at about 6 feet and a midlevel support at about 4 feet. Train and prune the vine to grow along these supports. Grape vines can be very heavy; if you are growing more than one, consider using posts at intervals along the wire to keep it from sagging.

Though grapes are primarily a plant that needs little care, pruning is important to ensure healthy vines and tasty grapes. In the first three years, the vines will need to be pruned according to future growth patterns and ease of harvest. Pruning should take place in late winter, sometime in February or March.

Different types of grapes can require different pruning methods; the method described here is called "spur pruning" and is easier than "cane pruning." Research this requirement before purchasing grape vines.

After planting, prune the vine back to one strong central stem and one side shoot. The side shoot should be kept short, as it is a fall-back option, in case the primary shoot dies. Once the vine has grown to about five feet, cut it back to just below the first wire. Remove all fruits to give the plant a chance to get established.

In the second year, the green stems from the first year will be hardened and brown. These are now called "canes." Allow one cane per side for each of the supports. At the end of winter, prune lateral vines back to two buds each. Remove any fruit.

In the third and successive years, prune the vines hard for control and production. Remove any canes that are growing outside the primary shape. Next, prune back existing wood to "spurs" or second year woody growth, leaving two buds in place. From these spurs, tender shoots will emerge bearing grapes.

Reading about pruning grapes can make it seem like a much more daunting task then it actually is. This description is a simple way to get started.

pests and diseases

Black rot; Botrytis; Downy mildew; Powdery mildew; Grape berry moths; Caterpillars; Japanese beetles

These varieties have been chosen because they respond well to spur pruning. However, there are many others that are tasty and would be well suited for backyard growing. These are divided into table and wine grapes, with a special mention for grapes that grow well in the South.

Table grapes: 'Red Flame', 'Tokay', 'Emperor', and 'Black Manucca'

Wine grapes: 'Pinot Noir', 'Merlot', 'Blanc du Bois'

Grapes for the South: 'Blanc du Bois' and 'Black Spanish'

Grapes must be harvested when ripe as no further ripening occurs after picking. The grapes that you see at the market are already ripe and ready to eat.

At home, it is easy to determine when yours are ready to eat. Color change can be an indicator, though most grapes change colors before they are truly ripe. You can also check the seeds to see if they have changed from green to brown. But the ultimate test of ripeness is sugar levels. Home growers can accurately gauge it by eating the fruit. Just pop a grape in your mouth and give it a taste. It is a good idea to check multiple places on the vine to ensure grapes haven't ripened unevenly.

JEAN ANN VAN KREVELEN

Grapes are super easy to grow, and sometimes that's a problem. They keep growing and growing and growing. I spend a good portion of my summer hacking back the new green shoots as they try to attack the raspberries. This is one fruit that requires a healthy dose of tough love to keep it under control.

| planting and growing | varieties | produce selection and harvest | **preparation methods** |

- **Jams/Jellies/Compotes:** Grapes are the quintessential fruit for preserves of all kinds. Though most often seen as a jelly, grapes can also be used to make jams and compotes. These can be used in a wide variety of ways. By varying the amount of sugar, compotes and jellies can serve as a topping for toast and muffins or spicy-sweet chutney as a side for pork.
- **Baking:** Grapes, and more often raisins, are used in all kinds of baked goods. Generally, most baked goods that call for grapes require removing the skin. Skin removal is relatively easy: either grasp and pinch the end opposite the stem, or use a food mill after cooking. Often, raisins are used instead of grapes—they're less work and have fantastic flavor!

- **Fresh:** Grapes are fantastic when fresh! Each variety has its own complexity and character. Forget old-school fruit salads, and try a more daring combination like gorgeous red grapes with Manchego cheese.
- **Juice:** Grape juice is common in most households, as is wine. What separates them is a fermentation process during which yeast converts sugars into ethanol, making it an alcoholic beverage. Both grape juice and wine can be made at home, just make sure you follow the correct steps.
- **Flavoring for Grains:** A handful of raisins give grains a big boost in the flavor department. Use both in savory grain dishes as well as hot cereal dishes for breakfast.

| preserving |

Canning; Dehydrating; Freezing

DID YOU KNOW?

Grapes have been around since 6,000 B.C. That's about the time humans invented the brick . . . which gives you an idea of their staying power! How about a lovely side of grapes for your woolly mammoth steak?

Curried Chicken Salad

The addition of grapes makes this recipe especially flavorful.

3 roast chicken breasts, diced

½ cup Greek-style yogurt

½ cup sour cream

1 rib celery, diced

1 small yellow onion, diced

1 red bell pepper, diced

2 cups grapes, washed and stems removed

1 tsp. curry powder

Salt and fresh-ground black pepper to taste

- Combine the chicken, yogurt, sour cream, celery, onion, bell pepper, grapes, and curry powder in a large bowl. Stir well to blend. Salt and pepper to taste. Chill 30 minutes, and serve.

Panettone Bread Pudding

2½ cups half and half

3 large eggs, beaten

¾ cup sugar

2 Tbsp. spiced rum

2 tsp. vanilla paste

1 tsp. ground cinnamon

Pinch of salt

16 oz. panettone (bread), cubed

½ cup raisins

2 Tbsp. chopped candied ginger

Whipped cream for serving

- In a small bowl, whisk the half and half, eggs, sugar, rum, vanilla, cinnamon, and salt.
- Place the panettone in a 9 x 13-inch pan. Sprinkle raisins and candied ginger on top. Pour the cream-egg mixture over the top. Refrigerate 1 hour to give the bread a chance to absorb the liquid. Bake in a preheated 350° oven for 40 minutes, or until the custard is firm and the top is golden brown. Serve with a dollop of whipped cream.

Stuffed Grape Leaves

Grape leaves are used in many Mediterranean dishes. The key step is to harvest the leaves when they are young, early in the season. Choose those that are nearly full size and are free of blemishes. Remove the stem and wash well with cold water.

1 pound lamb, venison, or beef

$\frac{1}{3}$ cup uncooked long grain rice

2 cloves garlic, minced

1 medium yellow onion, diced

1 egg, whisked

$\frac{1}{4}$ tsp. ground cinnamon

$\frac{1}{4}$ tsp. ground allspice

Salt and fresh-ground black pepper to taste

25 or so grape leaves, cleaned and stems removed

1 bunch mint sprigs

2 large lemons, zest and juice

8 oz. canned diced tomatoes

- Combine the meat, rice, garlic, onion, egg, cinnamon, allspice, salt, and pepper in a medium bowl. Using your hands or a fork, mix until combined. Don't overmix.

- Line the bottom of a stockpot with the grape leaves. One grape leaf at a time, place about a tablespoon of the meat mixture along the center of the leaf. Fold the sides in and the ends over. Add sprigs of mint on top of each layer of rolls. Stack them tightly in the pot. Layer any unused grape leaves over the top of the stuffed ones.

- Add the lemon zest and juice, tomatoes, and enough water to cover the grape leaves. Bring to a boil, and then reduce to a simmer. Cook until the leaves are tender, 1 to 1½ hours.

Vegetarian Stuffed Grape Leaves

2 8 oz. cans chickpeas, rinsed and drained

3 cloves garlic, minced

1½ tsp. tahini

¼ tsp. cayenne pepper

Salt and fresh-ground black pepper to taste

1 Tbsp. olive oil, or more if needed

25 grape leaves, prepared as described in the previous recipe

1 bunch mint sprigs

2 large lemons, zest and juice

8 oz. canned diced tomatoes

- Combine the chickpeas, garlic, tahini, cayenne pepper, salt, and pepper. Mash well. Add enough of the olive oil to create a paste that will stick together. Mix well. Fill and fold each leaf as described in the Stuffed Grape Leaves recipe on the previous page, layering in a stockpot. Add the mint sprigs, lemon, tomatoes, and enough water to cover the grape leaves. Simmer over very low heat for 2 hours, or until the grape leaves are soft.

Grape Juice

This is an easy-to-make juice, but it does require a couple of steps. This recipe varies depending upon the quantity of grapes and their sweetness. Just remember that it takes quite a lot of grapes to make juice in any quantity. Try starting with 15 pounds of grapes for your first foray.

- Wash and stem the grapes. Mash the grapes by adding them to a food processor and pulsing a few times, or crush with a potato masher. Add the grapes to a large stockpot to cook to release the liquids. Bring to a simmer over medium heat, stirring occasionally to prevent burning. Add sugar to taste; the amount depends upon the sweetness of the grapes. Cook 10 minutes. Remove from the heat. Line a large-mesh sieve with two layers of cheesecloth. Place over a large bowl. Press the grapes through the sieve to strain. Chill and enjoy!

Asian Pear and Raisin Chutney

½ cup rice wine vinegar

½ cup water

½ cup dark brown sugar

1 orange, zest only

1-inch piece fresh ginger, peeled

¼ tsp. ground cinnamon

¼ tsp. ground allspice

Pinch of salt

2 Asian pears, peeled and cubed

½ cup raisins

¼ cup currants

- Combine the vinegar, ½ cup water, brown sugar, orange zest, ginger, cinnamon, allspice, and salt in a medium saucepan. Cook over medium heat until the sugar dissolves. Remove from the heat and add the pears, raisins, and currants. Cool to room temperature and remove the ginger. Stir the mixture and store in the refrigerator up to 1 week.

Champagne Grape and Tomatillo Salsa

This refreshing salsa is an excellent accompaniment to fish, chicken, and pork dishes.

1 Tbsp. champagne vinegar

1 bunch basil, chopped

1 bunch flat leaf parsley, chopped

2 Tbsp. olive oil

Salt and fresh-ground black pepper to taste

5 tomatillos, husked, washed, and diced

½ medium red onion, diced

1 cup champagne grapes

1 cup yellow currant tomatoes

- In a medium bowl, whisk the vinegar, basil, parsley, olive oil, salt, and pepper. Add the tomatillos, onion, champagne grapes, and tomatoes. Toss to coat and serve.

Concord Grape Crumble

Concord Grape Crumble

5 cups red Concord grapes, skins
   removed
1 cup sugar
1 lemon, zest and juice
1/4 cup flour
Pinch of salt

Crumble Topping
1/4 cup flour
1/3 cup rolled oats
1/4 cup light brown sugar
Pinch of salt
4 Tbsp. butter

- Preheat the oven to 375º. Put the grape pulps in a medium saucepan. Save the skins. Bring the grapes to a boil; reduce heat to simmer 5 minutes. Press the grapes through a food mill to remove the seeds. Add the skins, sugar, lemon zest and juice, flour, and salt. Stir to combine.

- In a small bowl, combine the flour, oats, brown sugar, and salt. Use a fork to cut in the butter until the mixture resembles coarse meal. Pour the grape mixture into an 8-inch square pan. Top with the crumble mixture. Bake 25 minutes. Remove and let the grape crumble sit so that it becomes firmer, 15 to 20 minutes. Serve with vanilla ice cream.

 information:// Nutrition

Ancient Romans were right to eat grapes. These fruits have health benefits we're only just beginning to understand.

For slightly more than 100 calories, a cup of raw grapes provides 25 percent of the daily vitamin C and K needs. There are also small amounts of nearly every other nutrient.

Grape skins and seeds—along with red wine— are rich sources of a natural compound called resveratrol. This powerful phytochemical is believed to reduce cardiovascular disease and

inhibits the growth of various types of cancer cells. Resveratrol also lengthened the life spans of laboratory animals in research conducted by Harvard University Medical School.

Grapes contain antioxidants that may prevent cardiovascular disease by reducing LDL (bad cholesterol) and increasing HDL (good cholesterol). One Spanish study discovered people who drank 100 ml of red grape juice daily for two weeks greatly reduced their levels of LDL.

fruit:// Melon

planting and growing | varieties | produce selection and harvest | preparation methods

The sweet, juicy flesh of a perfectly ripened melon has long been associated with the celebration of summer. The long hours of sunlight and warm days and nights of the season are critical to the successful production of this crop. Southern gardeners often have great luck growing a wide variety of melons.

Traditional wisdom suggests that these plants grow best when planted in small hills. Although melons will grow in a variety of configurations, this method addresses several cultural requirements in one neat little package. Essentially, mounding creates a mini-raised bed, which improves drainage and air circulation and warms the soil. Add full sun, warm temperatures, nutrient-rich compost, and consistent watering and you have the basic elements needed to grow any kind of melon.

There are two primary issues that tend to make growing melons a challenge. The first is space. There are some compact varieties that exist, and those are an excellent choice for small spaces. But ultimately, this is a vining plant and it will need a bit of room to grow.

If you have limited yard space, trellising is one way to add extra growing space. Trellises can be made from traditional materials, found objects, or even wire fencing. Give the fruit extra support by using netting or pantyhose to encircle the melon; then tie it to a solid framework. This will prevent the melons from snapping off the vines as they grow larger.

The second issue is plant health. Although cultural conditions go a long way to combat ill effects, melons are members of the same family as cucumbers and squash, making them susceptible to similar pests and diseases. To give your melons the best chance possible, start with disease-resistant varieties. Keep a sharp eye out for pests and tackle any potential problems as they arise.

planting and growing | **varieties** | produce selection and harvest | preparation methods

Northern gardeners need to choose varieties that mature quickly. Start seeds 3 to 4 weeks before evening temps consistently stay above 55 to 60 degrees. Transplant seedlings out into hills.

Northern Gardens

Cantaloupe: 'Alaska', 'Minnesota Midget', 'Crane', 'Golden Jenny'

Honeydew: 'Earlidew', 'Eclipse', 'Creme de Menthe'

Watermelon: 'Golden Crown Hybrid', 'Blacktail Mountain', 'Diana', 'North Star'

Southern Gardens

Cantaloupe: 'Burrell's Jumbo', 'Hearts of Gold', 'Pride of Wisconsin'

Honeydew: 'Rocky Ford', 'Double Dew', 'Morning Dew'

Watermelon: 'Moon and Stars', 'Black Diamond Yellow Flesh', 'Orangelo'

planting and growing | varieties | **produce selection and harvest** | preparation methods

Whether you are at the market or at home, choosing a ripe melon can be a challenge. Cantaloupe, honeydew, and watermelon do not ripen once harvested and their flavor and texture can rapidly decline. Choose the freshest melons and eat within a day or two.

Honeydew and cantaloupe have a wonderful fruity aroma when they're ripe. Melons should not be rock hard and should give a bit with gentle pressure. Pick those that are heavy for their size. Melons that are too soft are overripe and should be avoided.

Cantaloupes harvested off the vine should easily release, or slip. Look for yellow netting where the melon has lain on the ground. Honeydews do not slip and must be cut from the vine. Check the skin of this melon as it changes from hairy to smooth when ready to harvest.

When harvesting watermelons at home they should slip easily from the vine. Watch for other indicators such as cracking in the stem right above the mature fruit or browning of the tendril closest to the fruit. Watermelons have a pale area where they have lain on the field. This spot should not be white, but should be cream or yellow in color. Many people swear by thumping watermelons to determine ripeness. When thumped, watermelons should sound hollow, not solid. This method won't help you determine if the melon is overripe, however.

pests and diseases

Powdery mildew; Downy mildew; Bacterial wilt; Cucumber beetle; Aphids; Squash vine borers

DID YOU KNOW?

Melon vines have both male and female flowers, but rely on pollinators to set fruit. Male flowers appear and disappear and it is the female flowers that create the resulting melon.

JEAN ANN VAN KREVELEN

A fun adult beverage made in its own carrying container can be easily created from one of my favorite melons. The "vodka watermelon" has made an appearance at many home parties. Here's how it works: Chill the watermelon. Next, cut a square plug out of the top of the melon. Pour good-quality, chilled vodka into the melon in small amounts; let it stand until the vodka is absorbed. Add vodka until the melon won't absorb any more. Pop the plug back in and head out to your neighbor's house. When you arrive, slice the watermelon and serve.

| planting and growing | varieties | produce selection and harvest | preparation methods |

Some types of melons are more versatile in their ability to be used in different dishes. Fruits with very soft inner flesh, such as watermelon, won't stand up to recipes that require a lot of handling.

- **Chutneys/Pickles:** Melons with firm flesh are used in a variety of chutney recipes and make a great accompaniment to fish. Watermelon rinds can also be pickled and served as a sweet-tart condiment.
- **Fresh:** Clearly, melons are at their absolute best when eaten at the peak of ripeness as a stand-alone or star ingredient. They can be added to any number of fresh food recipes. In addition to many different salads and dressings, they are also tasty wrapped with prosciutto or served up for breakfast.
- **Pies/Cakes:** Believe it or not, melons are used as the filling for many different types of pies and cakes.
- **Jams/Jellies/Gelatin:** Melons can be used in preserves and to flavor gelatin. Though we don't often think of storing and using this sweet fruit in this way, it is a good option for a big harvest. Preserve the taste of summer to enjoy year-round!
- **Juice:** Melon juice is very flavorful and very sweet. When making a serving, try mixing it with one-half tonic water or one-half of another type of juice. It also makes a great backdrop for a variety of frozen drinks that utilize light colored alcohol, such as vodka, rum, and gin.
- **Sorbet/Granita:** Melons are a classic fruit in sorbets and granitas. If the melon is very ripe, it can be the only ingredient in a granita. Just whir it in a blender, pour it into a pan, and pop it in the freezer. Use a fork to scrape and mix it every 30 minutes as it is freezing. Repeat the process for 4 hours . . . easy!

preserving

Freezing

Watermelon, Red Onion, and Feta Salad

1 medium watermelon, seeded and cubed
$\frac{1}{2}$ red onion, chopped
1 bunch mint (or basil), chopped
2 Tbsp. olive oil
1 Tbsp. balsamic vinegar
Sea salt and fresh-ground black pepper to taste
4 oz. feta cheese, crumbled

- Place the watermelon in a large bowl. Add the onion and mint; stir to combine. Refrigerate until chilled. In a small bowl, combine the olive oil, vinegar, sea salt, and pepper; stir to combine. Add the feta and the vinaigrette to the watermelon. Toss gently and serve.

Honeydew Mint Fizz

1 honeydew, seeded and cubed
1 bunch mint, $\frac{1}{4}$ cup chopped
$\frac{1}{8}$ tsp. grated fresh ginger
Pinch of salt
6 oz. lime vodka
Ice cubes
Tonic water

- Put the honeydew into a blender. Add ¼ cup of the mint, ginger, salt, and vodka. Whir to combine and adjust the ingredients to taste. To make one serving, fill a glass with ice cubes. Pour the honeydew mixture into the glass, three-fourths full, and fill the remainder with tonic water. Stir to combine. Serve with swizzle stick of the mint.

(Shared by Kim Pinkerton) Watermelon Popsicles

This is such an easy treat to prepare for your family during hot summer months. It's also a great way to use that large, sweet watermelon taking up room in your pantry or refrigerator. Our kids (my husband being the biggest of them all) loved all of my experiments with fruit popsicles, and I enjoyed making these refreshing, healthly snacks for them. Melons are usually yummy enough to freeze without any additions. Try this recipe with other fruits such as peaches, berries, or apricots; and add yogurt and/or bananas for a creamier popsicle. If needed, add a natural sweetener such as honey or agave nectar.

1 watermelon, seeded and coarsely cubed

- In a blender or using a hand mixer, purée the watermelon. Spoon into popsicle molds, paper cups, or ice cube trays; freeze. When the fruit purée is partially frozen, insert a popsicle stick and freeze until firm.

Casaba Melon Salad

1 Casaba melon, flesh in julienne strips
2 cups jicama, cleaned and in julienne strips
1 napa cabbage, shredded
1 medium red onion, thinly sliced
1 bunch basil, leaves cut in a chiffonade (thin strips)
1 tsp. fresh thyme leaves
2 limes, zest and juice
1 tsp. honey
Salt and fresh-ground black pepper to taste
$1/2$ cup extra virgin olive oil

- In a large bowl, combine the melon, jicama, cabbage, and onion; stir. In a small bowl, combine the basil, thyme, lime zest and juice, honey, salt, and pepper. Whisk the herb mixture constantly while adding the olive oil in a slow stream. Pour the dressing over the melon salad mixture; toss gently to combine.

Watermelon Popsicles

Casaba Melon Salad

Angel Food Cake with Cantaloupe Glaze

Angel Food Cake with Cantaloupe Glaze

It is important to use a 10-inch tube pan to make sure the cake bakes properly.

Cake	Cantaloupe Glaze
12 egg whites	1 small cantaloupe, seeded and chopped
1½ tsp. cream of tartar	
1 tsp. vanilla extract	¼ cup sugar (adjust for sweetness of melon)
1½ cups sugar	1 sprig fresh mint
1 cup cake flour	Pinch of salt

Fresh berries and whipped cream for serving

- Preheat the oven to 375°. When separating the eggs, take care to keep as much yolk as possible out of the whites. Save the yolks for a custard or crème brûlée recipe. Pour the egg whites into a very clean and dry mixing bowl.

- Whip the egg whites, adding the cream of tartar and vanilla after the eggs start to look frothy. Slowly add the sugar, continuing to whip until soft peaks form. Gently fold in the flour, a bit at a time. It is important not to deflate the eggs by adding too much flour too quickly or by stirring the mixture too much.

- Pour the batter into the tube pan. Make sure the pan is completely oil free; any fat will prevent a light, fluffy cake from forming. Bake 35 minutes or until a toothpick inserted comes out clean. Cool in its pan on a wire rack.

- While the cake is baking, make the glaze by adding the melon, sugar, mint, 2 tablespoons water, and salt to a medium saucepan. Cook over medium heat until the melon is completely soft and the sugar has dissolved. Remove the mint sprig. Pour the melon mixture into a blender; blend until smooth.

- When the cake has cooled completely, run a knife around the edges to loosen. Remove the cake from the pan and place on a serving platter. With a long wooden skewer, poke holes along the top of the cake. Spoon the cantaloupe glaze over the top of the cake, letting the cake absorb the glaze. Don't add too much or the cake will become soggy. Serve with fresh berries and whipped cream.

Melon Sorbet

Melon Sorbet

$\frac{1}{2}$ cup water

$\frac{1}{2}$ cup sugar

Pinch of salt

3 cups firm-flesh melon (any kind, such as cantaloupe or honeydew), seeded and chopped

- In a small saucepan over medium heat, stir ½ cup water, the sugar, and salt until the sugar has dissolved and a syrup has formed. (This is called simple syrup.) Add the melon to a blender and process until smooth. Add enough of the simple syrup to sweeten to taste. Pour into an ice cream maker and freeze until the sorbet has the texture of soft-serve ice cream. Serve immediately or freeze until the sorbet is fully hardened.

Lobster and Honeydew Salad

2 limes, zest and juice

1 small shallot, diced

Salt and fresh-ground black pepper to taste

2 Tbsp. vegetable oil

1 lb. cooked lobster, cut into bite-sized pieces

1 cup honeydew, cubed

1 mango, diced

1 handful cilantro or basil, chopped

Lobster and Honeydew Salad

- In a large bowl, whisk the lime zest and juice, shallot, salt, and pepper. Add the oil in a stream, whisking constantly, to combine. Add the lobster, honeydew, mango, and cilantro. Toss to coat. Chill for 1 hour and serve.

Cantaloupe Blackberry Smoothie

Cantaloupe Blackberry Smoothie

1 cantaloupe, peeled, seeded, and cubed
1 cup blackberries
1 small bunch fresh mint
1 small bunch fresh sweet basil
1 lime, zest and juice
Pinch of salt
Honey
Ice cubes
Light rum or vanilla vodka, optional

- Put the cantaloupe, blackberries, mint, basil, lime zest and juice, and salt into a blender. Whir to combine. Taste and add honey for sweetness and depth of flavor. Add 3 cups ice and blend until frothy. Serve immediately.

- For an adult smoothie, try adding light rum or vanilla vodka.

information:// Nutrition

Make space on your plate for melons. These fat-free, high-fiber fruits have lots of water, yet they still contain high levels of vitamins, minerals, and antioxidants.

One cup of cantaloupe has a whopping 120 percent of your daily vitamin A needs and 108 percent of vitamin C requirements. There are decent amounts of folic acid, other B vitamins, and every mineral, especially potassium.

Honeydew doesn't have as many nutrients as cantaloupe. Still, a cup provides 53 percent of vitamin C requirements, as well as many other nutrients, for only 64 calories.

Watermelon is 92 percent water, and has vitamins A, B6, C, and thiamin, not to mention traces of most other nutrients. It's especially high in lycopene, a red pigment that occurs naturally in plant tissues. This powerful antioxidant is believed to prevent certain cancers and heart disease. Watermelon has about 40 percent more lycopene than raw tomatoes, another excellent source.

fruit:// **Rhubarb**

planting and growing | varieties | produce selection and harvest | preparation methods

Rhubarb is an amazing plant that, when grown in the right cultural conditions, requires very little care. Not only is it edible, its appearance and form change significantly from first emergence to dormancy, making it a fun addition to an ornamental bed. But, it is important to remember that only the stalks are edible and *its leaves are poisonous.*

Technically, rhubarb is a vegetable, but in recipes it is almost always treated as a fruit. Like many fruits, it is a perennial that can be harvested for 10 to 15 years. Site selection is important, since this plant does not like to be moved or have the surrounding soil cultivated.

Plant crowns in early spring in well amended soil. Provide consistent moisture and add a layer of compost each growing season. In the first year, do not harvest any stalks, and only harvest a few stalks in the second. In following years, don't remove more than one-half of the plant at a time and stop harvesting when stalks start to reduce in size.

Mature plants are good candidates for dividing. In early spring, loosen the soil around the perimeter of the plant with a garden fork. Then, use a spade to dig up the crown and root system. Use a knife or very sharp spade to cut the crown into pieces that contain at least one bud and a strong root network. Replant immediately to ensure the greatest likelihood of success.

planting and growing | **varieties** | produce selection and harvest | preparation methods

Rhubarb comes in three different colors: green, pink (speckled), and red. There are also varieties that are solely for ornamental purposes; be sure you choose one that is edible.

Green: 'Riverside Giant', 'Green Victoria'
Pink (speckled): 'Victoria', 'German Wine', 'Sunrise'
Red: 'Cherry Red', 'Crimson Red', 'Valentine', 'MacDonald'

pests and diseases

Crown rot; Verticillium wilt; Corn borer; Cabbage worm; Rhubarb cucurlio

JEAN ANN VAN KREVELEN

I am in love with rhubarb! It is a workhorse in the garden. This plant needs little care and produces bumper crops each year. It is also an excellent addition to a decorative border, mutating through various forms, some alien in appearance. Overall, it is hard to find a "fruit" with a bigger bang for the buck.

planting and growing · varieties · produce selection and harvest · preparation methods

Rhubarb is easy to select at the farmers' markets or grocery stores. Choose crisp, healthy-looking stalks with vibrant color. It cooks down quite a bit, so be sure to purchase enough for your recipe.

Harvest rhubarb by gently tugging the stalk loose from the ground. Remove leaves and add them to the compost pile. Store rhubarb in a refrigerator for up to a week or so; don't clean until ready to use in a recipe.

preserving

Freezing; Canning; Vacuum sealing

planting and growing · varieties · produce selection and harvest · preparation methods

Rhubarb can be coupled with a wide variety of fruits or left on its own. The only real preparation requirement is adding enough sugar to counter its intense tartness. Though it is somewhat stringy and fibrous when raw, it easily breaks down when cooked.

- **Baking:** As mentioned, rhubarb is a fantastic component in baked goods. Its acidic nature combines with baking soda to form an effervescent leavening agent. Add cooked rhubarb to breads, cakes, muffins, and pancakes.

- **Jams/Compotes:** Rhubarb is a great component in jams and compotes. It is most often paired with strawberries, but it can be a partner to cherries, blueberries, and other fruits that don't overwhelm its delicate taste. Try it as a topping for waffles, biscuits, and ice cream.

- **Fillings:** Also known as the "pie plant," rhubarb is fantastic as a filling for pies, crisps, cobblers, and tarts. It can be a wonderful counterpart to other fruits as long as you are careful not to overwhelm its delicate flavor.

- **Sauces:** Rhubarb can make a great sauce, particularly since its color guarantees a vibrant finish. Sauces will need to be balanced with a bit of sweetness, which makes it a great pairing for lighter meats such as pork, chicken, and turkey.

- **Drinks:** Rhubarb imparts a tart flavor that is completely unique. It is particularly tasty when used to make a simple syrup and added to a variety of juices and mixed drinks. It can also be used in frozen drinks and smoothies.

Rhubarb-Cherry Ice Cream

Rhubarb-Cherry Mixture

4–5 stalks of rhubarb, chopped

1 cup cherries, pitted

1 cup sugar (depending upon the sweetness of the cherries)

Pinch of salt

- Combine the rhubarb, cherries, sugar, and salt in a medium saucepan over medium heat. Add a splash of water to the saucepan to prevent burning. Stir regularly to prevent the sugar from burning. Cook until the rhubarb and cherries have softened to applesauce consistency. Remove from the heat.

Ice Cream Base

1½ cups half and half

2 eggs

½ tsp. vanilla

Pinch of salt

- In a medium saucepan over medium-low heat, gently heat the half and half without letting it come to a boil. In a separate small bowl, whisk the eggs, vanilla, and salt. Slowly add the egg mixture into the saucepan with the half and half, constantly whisking. Cook until the ice cream base starts to thicken, stirring often. Add the rhubarb-cherry mixture. Remove from the heat. When the ice cream base has cooled a bit, refrigerate until completely chilled, 5 hours or longer. Make into ice cream using the manufacturer's directions for your ice cream maker.

DID YOU KNOW?

Rhubarb is highly acidic and has an amazing effect on baked goods. When you add cooked rhubarb to a recipe containing baking soda, the result is positively effervescent! The chemical reaction creates bubbles of carbon dioxide, making your baked goods light and fluffy.

Variations on Rhubarb Pie

Certainly, rhubarb makes a great pie filling, but it also plays well with other fruits in pies. Below is a basic rhubarb pie recipe with suggestions for alternate fruit combinations.

Pastry dough for a 9 inch pie plate, top and bottom crust

4 cups of rhubarb, cleaned and chopped

1 ½ cups of sugar

3 Tbsp flour

1 tsp cinnamon

½ tsp salt

1 Tbsp cream

- Preheat oven to 450°. In a small bowl, mix sugar, flour, cinnamon, and salt together. Spread a fourth of the mixture across the bottom of the pie crust. Add rhubarb on top, followed by the rest of the mixture. Add the top crust, cutting a few slits to allow the steam to escape. Brush with cream and sprinkle sugar across the top of the crust. Bake for 15 minutes and reduce temperature to 350°, bake for an additional 40 minutes.

Variations (Shared by Daniel Gasteiger)

Strawberry-Rhubarb

Strawberry rhubarb is great in a proportion of ⅓ strawberries to ⅔ rhubarb, as well as a ratio of ½ and ½. Sugar is adjusted to a bit more than a cup... perhaps 1¼ cups... and about six tablespoons of flour as thickener.

Sour Cherry-Rhubarb

Sour Cherry Rhubarb works well with about ⅔ cherries and ⅓ rhubarb. Add 1½ cups of sugar and ½ cup of flour together with the fruit.

Sweet Cherry-Rhubarb

A strikingly fine flavor combination with a mix of ⅓ cherries to ⅔ rhubarb. Use 1¼ cups of sugar and 6 Tablespoons of flour. I can't imagine a proportion of cherries to rhubarb that wouldn't taste grand.

Peach-Rhubarb

Use a 50-50 mix of rhubarb and peaches, with 1¼ cups of sugar and ⅓ cup of sugar, it's very satisfying.

Brined Turkey Breast with Rhubarb-Orange Compote

$1/2$ gallon water

$1/4$ cup kosher salt

2 oranges, zest and juice only

1 bunch fresh sage leaves

6 bay leaves

Handful of whole peppercorns, freshly cracked

4 cloves garlic, smashed

2 turkey breasts

Olive oil

■ Place a large stockpot on medium heat; add water and salt. Stir until the salt is dissolved. Add the orange zest and juice, sage, bay leaves, peppercorns, and garlic. Let cool completely. Immerse the turkey breasts in the brine, cover, and refrigerate 6 to 8 hours.

■ When you are ready to roast the turkey, preheat the oven to 400°. Remove turkey from the brine and pat dry. Place the breasts on a baking sheet and drizzle with the olive oil. Roast until a thermometer inserted into the thickest part reaches 165°. (The amount of time varies significantly depending upon the weight of the turkey breast. Using a thermometer is the safest way to gauge the doneness of the meat.)

Rhubarb-Orange Compote on next page

Rhubarb-Orange Compote

2 cups chopped rhubarb

1 orange, zest and juice only

1 tsp. dried sage

$1/3$ cup sugar

1 tsp. grated ginger

Pinch of salt

- In a medium saucepan, combine the rhubarb, orange zest and juice, sage, sugar, ginger, and salt. Cook over medium heat until the rhubarb falls apart. Serve with the brined roasted turkey.

Rhubarb, Strawberry, and Thyme Sorbet

$1/2$ cup water

2 cups rhubarb, chopped

1 cup strawberries, chopped, hulled

$3/4$ cup sugar

1 tsp. fresh thyme, finely chopped

Pinch of salt

- In a small saucepan, add ½ cup water and cook the rhubarb, strawberries, sugar, thyme, and salt until the sugar has dissolved and it forms a syrup. Add to a blender and process until smooth. Pour into an ice cream maker and freeze until sorbet has the texture of soft-serve ice cream. Serve or place in the freezer until fully hardened.

Rhubarb Cake with Citrus Glaze

Compote

8 stalks rhubarb, chopped into ½-inch pieces

1½ tsp. butter

Pinch of salt

4 Tbsp. sugar

1 tangerine, zest and juice only

- Sauté the rhubarb over medium-low heat in a large saucepan. Add the butter, salt, sugar, and tangerine juice and zest. Cook, stirring frequently; do not let it burn or brown. Let the rhubarb reduce until it becomes the consistency of applesauce; ensure that you have at least 1½ cups for the recipe. Remove from the heat to cool.

1 cup milk	1 tsp. salt
1 tsp. lemon juice	1 tsp. baking soda
1 tsp. vanilla	1½ cups of the rhubarb compote
1¾ cups brown sugar, divided use	½ cup chopped walnuts
⅔ cup vegetable oil	½ tsp. ground cinnamon
1 egg	1 tsp. melted butter
2½ cups all-purpose flour	

Cake

- Preheat the oven to 350 degrees and grease a bundt pan. In a large mixing bowl, combine sugar, oil, and vanilla, mix to combine, in a separate bowl, break the eggs and whisk, add a bit of the compote while whisking to temper, add remaining compote while whisking. Then add the mixture to the mixing bowl and stir to combine.
- Next add flour, cinnamon, nutmeg, ginger, baking soda, baking powder and salt. Mix to combine. Pour the mixture into a bundt pan and bake for 45-55 minutes or until a knife inserted into the center comes out clean.

- If you want to add a glaze, a really simple confectioner's sugar and tangerine juice combination is divine!

Rhubarb Bread

1 cup milk

1 orange, zest only

²/₃ cup vegetable oil

1 egg

1 tsp. vanilla

1³/₄ cups brown sugar, divided

2¹/₂ cups all-purpose flour

2 tsp. baking powder

¹/₂ tsp. baking soda

1¹/₂ cups rhubarb, chopped

¹/₂ cup walnuts, chopped

Streusel Topping

¹/₂ tsp. ground cinnamon

1 tsp. melted butter

- Preheat the oven to 325° and prepare two 9 x 5-inch loaf pans by greasing them. In a small bowl, whisk the milk, orange zest, oil, egg, and vanilla. In a large bowl, mix 1½ cups of the brown sugar, flour, salt, baking powder, and baking soda. Add the milk mixture to the flour mixture and stir just until combined. Fold in the rhubarb and walnuts. Pour the batter into the prepared loaf pans. In a small bowl combine ¼ cup of the brown sugar, cinnamon, and butter, mixing thoroughly. Sprinkle the streusel on top of the loaves. Bake 40 minutes or until a toothpick inserted into the center of a loaf comes out clean.

 information:// Nutrition

Rhubarb deserves our respect. This vegetable, which is typically treated as a fruit, is a healthy, low-calorie addition to your recipes.

You'll find rhubarb is 95 percent water. Yet it also contains vitamins C and K, plus traces of most other vitamins and minerals, including calcium, potassium, and manganese—all for only 26 calories a cup.

Just like cranberries, rhubarb is generally cooked prior to eating. The fruit's tart flavor means you'll need to add honey, sugar, or some other

sweetener to your dish. By adding sweet fruits like strawberries or raspberries to your recipe, you'll be able to reduce the amounts of higher-calorie honey or sugar quite a bit.

Always remember: Never eat rhubarb leaves. Along with an unknown toxin, the leaves contain high amounts of oxalic acid, a toxic and potentially deadly poison. Only the stems should be eaten.

fruit:// **Strawberry**

| planting and growing | varieties | produce selection and harvest | preparation methods |

Strawberries are one of the most adaptable fruits, and are found growing across the United States. They are well suited for container gardening and for growing in beds. They are easy to care for, bear fruit within the first year, and reproduce quickly, making them extremely cost efficient.

There are three different types of strawberries. Junebearing strawberries produce their crop all at once, usually around June, with no fruit for the remaining season. Everbearing strawberries produce two crops, a larger one in June and a small crop toward the end of summer, with a scattering of berries between the two. Day-neutral berries are not dependent on day length and can produce a steady crop from June until frost.

One of the easiest ways to grow Junebearing strawberries is in the "matted row" system. Start by choosing a sunny site with excellent drainage. This is another fruit that prefers soil to be a bit acidic and very well amended. Be sure to clear the area of all weeds, as strawberries don't do well facing competition for resources.

Plant strawberries about 2 feet apart in rows, and create paths in-between that are 3 feet wide.

Strawberries will send out runners to produce new plants. Remove any that spread to the path between rows during the growing season. Immediately after the plants stop producing fruit, set your lawn mower at 2½ inches in height and mow the entire bed. Use a tiller to turn under the outer row of plants, essentially paring back the row close to its previous size. Water and fertilize well.

This is a good system for Junebearing strawberries as they spread aggressively via runners. For day-neutral and everbearing, reduce plant spacing to one foot apart and till sides of a bed only when strawberries have spread significantly.

Strawberries need consistent water to produce a good crop. One inch of water is a good standard. Help conserve moisture and weeds by mulching well with straw.

JEAN ANN VAN KREVELEN

varieties | planting and growing | produce selection and harvest | preparation methods

There are many varieties of strawberries available today. Keep in mind that strawberries have very shallow root systems, so northern gardeners will want to choose a variety that is suited to cold climates. Other characteristics to look for include drought resistance, disease resistance, size, and taste.

Junebearing: 'Dunlap', 'Earliglow', 'Allstar', 'Surecrop'

Everbearing: 'Ozark Beauty', 'Superfection', 'Ogallala'

Day-neutral: 'Tristar', 'Tribute' Cold Climates: 'Redchief', 'Guardian', 'Sunrise'

Extremely Hot Climates: 'Tioga', 'Florida 90'

Many people don't think of strawberries and pie together, but my grandfather is absolutely nuts for the "Hot Strawberry Pie" my mom makes. It is filled to the brim with sweet, luscious berries, a bit of sugar, and little else. Add a flaky, homemade piecrust, top with some vanilla ice cream or sweetened whipped cream, and it is downright heavenly!

planting and growing | varieties | **produce selection and harvest** | preparation methods

When selecting berries at a store, look for those that are completely red and unblemished. Strawberries have a short shelf life to start with; any with damage will very quickly be unsuitable for eating. Also check for mold and obvious signs of decay; needless to say, these are not berries you want to eat.

If you are at a store or farmers' market that offers tastings, give the strawberries a try. Actually tasting this fruit is the only sure way to know if you have a high-quality, sweet berry or one that looks beautiful but has little in the way of taste.

Strawberries freeze very well. Look at your local market for those that have been individually frozen, not concentrates or big clumps. Buying berries that have been frozen at the peak of ripeness can result in a sweeter, fuller tasting berry than buying them fresh.

To harvest, look for berries that are completely red, an indication of ripeness. This is a fruit that will not ripen once picked, so avoid those that have any hint of green. Likewise, harvest all fruit once it has completely ripened. Strawberries do not hold on the vine for very long. Remove from the vine by cutting the stem rather than pulling the fruit. This will help avoid damage to the plant.

planting and growing | varieties | produce selection and harvest | **preparation methods**

Strawberries are an adaptable fruit that can be used in a number of recipes. As do all berries, they lose their shape quickly when heat is applied, which means volume will reduce greatly. This is particularly important to remember when using strawberries in baking.

- **Baking:** Strawberries are not often at the top of the list for inclusion in baked goods. This may be due partially to the reduction in volume and the amount of liquid they release during baking. Using a thickening agent, like cornstarch or flour, or precooking the berries will help address this concern. Try strawberries in pies, muffins, and scones.
- **Jams/Jellies/Compotes:** Strawberries are fantastic in preserves of any kind. One thing to keep in mind is that when ripe, they can be very sweet and may not need as much sugar as other fruit. If you are using traditional canning methods, these often require large amounts of sugar in order to set well. However, there are low-sugar pectin products and they are great for very sweet fruits.
- **Dried:** Drying strawberries concentrates the flavors and creates an outstanding flavor component for cereals, baked goods, and granola mixes.
- **Fresh:** Fresh strawberries are eaten in all manner of ways, including dipped in chocolate or whipped cream. Without a doubt, they are the most luxurious and sensual fruit in the home garden.
- **Sauces:** Because of their high sugar content, strawberry-based sauces are often used in conjunction with desserts. Use this sauce to brighten up the color of a plate, adding visual as well as flavor appeal. Highlight the flavor of strawberries by pairing them with a relatively neutral canvas like mascarpone, cheesecake, or vanilla ice cream.

DID YOU KNOW?

Junebearing strawberries benefit from removing the first year's blossoms and delaying harvest until the next year. Everbearing and day-neutral should have blossoms removed for the first three months, making it possible to have a late-summer harvest.

preserving

Canning; Freezing; Dehydrating; Vacuum packing

Mascarpone Crostata with Strawberries and Apples

A crostata is an Italian fruit pie/tart concoction. It is super easy to make and makes great use of home garden fruits. Because you are working with fruits, which exude quite a lot of liquid, it is best to use parchment paper or a silicon sheet to line the baking pan.

Crostata Dough

1/2 cup whole wheat flour

1/2 cup unbleached all-purpose flour

1/2 cup cold unsalted butter, cubed

1/2 tsp. salt

1 Tbsp. sugar

2–4 Tbsp. ice water

- In the bowl of a food processor, add the whole wheat and all-purpose flours, butter, salt, and sugar. Pulse 10 to 15 times until the mixture becomes crumbly, with pieces the size of peas. With the processor running, add just enough ice water for the mixture to just start to form a ball. Do not overwork the dough. Turn out onto a floured surface and loosely form into a disk. Cover with plastic wrap and chill at least 1 hour.

Filling

3 tart pie apples (such as Gravenstein, Pippin, Braeburn, Rhode Island Greenings), peeled, cored, and sliced

1 tsp. lemon juice

1 pint strawberries, hulled and sliced

1/4 to 1/2 cup sugar to taste

1 tsp. ground cinnamon

1 tsp. vanilla

1 tsp. lemon zest

1/4 cup flour

1 tsp. salt

3 oz. mascarpone cheese

2 Tbsp. butter, melted

1 Tbsp. sanding sugar (white sugar)

- Preheat the oven to 400°. Place the apples in a medium bowl and sprinkle with the lemon juice (to prevent browning). Add the strawberries, sugar, cinnamon, vanilla, lemon zest, flour, and salt. Toss to combine and coat the fruits.

- Take the dough out of the refrigerator and let it warm for a few minutes. Place the dough on a floured surface. Roll to a 12-inch-diameter circle. Don't worry if it isn't perfect; it should not be an exact circle, but have more of a rustic look. Roll onto the rolling pin or fold into quarters to lay on a rimmed baking sheet. Using a spatula, slather the mascarpone from the center of the dough to the edges, leaving one-third of the outer edges uncovered.

- Pour the fruit mixture in the center of the dough. Gather and fold the edges of the crust up around the sides of the fruit. Because this is a rustic dish, the most important element is to contain the fruit on all sides. Make sure that the top edges are securely folded in so that the crostata doesn't fall apart during baking.

- Brush the melted butter over the crostata crust; sprinkle with the sanding sugar. Bake 40 to 45 minutes, or until the fruit has set and the crust is browned. Cool for 10 minutes before serving.

Strawberry Topped Cheesecake

Strawberry-Topped Cheesecake with Cinnamon Graham Cracker Crust (Shared by Shawna Coronado)

Prepare this recipe one day ahead so it will be well chilled for serving.

Graham Cracker Crust

20 whole graham crackers, crushed

$3/4$ cup cold unsalted butter, cubed

$1/2$ cup packed brown sugar

$1 1/2$ tsp. ground cinnamon

$1/2$ tsp. fresh rosemary, minced

$1/2$ tsp. salt

Strawberry Filling

4 8-ounce packages cream cheese, at room temperature

$1 3/4$ cups sugar

3 Tbsp. fresh lemon juice

$2 1/2$ tsp. vanilla

$1/2$ tsp. salt

3 Tbsp. all-purpose flour

5 large eggs, beaten

Sour Cream Topping

2 cups sour cream

3 Tbsp. sugar

$1/2$ plus $1/4$ tsp. vanilla

Also needed

1 18-ounce jar raspberry jelly

32 oz. fresh whole strawberries, hulled just before serving

- Preheat the oven to 350º. Prepare the pan by wrapping foil outside a 10-inch-diameter springform pan with 3-inch sides.

- Combine the graham crackers, butter, brown sugar, cinnamon, rosemary, and salt. Mix until the graham cracker crumbs begin to get sticky. Press the crumbs into the bottom and 2¾ inches up the sides of the springform pan. Bake crust for 12 minutes. Remove from the oven and cool.

- Beat the cream cheese, sugar, lemon juice, vanilla, and salt in a large bowl until smooth. Gradually add the flour. Add the eggs and beat just until blended. Pour the batter into the crust. Bake until the outer 2-inch edge of the cheesecake is puffed and slightly cracked, the center is just set, and the top is slightly brown, 50 to 60 minutes. Remove from the oven. Cool 15 minutes.

- Whisk the sour cream, sugar, and ½ teaspoon of the vanilla in a medium bowl to blend. Spoon the sour cream topping over the cheesecake, spreading to the edges. Bake five minutes until the topping is just set. Remove from the oven. Gently run a knife between the crust and the pan to loosen the sides. Cool the cheesecake in its pan on a wire rack. Refrigerate overnight (or at least 8 hours).

- To serve the next day, melt the raspberry jelly in a small, heavy saucepan over medium-low heat. Cool to barely lukewarm and stir in ¼ teaspoon of the vanilla.

- Release the springform pan sides from the cheesecake. Place the cheesecake on a serving plate. Arrange the strawberries, points facing up, on top of the cheesecake—fill the top of the cake entirely. Brush enough raspberry jelly over the strawberries to glaze them generously. Any remaining raspberry glaze can be warmed and used as an accompaniment.

Strawberry and Stone Fruit Coulis

Strawberry and Stone Fruit Coulis (Shared by Lisa Bell)

Coulis is nothing but a fancy French name for a fruit sauce—all it takes is a stone fruit of some sort (fresh peaches, apricots, nectarines, or plums) and fresh strawberries. Purée and add a bit of sugar to create this versatile base that can be enjoyed over ice cream or used in any number of delicious beverages or recipes.

1 pound fresh, very ripe stone fruits, pitted and chopped

1 pint strawberries, washed and hulled

3/4 cup sugar

3/4 cup freshly squeezed lemon juice

3 Tbsp. cornstarch

- Purée the stone fruits and strawberries in a food processor or blender. Pour the mixture into a large (multi-cup) measuring cup, adding enough water to equal 4 cups total. Transfer to a large saucepan; add the sugar and lemon juice. Cook over low heat, stirring constantly, for 2 to 3 minutes. In a small bowl, whisk the cornstarch and 1 tsp. water. Add the cornstarch mixture to the fruit purée and whisk until the mixture is combined. Stir until the mixture thickens enough to coat the back of a spoon.
- Press the mixture through a sieve or food mill to remove any fibers or bits of peel. Refrigerate or freeze until use.

Quick Tip: You can freeze the coulis in ice cube trays and add a cube or two to mixed drinks or lemonade for a tasty treat.

information:// Nutrition

Nothing says summer better than strawberries. Lucky for us, these sweet berries aren't just delicious; they're loaded with vitamin C. Just a half-cup of fresh strawberries delivers about 70 percent of your daily requirements. Strawberries also contain small amounts of almost all vitamins and minerals, including a healthy dose of manganese.

Strawberries have high levels of antioxidants, which may inhibit the growth of cervical, breast, and liver cancer cells. The berries are one of the richest food sources of ellagic acid, a phytochemical, which has been found to kill cancer cells in laboratory tests.

Ellagic acid may help the liver remove cancer-causing substances from the blood. The naturally occurring compound is also believed to promote wound healing and may help reduce heart disease, birth defects, and liver problems.

That's not all. Animals fed strawberry extracts daily showed big improvements in short-term memory during a recent study.

vegetable:// Asparagus

planting and growing

varieties

produce selection and harvest

preparation methods

Asparagus is one of the first vegetables to peek out of the soil after frigid weather has passed, making the fresh taste of asparagus a true rite of spring. And because it is pricey in the grocery stores, you can smugly eat to your heart's content, thinking of the money you save by growing your own.

Since asparagus is one of the few perennial vegetables and will continue to produce for 15 to 20 years, it is important to do a bit of planning before you plant.

Choose a sunny location for the bed. Make sure the soil is loose and nutrient-rich by amending with compost and rotted manure. Asparagus does not compete well with weeds, so now is the time to be obsessive about removing every last one.

Asparagus can be grown from seed or crowns. However, growing from seed will delay your first harvest by another year while the plants form roots. Instead, get a jump-start on your first harvest by planting one-year-old root crowns purchased from

a reputable retailer to ensure they are healthy and disease free.

Plant the crowns 5 to 6 inches deep at least 2 feet apart and in rows that are 2 feet apart. Cover the crowns with 2 to 3 inches of soil, firming the soil around them to eliminate air pockets.

In the first year, do not harvest any spears that appear, but rather allow the 3- to 5-foot ferns to form that will provide food to the developing crowns; in the second year, do the same.

In the third year, you can begin harvesting the spears for a six-week period, after which you must stop harvesting and allow the ferns to grow and feed the crowns. Don't cut back the ferns until they have completely died back in fall since they continue to feed the crowns while they are still green or even yellow.

varieties

Asparagus plants can be male or female. Many gardeners now prefer male plants since females produce seeds that take energy away from producing those delicious asparagus spears. Female plants must also be weeded to keep from becoming invasive. Fortunately, there are all-male hybrid varieties, which make for easier maintenance and have higher productivity.

All-Male: 'Jersey Centennial', 'Jersey Giant', 'Jersey King'

Disease Resistant: Rust: 'Martha Washington', 'Waltham Washington', Fusarium wilt: 'U.C.-72', 'U.C. 500'

Specialty: 'Purple Passion', 'Precoce d' Argenteuil'

Hot Climates: 'UC-157'

produce selection and harvest

Many people believe that the size of an asparagus stalk indicates how tender it will be. But this is not necessarily true. Small stalks start life as a small stalk and stay small. Large stalks start as a large stalk and stay large. Neither is an indicator of age or tenderness.

Freshness and maturity are the two characteristics that contribute to a delectable spear. At a grocery store, select stalks with firm, tightly closed tips that are of the same thickness for even cooking.

When harvesting at home, pick asparagus as soon as the spears are ready. In early spring, this might mean every day. Later in the season, it might be two to three times a day. Instead of cutting with a knife, which can harm the crown, grasp the asparagus at the base and gently snap it off the plant. Plunge the spears into cool water and rinse until all sand and debris is removed between the folds of the buds.

preserving

Freezing; canning

ROBIN RIPLEY

You can grow the white asparagus you see on fancy restaurant menus right at home. As the asparagus tips emerge from the ground, just mound soil around the spear to prevent light from reaching it (which will allow the spear to turn green). Harvest at the usual size. Voila! Gourmet asparagus!

planting and growing

varieties

produce selection and harvest

preparation methods

You can eat asparagus raw, pickled, just barely blanched, boiled, cooked on the grill, or baked. Just don't overcook asparagus to the point where it becomes mushy—the preparation method most responsible for turning kids into lifelong asparagus haters. Using a light touch with the heat and keeping recipes simple will bring out the best of this versatile veggie.

- **Blanched/Boiled:** If you decide to cook asparagus via blanching or boiling, clean the spears and remove the lower, tougher segments. Drop the spears into salted boiling water and cook for no more than 2 minutes. Remove and immediately plunge into an ice bath. Drain, dry, and serve.

- **Fresh/Steamed:** Asparagus is fantastic when served fresh or lightly steamed. Fresh asparagus simply needs to be cleaned and the woody lower end of the stem removed. It is wonderful when served with dips or added to salads. Lightly steaming asparagus softens the texture a bit and is helpful if it is a bit past its prime.

- **Grilled/Roasted:** Grilling or roasting intensifies the flavor of asparagus by giving the natural sugars a chance to caramelize. Remove the lower woody sections of the stems, coat in olive oil, salt and pepper, and pop onto a hot grill or on a baking sheet in a hot oven for just a few minutes. Don't overcook!

pests and diseases

Crown rot; Rust; Fusarium wilt; Asparagus beetles

- **Sautéing:** One of the most rewarding and speedy ways to prepare asparagus is to sauté it with butter, olive oil, or a few drops of sesame oil mixed with a bit of garlic, salt, and pepper. You can go from garden to table in about five minutes by keeping the preparation this simple.

DID YOU KNOW?

Asparagus is one of the very few land-grown vegetables that prefers salty soil, likely due to its adaptability to maritime climates. After the first year of a new bed, routinely apply sodium chloride (NaCl) at the rate of 2.5 pounds per 100 feet. This should be applied in spring before the spears show or around July 4. Do not use other kinds of salt, including table salt, as this can kill your plants.

Creamy Asparagus and Pea Soup

Serve this delicious soup with a crusty bread and cheese for a satisfying dinner on a cool spring night.

2 Tbsp. butter

1 large yellow onion, finely chopped

1 large clove garlic, crushed

About 1½ lbs. thin to medium asparagus, washed, tough ends removed, and chopped into 1- to 1½-inch pieces

1 lb. fresh or frozen shelled peas

2 medium potatoes, peeled and diced

8 cups chicken or vegetable stock

½ cup dry vermouth

1 tsp. salt

½ tsp. white pepper

¾ cup heavy cream

Fresh chopped chives, for garnish

- In a large soup pot over medium heat, melt the butter. Add the onion and garlic. Stir constantly until the onion is softened but not browned. Add the asparagus, peas, and potatoes to the soup pot. Toss with the onion and garlic mixture 2 to 3 minutes. Add the stock, vermouth, salt, and white pepper. Increase the heat and bring to a boil. Once it has reached a boil, lower the heat to simmer 30 minutes.

- Use an immersion blender or transfer the asparagus and pea mixture in batches to a blender. Purée until the soup is a smooth consistency. Return the purée to the soup pot and increase the heat to medium.

- In a separate bowl, mix ½ cup of the soup mixture with the cream. Transfer the cream mixture to the soup pot and blend. Heat the soup thoroughly. Garnish each serving with the chives before serving.

Asparagus Salad with Chervil Pesto

Chervil Pesto

1 cup fresh chervil, chopped

¼ cup shredded Romano-Pecorino cheese

¼ cup pine nuts, toasted

3 Tbsp. olive oil

1 clove garlic, crushed

Salt and fresh-ground black pepper

1 tsp. white wine vinegar

- Combine the chervil, Romano-Pecorino cheese, pine nuts, olive oil, garlic, salt and pepper to taste, and vinegar in a food processor. Process until it is well chopped and blended.

Asparagus Salad

2 bunches fresh asparagus, woody stems removed

3 cups corkscrew pasta, cooked

½ medium red onion, separated into rings

½ kohlrabi, peeled and cubed (can substitute jicama)

1 red bell pepper, seeded and chopped

- Blanch the asparagus in a large saucepan of boiling water no more than 2 minutes. Remove and immediately place into a bowl of ice water to stop the cooking. When the asparagus is chilled, remove it, dry, and cut into bite-sized pieces. Place in a serving bowl with the prepared pasta, onion, kohlrabi, and bell pepper. Add the prepared chervil pesto and toss well. Chill, covered, until serving.

Asparagus and Goat Cheese Tart

Vegetables become an entrée when they're incorporated into a savory filling such as this asparagus and goat cheese tart. Pair it with a hearty salad and serve the tart at room temperature for a satisfying warm-weather dinner.

Tart Pastry

1½ cups pastry or all-purpose flour
½ tsp. salt
8 Tbsp. cold butter
4 Tbsp. ice water

- Combine the flour and salt. Using a pastry cutter or your fingers, cut in the butter until the flour and butter mixture resembles coarse meal. Add the water and mix until a dough is formed. Shape the dough into a ball. Turn onto a lightly floured surface and knead a couple of times to ensure the water is evenly incorporated. Do not overknead.

- Roll the dough into a tight ball and press into a flat square. Using a rolling pin, roll the dough into a 12-inch circle or large enough for your baking pan. Gently pull up the crust and fit into a tart pan or pie pan, crimping the edges. Refrigerate the tart pastry shell while preparing the filling.

Tart Filling

1 Tbsp. unsalted butter
1 Tbsp. olive oil
1 medium yellow onion, finely chopped
1 lb. asparagus, washed and tough ends removed
4 eggs
½ cup milk
½ tsp. tarragon leaves, crushed
¾ tsp. salt
Fresh-ground black pepper to taste
6 oz. soft goat cheese, such as Montrachet, divided use

- Preheat the oven to 400º. Melt the butter in a medium skillet. Add the olive oil and onion. Sauté, stirring constantly, until the onion softens. Add the asparagus. Gently lift and turn the spears to cook evenly, about 3 to 4 minutes. Set aside.

- In a medium bowl, whisk the eggs, milk, tarragon, salt, pepper to taste, and 3 oz. of the goat cheese. Pour three-fourths of the egg mixture into the prepared tart crust. Arrange the asparagus and onion mixture on top, with spears forming spokes (trim the length of the spears if necessary). Pour the remaining egg mixture over the asparagus. Dot the top of the tart with the remaining 3 oz. of the goat cheese.

- Bake 40 minutes or until the middle of the tart is firm. Remove from the oven. Let the tart sit 10 to 15 minutes before serving for easier cutting.

Roasted Asparagus in Olive Oil

Roasted Asparagus in Olive Oil

Use a high-quality olive oil and a coarse salt, such as kosher salt, to make this simple recipe special.

About 1½ lbs. thin asparagus, washed and tough ends removed
2 Tbsp. extra-virgin olive oil
Salt
Lemon zest

- Preheat the oven to 450°. Toss the asparagus with the olive oil and spread the spears in a single layer on a large baking sheet. Roast for 12 minutes, rotating the spears by shaking the pan once or twice during roasting. Season to taste with the salt. Top with the lemon zest just before serving.

information:// Nutrition

Low in calories and high in fiber, asparagus is a healthy treat. One cup will provide 70 percent of your daily needs for vitamin K, which is essential for healthy bones.

Asparagus also contains decent amounts of vitamin C, vitamin A, folic acid, and iron—not to mention other B vitamins and minerals like calcium, magnesium, and zinc. Not bad for 27 calories per cup.

The vegetable is also high in compounds that may have anti-tumor benefits. These include glutathione, one of the body's most powerful antioxidants. Rutgers University research found that crude saponins in asparagus might actually inhibit the growth of leukemia cells.

A gentle diuretic, asparagus is soothing for the urinary tract and helps alleviate water retention. So, why does asparagus make your urine smell strange? The culprit is the amino acid asparagine, which derives its name from the plant and is completely harmless.

vegetable:// Beans

| planting and growing | varieties | produce selection and harvest | preparation method |

There are so many types of beans out there. Bush beans that only grow about knee high, pole beans that grow into long runners, beans eaten with the pod, beans eaten without the pod—even beans eaten with or without the pod. The important thing is to know what kind you have and how they are best grown, harvested, and stored . . . because, believe it or not, there are beans for drying, beans for eating fresh, and some that fit both purposes.

Whatever kind of beans you have, they should be planted after temperatures are in the 70s in an area that gets at least six hours of full sun a day. Make sure the soil has good drainage. For extra measure, work in generous amounts of compost and loosen the soil at least 8 inches deep.

As with peas, mixing the bean seeds with an inoculant or mixing the inoculant in the soil will boost production. The inoculant makes nutrition in the soil more readily available to the beans. It is likely that they will not need any other fertilizer as beans are "nitrogen fixing," which means that they naturally add nitrogen to the soil.

Direct sow bush beans 1 inch deep and 4 inches apart, allowing at least 12 inches between rows. If you're growing pole beans, make sure the supports are already in place, since beans have shallow roots and don't like to be disturbed. Directly sow pole beans 1 inch deep and 5 inches apart around the supports.

Make sure you keep the soil evenly moist while the beans are germinating and getting established. After that, just be careful of weeding around their shallow roots.

varieties

Beans are so easy to grow and there are so many varieties of them, you could spend your whole gardening life exploring the world of beans. Just remember that "green beans" are meant to be eaten fresh, not dried (and they can be any color). Want something a bit more exotic? Edamame, extensively used in Asian cooking and a flavorful snack all by themselves, are blanched and shelled soybeans.

GREEN BEANS
Pole: 'Kentucky Blue', 'Kentucky Wonder', 'Fortex', 'Rattlesnake Snap'
Bush: 'Maxibel', 'Yellow Wax', 'Royal Burgandy', 'Dragon Langerie'
DRYING BEANS
Pole: 'Snow Cap', 'Good Mother Stallard', 'True Red Cranberry'
Bush: 'Calypso', 'Jacob's Gold', 'Ireland Creek Annie'

produce selection and harvest

When purchasing fresh beans at the grocery stores look for firm beans with a bright color. Pass on any beans that are woody, stringy, or overdeveloped with broken pods. At the farmers' markets make sure you ask if the beans are "green" (which means they are meant to be eaten fresh) or if they are drying beans.

When harvesting fresh beans at home, check the plants regularly. This is a very quick-growing, high-production vegetable and a timely harvest

pests and diseases

Aphids; Corn earworms; Japanese beetles; Spider mites; Striped cucumber beetles; Cabbage loopers; Corn borers; Leaf miners; Mexican bean beetles; Anthracnose; Mosaic virus; Downy mildew; Bacterial blight; Rust

helps encourage new pod formation. Once a bean becomes overly mature, it is fibrous and woody. It's better to dry and save those for planting next year.

Harvesting dried beans is fairly simple. You can either harvest them when green and fully mature or allow them to dry on the vine. If you choose the latter, remove as soon as the outer shells become papery.

ROBIN RIPLEY

In the early years of my career and living on my own, I could barely make ends meet. But I was always satisfied eating rice and beans cooked with some sautéed onion and ground cumin—cheap, healthy, and delicious. Although I no longer have to count pennies as I did in my 20s, beans are still my favorite comfort food. I eat them every day!

preserving

Pickling; Freezing; Dehydrating; Vacuum

planting and growing | varieties | produce selection and harvest | **preparation methods**

Beans are probably the most versatile vegetable you can select.

- **Blanched/Steamed:** Green beans can be blanched and tossed directly into salads, soups, or other dishes. They are also fantastic when paired with a dip and served chilled for snacking.
- **Stir-fried/Sautéed:** Fresh beans can be stir-fried and table-ready in fewer than five minutes. Add a bit of olive oil, salt, and pepper and you are ready to go. Avoid overcooking to retain the flavor and nutrients.
- **Puréed:** Some of the starchier beans, such as white beans or black beans, can be puréed to make dips or even to give a creamy consistency to foods when you want to avoid dairy products.

- **Soups/Sides:** Dried beans are fantastic in soups and served as a side dish. Avoid the gaseous side effects of some beans, either by soaking them overnight in plenty of cool water or by bringing them to a boil for five minutes, turning off the heat and letting them stand for an hour. Be sure to discard the liquid in either case.
- **Meat Substitute:** Lentils, those tiny brown, red, or orange dried beans, cook in about 30 minutes and can be formed into patties to substitute for hamburger or into loaves as a meatloaf replacement. Experiment with your own combinations by adding sautéed celery, onion, carrots, breadcrumbs, and eggs. Flavorful seasonings to pair with these dishes include savory, sage, and thyme.

DID YOU KNOW?

Native Americans grew corn, squash, and pole beans together in one symbiotic relationship they called the Three Sisters. You can try this in your own garden. As the corn grows tall the squash spreads on the ground. The beans climb and twine among the corn. It's the perfect solution for small gardens.

Baby Lima Bean Salad

Baby Lima Bean Salad

It's a shame that lima beans get such a bad rap. Tender, young lima beans are an especially delectable treat, particularly when used in a salad, such as this one with fresh herbs.

½ cup extra-virgin olive oil

¼ cup white balsamic vinegar

1 tsp. dry mustard

3 Tbsp. chopped fresh herbs, such as basil, marjoram, and parsley

2 shallots, diced

3 cups baby lima beans, cooked

2 large tomatoes, diced

½ cup black olives, sliced

Salt and fresh-ground black pepper

■ Whisk the olive oil and vinegar in a large bowl with the mustard, herbs, and shallots. Mix in the lima beans, tomatoes, and olives. Season with salt and pepper to taste.

White Bean and Turkey Chili

Substituting white beans for red and turkey for beef makes this a new and tasty twist on traditional chili.

2 Tbsp. olive oil

1 large onion, diced

2 cloves garlic, minced

2 lbs. ground lean turkey

2 15-oz. cans or 3 cups cooked small white beans, rinsed and drained

8 oz. can tomato paste

1 28-oz. can whole tomatoes, cut into bite-sized pieces

2 cups vegetable or chicken stock

1 Tbsp. dried oregano

2 tsp. ground cumin

3 Tbsp. good-quality chili powder

1 Tbsp. unsweetened cocoa

2 tsp. salt

Greek yogurt, sour cream, chopped cilantro, or red onion, for garnish

- Heat the olive oil in a large stockpot over medium-high heat. Add the onion and garlic and sauté until the onions are soft and lightly browned. Add the turkey. Break the turkey into small pieces as it cooks. Stir in the beans, tomato paste, tomatoes, stock, oregano, cumin, chili powder, cocoa, and salt. Bring to a boil. Lower the heat to medium. Cover and cook for 1 hour, stirring occasionally. Garnish with the Greek yogurt, sour cream, chopped cilantro, or red onion when serving.

White Bean and Turkey Chili

Stir-Fried Green Beans

1 Tbsp. extra-virgin olive oil
1 Tbsp. sesame oil
2 cloves garlic, minced
1 tsp. dried red pepper flakes

8 oz. fresh green beans, tips and
  strings removed
Salt

■ In a heavy skillet, heat the olive oil, sesame oil, garlic, and red pepper flakes. Stir
constantly for a few seconds until the garlic is just tender. Add the green beans.
Toss the green beans evenly just until they are tender—about 3 to 4 minutes.
Remove from the heat, season with the salt, and serve immediately.

Three Sisters Salad (Shared by Helena Wolkonowski)

3–4 qts. white corn, cooked
1 cucumber, diced
4 fresh tomatoes, diced
2 cups green beans, trimmed, cut
  into 1-inch pieces, and blanched

1 green pepper, diced
1 red, yellow, or orange pepper, diced
1 medium zucchini, diced
1 medium yellow squash, diced
1 medium yellow onion, diced

Dressing
½ cup apple cider vinegar
½ cup olive oil
½ tsp. coriander
Fresh chopped cilantro

■ Mix the corn, cucumber, tomatoes, and prepared green beans in a large bowl.
In a skillet over medium heat, lightly sauté the peppers, zucchini, squash, and
onion. Add the sautéed vegetables to the corn mixture. Refrigerate.

■ To prepare the dressing, mix the vinegar, olive oil, coriander, and cilantro
to taste in a small bowl. Refrigerate. Combine the chilled corn salad and the
chilled marinade just before serving.

Roasted Potato and Green Bean Salad

4 medium Yukon Gold potatoes, cleaned and cubed

½ cup olive oil, plus more for coating baking sheets

Salt and fresh-ground black pepper

¼ lb. fresh green beans, cleaned and trimmed

1 shallot, minced

1 Tbsp. Dijon mustard

¼ cup balsamic vinegar

1 tsp. fresh thyme leaves, minced

- Preheat the oven to 400º. Place the potatoes on a couple of baking sheets. Drizzle with olive oil and sprinkle with the salt and pepper. Bake 45 minutes or until the potatoes are brown and well caramelized.

- Blanch the green beans by immersing them in a large saucepan of boiling water for 2 to 3 minutes. Remove the green beans from the saucepan and dunk them in a bowl of ice water to stop the cooking process. Drain and dry the green beans.

- In a large bowl, combine the shallot, Dijon mustard, vinegar, and thyme. Salt and pepper to taste and whisk to combine the ingredients. While whisking, add ½ cup of the olive oil in a stream. Continue whisking to blend the oil thoroughly into the dressing. Add the potatoes and green beans; toss to combine. Serve.

Roasted Potato and Green Bean Salad

Spanish-Inspired Hummus *(sidebar tab)*

Spanish-Inspired Hummus

Hummus is a very versatile dip. It is fantastic with raw vegetables and breadsticks and as a spread in sandwiches. For another option, reduce the liquid, roll it into balls, and deep fry. You will have the makings for an amazing falafel sandwich.

2 cups reconstituted or canned garbanzo beans, drained if canned

1 tsp. Spanish smoked paprika (available from mild to hot)

1–2 Tbsp. Spanish olive oil, plus more to coat the hummus

1½ Tbsp. tahini

1 lemon, zest and juice

1 clove garlic, chopped

6 oz. Spanish olives, pitted and chopped

- In the bowl of a food processor, combine the garbanzo beans, paprika, olive oil, tahini, lemon zest and juice, and garlic. Pulse a few times to combine. If the mixture is too thick, add a bit more olive oil or lemon juice to thin it. Add the olives and pulse once or twice to combine. Spoon the mixture into a serving dish. Top with a drizzle of excellent-quality Spanish olive oil.

 information:// **Nutrition**

Funny songs aside, beans deserve our respect. Snap beans and wax beans provide healthy amounts of vitamin C, fiber, and vitamin K. They also contain vitamin A, some B vitamins, and other nutrients.

Dried beans typically have less vitamin A and C than snap beans. But, they are loaded with iron, magnesium, and manganese, depending on the variety. These legumes also have B vitamins and various important minerals.

Researchers have discovered small red beans have even more disease-fighting antioxidants than blueberries. In fact, this humble bean topped the list of food sources for powerful antioxidants. Kidney and pinto beans were also highly ranked, with black beans further down the list.

One cup of boiled black beans provides 64 percent of your daily needs for folic acid – not to mention other healthy nutrients like thiamin, iron, and phosphorus.

planting and growing | varieties | produce selection and harvest | preparation methods

Cool-season vegetables like broccoli can usually be planted for spring or fall harvest. If you happen to live in a part of the country that has mild winters, you can also sow the seeds in fall for an early spring harvest. That gives gardeners an opportunity to have three harvests in a year . . . talk about flexibility!

Broccoli can be direct sown or planted as seedlings. You can either purchase them from a nursery or start them inside in the very early spring (six weeks before the average last frost for your area). Sow seeds in flats or in peat pots about ½ inch deep. Keep them in a cool, dark place until the seeds emerge. Place them on a sunny windowsill or under grow lights.

Broccoli should have full sun, but it will tolerate a bit of shade, particularly in the warmer parts of the country. Prepare the bed with plenty of compost, well-rotted manure, and lime to help with the uptake of calcium the broccoli will need as it grows.

Plant the broccoli seedlings 1½ to 2 feet apart in rows 3 feet apart. Keep the soil moist as it grows. Applying a layer of mulch can help retain water and keep the soil from drying out. Apply fish emulsion or another balanced organic fertilizer a few weeks into the growing season.

For a fall broccoli crop, start seeds in a shaded area or cold frame in May or June and transplant them into their final location in late summer.

After your harvest, leave the plants in place and they will produce smaller branches to the sides that can also be harvested and eaten.

planting and growing | **varieties** | produce selection and harvest | preparation methods

Most of us are familiar with the traditional green, large-headed broccoli. But there are other fantastic varieties, hybrids, and relatives that can expand your flavor options.
Standard: 'Waltham 29', 'Green Comet', 'Di Cicco'
Sprouting: 'Calabrese', 'Early Purple Sprouting'
Unusual Varieties: Green Romanesco: 'Minaret'; purple kale/broccoli hybrid: 'Peacock Broccoli'; harvest leaves only: 'Spigariello Liscia,' 'Leaf Broccoli'; broccoli rabe: 'De Rappa', 'Rapini'

planting and growing	varieties	**produce selection and harvest**	preparation methods

Freezing

The best broccoli is very dark green—almost purple. The head should be compact and tightly formed. Avoid any with signs of yellow buds emerging from the flower head. The stalks should be firm, not rubbery.

Harvesting broccoli at home is a cinch. Just be sure you do so before it starts to flower. Use a sharp knife to cut off the head below branching, where the stem becomes singular and solid. Once the main shoot is removed, smaller side shoots will continue to produce until the weather becomes too hot or too cold. There is also a variety of broccoli (sprouting broccoli) that doesn't form a large head, but instead has consistent production of smaller shoots.

ROBIN RIPLEY

Although I adore a salad, when I'm watching my weight I always opt for young, tender broccoli instead. At just 31 calories a cup, I can eat myself silly and not have to worry about whether I'll fit into those jeans the next day.

pests and diseases

Aphids; Flea beetles; Cabbage worms; Cutworms; Root maggots; Blackleg; Black rot; Clubroot

DID YOU KNOW?

The Italians were the first to embrace broccoli's true culinary potential and introduced it to the rest of the world. This vegetable made its debut in America thanks to the determination of two brothers from Messina, Italy. Stephano and Andrea D'Arrigio started growing small crops in San Jose, California, in the early 1920s.

planting and growing | varieties | produce selection and harvest | **preparation methods**

Broccoli can be prepared in several ways . . . experiment and find one (or more) that you like!

- **Raw:** One of the easiest methods of eating broccoli is simply to wash it and cut it into bite-sized pieces. In salads, broccoli is a dream since the florets soak up flavorful dressings.
- **Blanched/Steamed:** Another super-easy way to prepare broccoli is to blanch it in a pot of boiling water for a couple of minutes or steam it until it's tender.
- **Sautéed:** For a bit more flavor, try sautéing broccoli in olive oil with garlic, ginger, chilies, or lemon juice. Cook until just tender and finish with a sprinkle of Maldon salt or your favorite finishing salt.
- **Roasted/Grilled:** Broccoli is particularly tasty when brushed with olive oil, grilled or roasted in the oven, and topped with a bit of grated Parmesan or Asiago cheese. Or try adding a bit of sesame oil for an Asian flavor.

Roasted Broccoli and Cauliflower Salad

1 head broccoli, cleaned and cut into bite-sized pieces
1 head cauliflower, cleaned and cut into bite-sized pieces
6 Tbsp. olive oil, plus more to coat
Salt and fresh-ground black pepper
2–3 cloves garlic, skin left on
3 Tbsp. balsamic vinegar
1 Tbsp. whole-grain mustard

- Preheat the oven to 400°. Place the broccoli and cauliflower on a baking sheet; drizzle with some of the olive oil and sprinkle with salt and pepper. Toss to coat. Add the garlic to the baking sheet. Place the baking sheet on the top rack of the oven and bake 45 minutes. Depending upon the size of the vegetables, they may be ready or they may need a bit more time. The broccoli and cauliflower should be caramelized and softened. The garlic will be ready much sooner and should be removed from the oven when it's softened. When the garlic has cooled, remove the garlic from its skin.

- In a large bowl, whisk the vinegar, mustard, garlic, and salt and pepper to taste. Continue whisking as you slowly drizzle in the 6 Tbsp. of the olive oil. Add the roasted broccoli and cauliflower and toss to coat. Serve warm.

Roasted Broccoli and Cauliflower Salad

Broccoli Cheddar Soup

1 bunch broccoli (about ¾ pound), washed and chopped

2 Tbsp. butter

1 large yellow onion, chopped

1 red pepper, seeded and chopped

2 medium potatoes, peeled and chopped

5–5½ cups chicken broth

½ cup dry white wine, optional (if you do not use wine, use ½ cup more stock)

1 tsp. dry mustard

1 tsp. ground cumin

Salt and fresh-ground black pepper

³/₄ cup heavy cream

2 cups freshly grated Cheddar cheese

- In a large stockpot, bring water to a boil and immerse the broccoli 4 to 5 minutes. Drain and rinse in cold water to stop the broccoli from continuing to cook.

- In a large soup pot, melt the butter and add the onion, pepper, and potatoes. Stir constantly for 5 minutes. Add the stock, wine if you are using wine, mustard, cumin, and salt and pepper to taste. Bring the mixture to a boil. Lower the heat to simmer. Cook 25 minutes, or until the potatoes are very tender. Add the broccoli. Stir.

- Use an immersion blender or transfer the vegetable mixture in batches to a blender and purée until the soup is a smooth consistency. Return the purée to the soup pot and increase the heat to medium.

- In a small bowl, combine ½ cup of the hot soup mixture with the cream. Transfer the cream mixture to the soup pot and blend. Stir in the Cheddar cheese. Heat the soup thoroughly, but do not let it come to a boil.

(Shared by Shawna Coronado) Best Broccoli Quiche in the World

This is, without a doubt, one of my absolute favorite recipes for broccoli, ever! It is an adaptation from an old, old recipe I heard of from my grandmother. It tastes like veggie heaven.

1 lb. broccoli, cleaned and chopped into ½-inch pieces

1 medium yellow onion, peeled and sliced

2 Tbsp. butter

1 ready-to-use piecrust (bottom only), baked in quiche pan, and cooled

4 eggs

¾ cup cream

1¼ cups whole milk

1½ tsp. fresh thyme, minced

Salt and fresh-ground black pepper

½ lb. Swiss cheese, grated

- Preheat the oven to 375°. Place a baking sheet in the oven to preheat (this will be used under the quiche to catch any drippings).

- In a medium skillet over medium heat, sauté the broccoli and onion in the butter until the vegetables are tender. Put the broccoli and onion into the prepared piecrust.

- Whisk the eggs, cream, milk, thyme, and salt and pepper to taste in a medium bowl. Pour over the broccoli-onion mixture in the piecrust.

- Place the quiche pan on the baking sheet. Top the quiche with the Swiss cheese and lots of fresh-ground pepper. Bake 30 to 40 minutes or until a knife inserted in the center comes out clean. Cool 15 minutes before cutting for serving to allow the quiche to firm up well.

3 B's Salad

Keep the beet sticks on the small side as beets take longer to cook than broccoli and you want both vegetables to be done at the same time.

1 head broccoli, cleaned and chopped into florets
1 large beet, peeled and cut into matchsticks
½ cup olive oil, plus more for coating broccoli and beets
Salt and fresh-ground black pepper
1 shallot, peeled and chopped
1 tsp. Dijon mustard
1 tsp. dried oregano
⅛ cup white balsamic vinegar
2 cups cooked barley
½ cup shredded Parmesan cheese

- Preheat the oven to 400°. Place the broccoli and beets on a baking sheet. Drizzle with olive oil, and salt and pepper to taste. Roast 45 minutes or until the beets are soft and the broccoli is caramelized.

- In a large bowl, combine the shallot, Dijon mustard, oregano, vinegar, and salt and pepper to taste. Whisk to combine; slowly add the ½ cup of the olive oil while continuing to whisk.

- Add the roasted vegetables and barley. Toss to coat. Let the mixture stand for a few minutes to give the grain time to absorb some of the dressing. Top with the Parmesan cheese. Serve at room temperature.

Bodacious Tomato, Broccoli, and Cheese Tart

(Shared by Lisa Bell)

For this recipe, you will need enough dough to form a bottom crust for a 9-inch tart.

Tart Filling

1 Tbsp. olive oil

1 cup broccoli, chopped

2 large shallots, chopped

4 cloves garlic, minced

6 oz. farmer's cheese or cream cheese, softened

$\frac{1}{3}$ cup fresh chives or scallions, minced

1 large egg, lightly beaten

2 Tbsp. all-purpose flour

$\frac{1}{2}$ tsp. salt

$\frac{1}{2}$ tsp. fresh-ground black pepper

3 medium vine-ripened tomatoes, preferably red and yellow, cut into $\frac{1}{2}$-inch-thick slices

1 Tbsp. Parmesan cheese, grated

2 Tbsp. basil, thinly sliced

- Preheat the oven to 375°. Fit the dough over a 9-inch removable bottom tart pan. Position the overhanging dough to form an edge; crimp as desired. Prick the bottom with a fork. Line the tart shell with aluminum foil. Weight down with dry beans or rice. Bake 15 minutes; remove the foil and beans. Return the tart crust to the oven; bake until golden, 15 to 18 minutes. Remove and let cool. (Leave the oven on.)

- In a small skillet, heat the oil over medium heat. Add the broccoli, shallots, and garlic. Cook until golden, about 5 minutes. Remove from the heat; cool 5 minutes. In a large bowl, combine the broccoli mixture, farmer's cheese, chives, egg, flour, salt, and pepper. Mix well.

- Increase the oven temperature to 425°. Spread the cheese mixture in the tart shell. Bake until set, about 10 minutes. Remove from the oven. Arrange the tomato, alternating colors if possible, in concentric rings on top of the tart. Sprinkle with the Parmesan cheese. Return to the oven. Bake until the tomatoes are just softened and cheese is lightly browned, about 8 minutes. Let cool to room temperature. Just before serving, sprinkle with the basil.

Raspberry Ripple Ice Cream

Raw Apple-Sage Stuffing

Raw Apple-Sage Stuffing (Shared by Mike Lieberman, raw foodie)

1 head cauliflower, cut into bite-sized chunks

2 heads broccoli, florets only

1 red onion, chopped

3 ribs celery, sliced in large chunks

3 Granny Smith apples

4 Fuji apples

7–8 sage leaves

1 tsp. apple cider vinegar

Splash of olive oil

Splash of water

- Mix the cauliflower, broccoli, onion, and celery in a bowl. Dice 4 of the Fuji and Granny Smith apples and add to the bowl. Coarsely chop the remaining 3 apples and put in a blender with sage, vinegar, olive oil, and water. Process several times to liquefy. Pour the liquid over the vegetables. Toss to combine. Spread the mixture on a teflex sheet. Dehydrate on a dehydrator tray at 110° for 6 to 8 hours.

information:// Nutrition

In the nutrition world, broccoli is a superstar. Just one cup of raw broccoli contains 110 percent of your daily needs for vitamin C and 43 percent of vitamin A requirements. Plus, broccoli contains some B vitamins, including folic acid, as well as calcium, potassium, and other minerals.

Researchers have discovered that broccoli is loaded with phytochemicals. These healthy compounds may reduce the risk of diabetes, respiratory problems, heart disease, and several types of cancer, including lung, stomach, prostate, and breast cancers.

Of all the vegetables, broccoli and Brussels sprouts have the highest amounts of cancer–fighting compounds called isothiocyanates. Broccoli is also rich in sulforaphane, which is among the most powerful anti–carcinogens found in food.

To retain maximum nutrients, steam broccoli 3 to 4 minutes until tender but still firm. University of Illinois research discovered that gentle heat kills a sulfur-grabbing protein but allows broccoli to release the powerful antioxidant sulforaphane more effectively.

vegetable:// **Carrot**

planting
and
growing

varieties

produce
selection
and harvest

preparation
methods

The secret to success with carrots is the soil. Because those tender roots must reach down as they grow, the soil must be light and fluffy, free of rocks, clods, dense clay, or any other obstacles that will cause the carrots to fork, bend, or even stunt their tender growth. So take the time to dig a bed 12 to 16 inches deep in a sunny, well-draining location. If your soil is heavy clay, lighten it by adding sand.

This is one vegetable that doesn't like to be transplanted. Direct sow carrot seeds about an inch apart two to four weeks before the last average frost date.

You'll quickly learn that carrot seeds are tiny! Some gardeners mix carrot seeds with sand to make them easier to handle. If the wee seeds still are driving you mad, you can also just broadcast them over the entire bed. Cover the seeds with a half-inch of the same fine soil you've prepared in the bed.

Keep the carrot bed moist with a fine spray during the germination period, paying particular

attention on hot, dry days so that the seedlings won't have to fight their way up through a hard, dry surface crust.

As the carrots grow, be vigilant about thinning them so those that remain have room to grow. It's best to do this in stages, clipping the seedlings during the first stage so that you don't accidentally pull out its neighbor. Begin when the seedlings are about two inches high, thinning to one inch apart. Continue to thin the carrots as they grow whenever they begin to look crowded, adding the baby carrots to salads.

Unlike many of the vegetables we recommend, don't overfeed your carrots with compost or fertilizer high in nitrogen or you'll end up with beautiful greens but little in the way of actual carrots.

planting and growing | **varieties** | produce selection and harvest | preparation methods

Not all carrots are long and orange. In fact, Western carrots are divided by three primary characteristics: short, medium, and long. They also come in a variety of colors . . . a fact that many Americans don't know due to our infatuation with this orange icon.

Short: 'Parmex', 'French Round', 'Oxheart', 'Thumbelina'

Medium: 'Scarlet Nantes', 'Danver's Half Long'

Long: 'Sweetness III', 'Yellowstone', 'St Valery'

Color Variations: 'Atomic Red', 'Purple Haze', 'Dragon', 'Sinclair', 'Belgian White', 'Rainbow Mix'

pests and diseases

Carrot rust flies; Carrot weevils; Parsley worms; Nematodes; Leaf blight; Mosaic virus; Vegetable soft rot

ROBIN RIPLEY

Next time someone tells you to eat carrots to improve your eyesight, give them a short history lesson. It was the British air ministry in World War II that promoted the idea of carrots as sight boosters. Not only did it help dispose of a glut of carrots in the country as people munched them down, it also helped disguise the fact that British pilots' amazing "eyesight" was really due to radar.

planting and growing | varieties | **produce selection and harvest** | preparation methods

When shopping, look for firm, small to medium carrots without cracks or brown spots. If you purchase them with the tops on, remove the tops when you get home. This helps prevent the roots from wilting.

Carrots can be harvested at home once the root has started to develop. As you thin the carrots, test one or two to determine when the long thin root has started to fill out. Generally, carrots are ready to harvest between 6 and 8 weeks.

Only harvest as much as needed since carrots hold well in the ground. Seeds sown later in the season can stay in the ground all winter, if the ground in your area doesn't freeze completely.

planting and growing | varieties | produce selection and harvest | preparation methods

Carrots are an incredibly versatile vegetable. They can be sautéed, roasted, steamed, mashed, shredded—not to mention they can be used in both sweet and savory dishes. They also pair beautifully with a wide range of herbs and spices. Experiment with different combinations of tarragon, sweet paprika, cumin, curry, cilantro, parsley, and garlic.

- **Roasted:** Wash carrots thoroughly, chop, and toss onto a baking sheet. It isn't necessary to remove the skin of the carrot; unless you are serving them raw, no one will know the difference. Drizzle with olive oil, add salt and pepper, then roast them in an oven preheated to 400°. Carrots can take a while to cook. If you are in a hurry, remember that smaller pieces cook faster.
- **Mashed:** Have you ever had mashed carrots? They're delicious! The texture is much like sweet potatoes. Steam or boil the carrots until tender, mash, add a bit of butter and sea salt, and serve. Or try adding a bit of molasses or honey after mashing.
- **Sautéed:** Wash and chop carrots. Sauté them in a combination of butter and olive oil; add salt and pepper. Once the carrots start to soften, add a shot of dark honey or molasses. Let the concoction caramelize for 10 minutes or so, but be careful not to let the sugars burn.

preserving

Freezing; Dehydrating

DID YOU KNOW?

Those little carrots often sold as "baby carrots" may not be baby carrots after all. If they are labeled "baby-cut" carrots, they are whittled down from larger carrots specially developed for their color and sweetness. For true baby carrots, look for those labeled "baby carrots"—or grow your own.

Shepherd's Pie with Carrot and Sweet Potato Topping

This recipe is a wonderful variation on the traditional shepherd's pie. If you can't find lobster or oyster mushrooms, just use white button mushrooms, or whatever variety you like.

3 large sweet potatoes, pierced several times with a fork

3 carrots

Butter

Flour

1–1½ cups chicken stock

Salt and fresh-ground black pepper

1 yellow onion, chopped

1 lb. ground turkey

3 oz. lobster or oyster mushrooms, cleaned and chopped

4 cloves garlic, chopped

1 Tbsp. fennel seeds

1 tsp. dried rosemary

1 tsp. dried sage

3 kale leaves, stems removed and chopped

4 oz. frozen peas

3 bay leaves

- Preheat the oven to 400°. Wrap the sweet potatoes in foil. Wrap the carrots in foil with a sprinkling of water. Put the sweet potatoes and carrots in the oven. Roast until they are soft (check for doneness), 30 minutes to 1 hour. Remove from the oven and let cool 15 minutes. Scoop out the insides of the sweet potatoes into a bowl. Add the carrots. Mash together using a bit of butter and a splash of the stock to reach a good consistency. Season with the salt and pepper.

- Combine the onion, turkey, and mushrooms in a large sauté pan; sauté until the onion is caramelized and brown. Add the garlic, fennel, rosemary, and sage, and salt and pepper to taste. Move the pan contents to the side and add 1 Tbsp. butter and 1 Tbsp. flour to the center of the pan (mix to create a roux). Allow the roux to cook for a minute or so to eliminate the floury taste. Depending upon how much liquid is already in your pan, add 1 to 1½ cups of stock. You want enough liquid to create gravy, but not a soup. Add the kale, peas, and bay leaves. Bring to a simmer. Allow time for the gravy to thicken. When the gravy is thickened, cover the top of the mixture with the sweet potato/carrot mash. Bake 35 to 45 minutes until the flavors are combined and the top is crisp.

Beet, Carrot, and Cabbage Slaw

Slaw

3 medium yellow beets (substitute whatever variety you prefer), shredded

3 medium carrots, shredded

1 head cabbage, shredded

1/2 red onion, shredded

Dressing

3/4 cup white wine vinegar

2 Tbsp. Dijon mustard

1 tsp. honey

1 small shallot, minced

1 tsp. fresh thyme, chopped

Salt and fresh-ground black pepper

3/4 cup olive oil

■ Place the beets, carrots, cabbage, and onion in a large bowl. In a small bowl combine the vinegar, mustard, honey, shallot, thyme, and salt and pepper to taste. Whisk to combine. Slowly add the olive oil in a stream, whisking constantly to emulsify. Pour the dressing over the slaw. Toss to coat. Refrigerate 1 hour before serving.

Maple-Glazed Carrots

1 Tbsp. butter

1 lb. carrots, peeled and sliced into match sticks or diagonal rounds

4 Tbsp. maple syrup

Pinch of cinnamon

■ Melt the butter in a sauté pan over medium heat. Add the carrots and sauté 5 minutes. Add 1/4 cup of water, the maple syrup, and cinnamon. Cover and cook until the carrots are tender—about 10 minutes.

Italian Ragu Sauce

1 medium yellow onion, chopped
4 cloves garlic, chopped
2 medium carrots, finely grated
1 lb. ground beef
4 oz. mushrooms, chopped
1 tsp. fennel seeds
1 tsp. dried oregano
1 tsp. dried basil
1 tsp. dried rosemary
1 tsp. dried thyme

1 tsp. red pepper flakes
1 tsp. sugar
Salt and fresh-ground black pepper
1 Tbsp. tomato paste
1 8 oz. can tomato sauce
1 16 oz. can diced tomatoes*
2 bay leaves
2 Tbsp. anchovy paste, if desired
Pasta

- Sauté the onion, garlic, and carrots in a medium pan over medium heat. Cook until softened. Add the beef, mushrooms, fennel, oregano, basil, rosemary, thyme, red pepper flakes, sugar, and salt and pepper to taste. Cook until the meat is browned. Add the tomato paste, tomato sauce, tomatoes, bay leaves, and anchovy paste. (The anchovies add a bit of depth to the sauce, but if you fear the fish, feel free to skip.) Simmer over low heat 30 minutes or longer. Tomato sauces like this one taste better if they are allowed to simmer; if you have time, let it go for an hour or so.

- Prepare the pasta of your choice and add to the pan containing the sauce. Give the pasta a chance to absorb the sauce. This really brings the pasta to life— so don't skip this step!

Thai Noodle Salad with Zucchini and Carrots

This recipe tastes good whether warm, cold, or at room temperature. Because it doesn't have any mayonnaise or egg-based dressing, it is great for a picnic or lunch on the go.

2 medium zucchini, grated

2 medium carrots, grated

4 scallions, cleaned and chopped (white and light-green parts only)

Olive oil

4 cloves garlic, peeled but not mashed

Fresh-ground black pepper

Red pepper flakes

Tamari

1 package rice noodles, prepared according to package directions and drained

1½ cups fresh basil, chopped

1 Tbsp. rice wine vinegar

2 oz. whole roasted peanuts

2 oz. whole roasted cashews

Pinch of sea salt

- Add the zucchini, carrots, and scallions to a large sauté pan. Add a little olive oil to the pan. Sauté over medium heat for 2 to 3 minutes. Add the garlic, black pepper, red pepper flakes, and tamari. Cook until the garlic is just tender. Remove the garlic and drop the cloves into the bowl of a food processor. Add the prepared noodles to the sauté pan, turning to coat. Set aside.

- In the bowl of the food processor containing the garlic, add the basil, vinegar, peanuts, cashews, and salt. Add about a tablespoon of olive oil. Process in short pulses to create a sauce. Pour the sauce over the noodle-vegetable mixture. Toss to coat and serve.

Curried Carrot Soup

2 Tbsp. butter

1 medium leek, cleaned and thinly
   sliced (white and light-green part
   only)

1 lb. carrots, thinly sliced

2 large potatoes, thinly sliced

$\frac{1}{2}$ cup dry sherry

3 cups vegetable stock

1 tsp. good-quality curry powder

$\frac{3}{4}$ cup heavy cream

Cilantro for garnish

- In a heavy stockpot over low heat, melt the butter and sauté the leek until softened; about 5 minutes. Add the carrots and potatoes. Toss 2 to 3 minutes. Add the sherry and sauté 5 minutes. Add the stock and curry powder. Cover and simmer about 40 minutes on medium-low heat.

- Add a bit of the soup to the cream and mix well before adding the cream to the soup mixture. Process the soup with an immersion blender or in batches in a blender until smooth. Garnish with cilantro before serving.

 information:// Nutrition

Your mother was right. You should eat your carrots. One cup of raw carrots (52 calories) has more than 20,000 IUs of vitamin A, about 428 percent of your daily needs.

A nutritional powerhouse, carrots also contain vitamin C, several B vitamins, potassium, and vitamin K, not to mention other nutrients.

Carrots also have loads of carotenoids. These powerful compounds—which include beta-carotene and alpha-carotene—derive their name from carrots and are responsible for the pigment

of many deep-orange vegetables. Carotenoids may significantly reduce the risk of lung, bladder, prostate, colon, and breast cancers. Eating carrots may also help protect your eyesight and prevent cataracts due to high levels of two powerful antioxidants called lutein and zeaxanthin.

Cooking carrots gently allows various nutrients to be more easily absorbed, although raw carrots are also healthy. Maximize your absorption of carotenoids and vitamin A by adding a little healthy fat, such as olive oil.

Curried Carrot Soup

vegetable:// **Cucumber &
Squash**

planting and growing | varieties | produce selection and harvest | preparation methods

If you're a beginning gardener and want to feel that flush of success that comes from being inundated with fresh produce, grow cucumbers and squash. With just a few plants you'll have enough to feed your family, your friends, and your friends' friends.

Both cucumbers and squash need warm weather and full sun. You can either sow cucumbers directly or begin the seeds indoors in peat pots four weeks before transplanting outside. Summer squash can easily be sown directly outdoors, but you may wish to start winter squash indoors four weeks before planting because of their longer time to maturity.

Squash and cucumbers are heavy feeders, so prepare the soil by adding liberal amounts of compost. For either squash or cucumbers, mound soil in hills or in rows and plant seeds in clusters of three. Space cucumber clusters three feet apart. Give squash a bit more room, about five or six feet, since the vines will sprawl on the ground as they grow.

If space is at a premium, both cucumbers and squash can be trained to grow up a fence, trellis, or other vertical support. The vines will attach to the trellis via tendrils, but they may need some assistance to get them started. Cucumbers are small enough that you won't need to offer any additional support, but larger squash varieties are heavy enough either to pull the vine off the trellis or the fruit off the vine. In order to prevent that, use a nylon stocking or other soft, flexible fabric to encircle and tie the squash directly to the support.

Keep the growing vegetables, especially the cucumbers, well watered—but not standing in puddles—during dry weather. Cucumbers under stress from underwatering or even poor soil become bitter and unpalatable. So feed and water generously!

Winter squash will take much longer to mature than summer squash. To keep them from rotting, nestle the squash in mulch or perch them on a low piece of plastic or wood.

planting and growing | **varieties** | produce selection and harvest | preparation methods

There are two types of cucumbers—the longer, slicing varieties and the shorter varieties suitable for pickling. Of course, you can also slice and eat those pickling cucumbers too.

Slicing: 'English', 'Burpless', 'Diva', 'Sweet Slice', 'Sweet Success'

Pickling: 'Eureka', 'Carolina', 'West India Gherkin'

Specialty: 'Armenian Yard Long', 'Lemon', 'Suyo Long'

There are two types of squash—summer squash, which should be enjoyed fresh during growing season, and winter squash, which can be eaten fresh or stored for up to six months.

SUMMER SQUASH

Standard: 'Zephyr' (yellow straightneck), 'Horn of Plenty' (yellow crookneck), 'Black Beauty' (zucchini), 'Golden Scallop', 'Starburst', and 'White Patty Pan' (patty pan)

WINTER SQUASH

Standard: 'Table Gold' (Acorn), 'Blue Hubbard', (Hubbard), 'Early Butternut', (Butternut), 'Sugar Loaf' (Delicata), 'Tivoli' (Spaghetti)

pests and diseases

Squash *Squash vine borer; Cucumber beetle; Squash bug; Aphids; Blossom end rot; Downy mildew; Bacterial wilt; Mosaic virus; Anthracnose; Powdery mildew; Verticillium wilt*

Cucumber *Cucumber beetle; Anthracnose; Downy mildew; Powdery mildew*

planting and growing | varieties | **produce selection and harvest** | preparation methods

At the market, select cucumbers that are plump, firm, and deep green in color without any yellow or brown discolorations. Smaller cucumbers generally have fewer seeds.

Many grocery stores stock cucumbers coated in wax to preserve the moisture content. These should be peeled before serving. Unless you're skilled with a pairing knife, use a vegetable peeler to avoid wasting the flesh of the cucumber.

Squash should also be firm and without discoloration. Smaller summer squash are more flavorful and tender than larger squashes. Winter squash should have a harder exterior than summer squash, with no soft spots or evidence of rotting.

Although you may already have a refrigerator full of cucumbers and squash, keep harvesting when the veggies are ready or the plants will stop producing. Pick squash every day or they will grow to the size of baseball bats and become tough and inedible.

Winter squash is not harvested until it's fully ripened and vines have died back. Cut from the stems with a sharp knife. Wash with a solution of two tablespoons of white distilled vinegar to one pint of water to reduce the occurrence of bacteria; rinse thoroughly.

Dry the squash and place them on a screen, rack, or some device that allows good air circulation. Store in a warm, dry space until the outer shell has hardened to the point that it is difficult to make an indention with your fingernail. Squash prepared this way can be stored for up to five months in a basement or unheated garage that maintains a temperature of around 45 to 50 degrees.

ROBIN RIPLEY

One year I had a bumper crop of zucchini the same year my gardening friends did. We couldn't give the stuff away! As a joke, we started sneaking bags of it into the back seats of each other's cars until we all had to begin locking the doors. Then, we just left it on each other's doorsteps!

| planting and growing | varieties | produce selection and harvest | **preparation methods** |

■ **Raw:** Cucumbers and summer squash can be eaten raw in salads and with dips. Both have a crisp texture and mild flavor that really comes to life when they're eaten uncooked.

■ **Pickled:** Cucumbers and summer squash can also be pickled alone or with other vegetables. Keep in mind that if you are using a hot canning process, crispness will be reduced. If you prefer the snap of fresh veggies, try a cold pickling process instead.

■ **Sautéed/Stir-Fried:** Believe it or not, both summer squash and cucumbers can be sautéed until tender-crisp with shallots and lemon for a surprisingly good dish. Both are also tasty components in a number of Asian recipes, including stir-fries and lettuce wraps.

■ **Grilled/Roasted/Baked:** All kinds of squash can be grilled or roasted. Summer squash can be sliced, drizzled in olive oil, and grilled. It can also be cubed, tossed in olive oil, and roasted in the oven. Keep an eye on it; summer squash cooks

DID YOU KNOW?

The first blossoms that appear on squash plants are usually male. Female squash flowers will quickly develop a tiny swelling that resembles the miniature squash that it is. Although a few male squash blossoms are needed for pollination, you can harvest the other males, and even some of the females, and eat them raw, fried, stuffed, or incorporated into dishes such as quiche or frittatas.

very quickly. Winter squash can be cooked in the same way, once the outer skin is removed. Or, you can slice the squash in half, place both pieces on a baking sheet, and roast as described.

■ **Mashed/Puréed:** Winter squash is fantastic when it's mashed or puréed. It can either be baked or cubed and simmered in water or stock until tender. Transfer the cooked squash to a bowl, add a bit of butter and salt, and mash. To purée, drain cooked squash and reserve a cup of the cooking liquid. Put squash in the bowl of a food processor and pulse. Add liquid to loosen mixture to desired consistency. Winter squash can be substituted for mashed potatoes and also incorporated into pies, soups, and even breads.

| preserving |

Canning; Dehydrating; Freezing; Vacuum

Asian Cucumber Salad

Many people are so accustomed to the ubiquitous cucumber paired with vinegar salads that they are surprised by the flavorful and exotic taste of this Asian version made by switching the types of vinegar and oil.

3 medium cucumbers, peeled, seeded, sliced lengthwise and then sliced
  crosswise in thin slices
1 Tbsp. kosher salt
3 Tbsp. rice wine vinegar
3 Tbsp. toasted sesame oil
$1/2$ tsp. sugar
$1/4$ tsp. hot red pepper flakes
$1\frac{1}{2}$ Tbsp. sesame seeds, toasted in a skillet until golden brown

- Toss the cucumbers with the salt and place in a colander in the sink. Place an ice-filled bag on the cucumbers to drain for 45 minutes to 1 hour. (The ice bag will weight the cucumbers to help their liquid drain.) Whisk the vinegar, sesame oil, sugar, and hot pepper flakes until blended and the sugar is dissolved. Rinse the cucumbers and pat them dry with paper towels. Toss the cucumbers with the dressing. Top with the sesame seeds and serve immediately.

Butternut Squash and Brown Rice Risotto

Keep in mind the following tips as you prepare this dish:
- Brown rice always takes longer to cook than white rice; this is not a fast risotto recipe.
- You can cheat a bit and start the recipe using a traditional risotto method, then about 30 minutes later, add enough liquid to cover the rice, cover the pot and cook another 15 to 20 minutes and you will achieve a similar result.
- You can avoid all of this by using standard short grain white rice, like arborio, but the flavor combo of the butternut squash and brown rice is outstanding. Or, peel, cube, and roast the squash and add to cooked brown rice. Delicious!
- Salt at the end of the cooking process. This recipe calls for reduced stock and Parmesan…if you aren't careful, you will have a salt lick by the time you are through.

1 butternut squash, peeled and cubed	2 bay leaves
6 cups chicken stock	1 Tbsp. fennel seeds
Olive oil, good quality	1 tsp. rubbed sage
3 Tbsp. butter	$\frac{1}{2}$ cup grated Parmesan cheese
1 large yellow onion, sliced	Salt and fresh-ground black pepper
4 cloves garlic, sliced	Grating of nutmeg
2 cups short grain rice, brown or white	

- Place the squash in a large bowl. Add a bit of water, cover with plastic wrap, and microwave until squash is fork tender. Mash, but don't eliminate all the texture; set aside. Pour the stock into a stockpot and bring to a simmer. Reduce the heat and cover with a lid. You don't want the stock to evaporate, just to stay warm.

- Combine olive oil to coat the pan and the butter in a medium sauté pan over medium-low heat. Sauté the onion and garlic slowly to caramelize. Once the onion is soft and caramelized, add the rice, bay leaves, fennel seeds, and sage. Toast the rice for a few minutes.

- Add the warmed stock, a couple of cups at a time, stirring to incorporate. Continue to add stock as the rice absorbs the liquid until the rice stops absorbing readily and/or when the rice is tender and has a creamy consistency.

- Fold in the prepared squash and the Parmesan cheese. Heat through. Adjust the seasonings with the salt and pepper. Add a few gratings of nutmeg. Finish with a light drizzle of the olive oil.

Butternut Squash and Brown Rice Risotto

Roasted Summer Squash Dip

3–4 summer squash, cleaned and cut into chunks
2–3 cloves garlic, skin on
Extra-virgin olive oil
Salt and fresh-ground black pepper
1 tsp. fresh thyme leaves, chopped
1 lemon, zest and juice
Vegetable sticks, crackers, or pita for serving

- Preheat the oven to 350°. Place the squash and garlic on a baking sheet, drizzle with olive oil, and salt and pepper to taste. Toss to coat. Roast 25 minutes or until the squash and garlic have caramelized. Remove from the oven and let cool.

- Now, this by itself is a great way to prepare squash. You could certainly stop right there, slip the garlic out of its skins, chop, and eat. But if you want to make the dip, remove the garlic from its skins. Combine the garlic, squash, thyme, and lemon zest and juice to the bowl of a food processor. Process in short pulses until it develops a smooth consistency. Slowly add more olive oil to loosen mixture a bit and add flavor. Serve with noshing snacks (veggies and crackers, for example) or use as spread in pitas and sandwiches.

Cucumber Yogurt Salad

This is an amazingly versatile dish that can be eaten alone, used as a dip for other vegetables, or as a topping on lentils and rice or other bean dishes. This sauce is also a great accompaniment for Greek dishes made with lamb or falafel.

1 clove garlic

1 tsp. salt

3 cups plain Greek or other plain yogurt

2 cucumbers, peeled, seeded and diced

1 Tbsp. chopped fresh mint, optional

■ With a mortar and pestle or in the bottom of a small bowl, mash the garlic with the salt. Add the yogurt, cucumbers, and mint, if desired. Mix well.

Cucumber Yogurt Salad

Cucumbers have a high water content, which can keep them from absorbing the flavors or dressings of other foods. To make them more amenable to absorbing flavors, slice the cucumbers, sprinkle them liberally with kosher salt, and place them in a colander. Weight the cucumbers with a bag of ice to keep them cool and to press out the excess moisture, for about an hour. Rinse well to remove the salt and pat dry with paper towels.

 information:// Nutrition

You can enjoy squash in summer or winter. But there are big nutritional differences between the varieties.

Summer squash, such as zucchini, has traces of most vitamins and minerals. A cup of raw zucchini contains about a third of your daily vitamin C requirements, as well as some B vitamins and minerals like potassium. Squash also contains lutein and zeaxanthin, two antioxidants known for protecting the eyes.

Winter squash is a nutritional powerhouse. Eat a cup of baked butternut squash and you'll get half your vitamin C daily requirements and 457 percent of vitamin A needs. There are also B vitamins and plenty of minerals, particularly magnesium and manganese.

That's not all. Winter squash has loads of betacarotene, alpha-carotene, and other carotenoids, which boost immune systems and fight against infections and cancer.

Cucumbers are refreshing for summer. They aren't high in nutrients, but they don't have many calories, either. A half-cup has about 8 calories.

vegetable:// Cool-Season Greens

planting and growing | varieties | produce selection and harvest | preparation methods

It's amazing the bounty of groceries you can grow even when it's too cold to feel like stepping outside. But pop some cool-season greens into the ground, such as collard greens, mustard greens, Swiss chard, curly and flowering kales, and you'll be able to harvest early and often in spring and even well into winter.

You can begin seedlings indoors about four weeks before you plan to transplant outside, but if the soil is workable in late winter or early spring, you can start any cool-season green directly in the garden. Start your seeds as soon as the ground can be worked—about four weeks before the last average frost date. For a fall crop, you can begin the seeds in late summer—late July or August—for greens that will carry you well into winter.

Choose a sunny location for your greens bed. Most cool-season greens are not particular about the soil, but it's best to add some compost or well-rotted manure to the bed. If your soil is particularly acidic, you can also work in some lime.

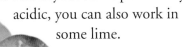

Sow seeds for most cool-season greens about one-half inch deep in furrows a few inches apart. As they grow, continue to thin the seedlings of larger greens, such as collards and kale, until they are two to three feet apart. You can use these baby greens in salads. Spinach can be more closely planted, but it should not be allowed to become crowded or it will bolt too quickly.

The roots of most greens are shallow, so make sure the plants have constant moisture. If necessary, add a layer of mulch to help hold in moisture and keep the roots from drying out. Once the plants are growing, they will appreciate a shot or two of fish emulsion fertilizer.

planting and growing | **varieties** | produce selection and harvest | preparation methods

SPINACH is somewhat temperamental and will bolt if it is too crowded. It will also bolt as the days lengthen in spring or if the weather is too hot.

Varieties: 'Bloomsdale Longstanding', 'Olympia', 'Tyee'

SWISS CHARD is an amazing producer, surviving from early spring through the hot summer and well into winter.

Varieties: colored stems, 'Bright Lights', 'Yellow Lights'; white stems, 'Montruso', 'Fordhook Giant'

KALE is an easy-to-grow, easy-to-eat green. It comes in a variety of textures and colors.

Varieties: 'Winterbor', 'Red Russian', 'Nero Di Toscana' or 'Dinosaur', 'Dwarf Blue Curled Scotch'

COLLARDS have long been a staple in southern gardens.

Varieties: 'Vates', 'Georgia Southern' (Creole), 'Morris Heading'

Unfortunately, these greens have hogged the spotlight for much of America's culinary history. But there is a whole wide world of greens out there, and if you are feeling adventurous, try some of these…you won't regret it!

Varieties: 'Bok Choy', 'Giant Red Mustard', 'Tatsoi', 'Osaka Purple Mustard', 'Huazontle' (Red Aztec Spinach)

pests and diseases

Cabbage loopers; Cabbage worms; Cutworms; Flea beetle

ROBIN RIPLEY

When I was a kid, my mom would occasionally declare "Meatless Day." On this dreaded day she would cook a big pot of beans, prepare some collard greens, and bake cornbread. I absolutely hated that meal as a kid. Thankfully, I have grown wiser as I have grown older. Today it is comfort food!

planting and growing | varieties | **produce selection and harvest** | preparation methods

Greens at the grocery store or farmers' markets should be robust in color. They should appear vibrant with no signs of yellow, brown, or decay. Avoid greens that appear wilted or shriveled.

Spinach can be purchased frozen at the store. When using it in recipes, make sure you defrost it and squeeze as much liquid as possible from it. If you don't, you are likely to have a soupy mess.

Harvest at home anytime during the growing cycle. Snip off leaves and stems with a pair of scissors to prevent damage to the plant. Greens don't keep for long in the refrigerator, so harvest them just before using. Or harvest just before bolting, blanch for a couple of minutes, drop in an ice bath, and drain very well; freeze for future use.

Cabbage can be harvested as soon as a head forms. Cut the head from the stalk in order to encourage the plant to produce mini cabbage shoots for later harvest.

To extend the harvest of fall plants, mulch around the roots and the base of the plant to keep the greens producing. If you live in a very cold climate, add up to twelve inches of straw and a plastic cover to prevent the ground from freezing.

| planting and growing | varieties | produce selection and harvest | **preparation methods** |

Because cool-season greens vary greatly in their flavors and textures, you can always find one that suits your palate and your recipe.

- **Raw:** Other than spinach, an ubiquitous salad bar staple, most people think all greens should be cooked. In fact, most greens, including Swiss chard, mustard greens, and kale, can be eaten raw when the leaves are picked when they are young and tender.
- **Steamed:** A great way to prepare greens is by steaming. This can be done in an actual steamer or with half an inch of water in a pan (with a lid) on the stove.

- **Sautée/Stir-Fried:** Greens are often sautéed in olive oil. Spinach is wonderful sautéed with sliced garlic and a bit of balsamic vinegar.
- **Boiled:** Many people prefer the traditional method of boiling their greens with a ham bone or even with a few hot peppers. In the South it is common to serve greens with a bottle of vinegar for people to use to flavor the greens at the table.
- **Sneaky Greens:** If your family is greens-averse, try adding ribbons of greens to soups, casseroles, or even to mashed potatoes. They will never know the difference.

| preserving |

Freezing; Vacuum packing

DID YOU KNOW?

Many cool-season greens are cut-and-come-again vegetables. Rather than harvesting the whole plant, simply harvest the largest outer leaves and allow the plant to continue to grow. Most cool-season greens will continue to produce for weeks with this treatment.

Swiss Chard and Spaghetti

This dish is so delicious and easy; it will probably become part of your regular menu at home. If you use Swiss chard with red stems, the pasta takes on a lovely pink hue. Serve it with a crusty bread and salad for a hearty meal. Make sure to cook up a bunch so you can have leftovers the next day for lunch.

About 1½ lbs. Swiss chard, washed carefully, stems chopped, leaves
  reserved

2 Tbsp. butter

2 Tbsp. olive oil

2 cloves garlic, minced

1 tsp. dried red pepper flakes

8 oz. thin spaghetti, cooked according to package directions (al dente),
  drained

Salt

Parmesan or Asiago cheese

- Roll the Swiss chard leaves lengthwise into a tight bundle and slice into 1-inch ribbons.

- In a large skillet over low heat, melt the butter, and add the olive oil. Add the garlic. Stir the garlic constantly until it is soft, being careful not to let it burn. Add the red pepper flakes and stir. Add the stem pieces of the Swiss chard and sauté 3 to 4 minutes, until the chard is fairly tender. Add the Swiss chard leaves and toss until it is wilted and tender. Add the prepared pasta and toss to incorporate into the chard mixture. Season with salt to taste. To serve, top the pasta with the Parmesan cheese.

Brazilian Collard Greens

If you grew up in the South you probably think collards take hours to cook and involve a hambone. This version can be made in less than 10 minutes, retains more of the vitamins, and is just delicious.

2 Tbsp. olive oil

1 clove garlic, minced

1 large bunch collard greens, washed, leaves rolled into tight bundle and sliced into ½-inch ribbons

Salt and fresh-ground black pepper

- In a large skillet over medium heat, combine the olive oil and garlic. Stir about 1 minute. Add the collards and toss until tender, about 5 minutes. Season to taste with the salt and pepper.

Wilted Spinach Salad

The spinach in this salad is wilted with hot oil to bring out its flavor and deepen its color. After trying this version of a spinach salad you may never be satisfied with a raw spinach salad again.

4 Tbsp. olive oil

1 clove garlic, minced

1 small red onion, diced

2 lbs. spinach leaves, washed carefully and stems removed

6 oz. feta cheese, crumbled

2 Tbsp. red wine vinegar

Fresh-ground black pepper

Kalamata olives, optional

- In a large stockpot, heat the olive oil and quickly sauté the garlic. Add the onion and stir for a few seconds. Keep the stockpot on the heat until the oil is very hot, but be careful not to let it smoke. Add the spinach and toss quickly. It will make a frightful sound, but keep tossing to cover the leaves evenly with the hot oil. Remove from heat and pour into serving bowl. Add the vinegar and feta cheese and season with pepper. Garnish with the kalamata olives, if desired.

Brazilian Collard Greens

Wilted Spinach Salad

Grandma's Stuffed Cabbage

Grandma's Stuffed Cabbage (Shared by Kim Pinkerton)

This simple and nourishing meal comes from a recipe passed down through our family. My mom often made this hardy dish on weekends to feed our large family. There are many variations of this dish, but this one is easy and delicious. All ingredients are approximate since the recipe was never written down, so you can adjust seasonings and amounts to suit your taste. It's especially good in winter, when fewer seasonal vegetables are available.

1 head green cabbage, cored
1½ lb. ground beef
½ lb. sausage
½ cup uncooked long grain rice
1 small onion, chopped
2 eggs
1 clove garlic, minced
¼ tsp. ground caraway seed
Salt and fresh-ground black pepper
Ketchup or tomato juice

- Scald the cabbage in a pan of water for a few minutes until you can peel the leaves off. Set the cabbage aside. In a large bowl, combine the beef, sausage, rice, onion, eggs, garlic, caraway seed, and salt and pepper to taste. My mom says to mix it all with your hands.

- Form the mixture into golf-ball-sized meatballs. Fold a cabbage leaf around each meatball. Stack them in a stockpot. Cover with water and simmer, with a lid partially on, for 2 hours. The liquid will cook down so add enough ketchup to cover and cook another 30 minutes. Variation: Cook using only tomato juice without any of the water, if you prefer.

Spinach and Tomato Frittata

Though spinach and tomatoes are not in season at the same time, they both store exceptionally well. Just substitute canned or frozen tomatoes and frozen spinach, depending upon the time of year.

8 large eggs

Splash of milk

Salt and fresh-ground black pepper

Olive oil

1 small onion, chopped

2 cloves garlic, minced

1 cup fresh spinach,* cleaned and chopped

1 tsp. dried oregano

1 tsp. dried rosemary

Pinch of red chili pepper flakes, optional

1/2 cup feta cheese, crumbled

1 tomato, seeded and chopped*

*If you use frozen spinach, be sure to defrost it, place in a kitchen towel, and squeeze to remove all moisture. If you use canned or frozen tomatoes, drain as much liquid as possible.

■ Preheat the oven to 400°. In a medium bowl, whisk the eggs, milk, and salt and black pepper to taste until the yolks are broken and the eggs are incorporated. In an ovenproof pan over medium heat, add olive oil to coat the pan. Add the onion, garlic, spinach, oregano, rosemary, and red pepper flakes, if desired. Sauté.

■ Pour the prepared eggs over the spinach mixture. Use a spatula to ensure the mixture is even and to lift contents of pan so any uncooked egg mixture can reach the bottom of the ovenproof pan. Top with the feta and tomato. When the eggs are starting to set, put the pan into the oven. Bake 10 to 15 minutes or until top is golden and the center doesn't move. Remove from the oven and let stand for a few minutes before serving.

Crispy Kale

Crispy Kale

This recipe has three ingredients. Just three . . . but it is so yummy! And, it is a great way to get your kids to eat their veggies. Serve this instead of potato chips or as a fun side at dinner.

5 kale leaves, stems removed and chopped
Olive oil
Good-quality sea salt

- Preheat the oven to 350º. Place the kale on a baking sheet. Drizzle with olive oil and salt; toss to coat. Bake 10 minutes. Remove from the oven and toss again for maximum crispness. Bake 10 to 15 minutes more. The kale is done when it's completely crispy.

 information:// Nutrition

When it comes to nutrition, dark leafy greens really top the charts. These vegetables are simply loaded with vitamins, minerals, and antioxidants.

The nutritional king is kale. One cup of raw kale contains more than 10,000 IUs of vitamin A—or 206 percent of your daily needs—as well as 134 percent of vitamin C and 684 percent of vitamin K requirements. It also has B vitamins, potassium, calcium, and other minerals.

Mustard greens have less vitamin A, C, and K than kale, but they still offer impressive amounts.

These greens are excellent sources of folic acid, along with other nutrients. Best of all, a cup is about 15 calories.

Swiss chard and collard greens are other low-calories sources for many of these vitamins and minerals.

All these vegetables are rich in cancer-fighting phytochemicals—not to mention, the eye-strengthening carotenoids called lutein and zeaxanthin.

vegetable:// Lettuces & Salad Greens

| planting and growing | varieties | produce selection and harvest | preparation methods |

If you're paying $4 for a bag of salad greens in a grocery store, you'll be glad to know that growing your own will not only save you money, it's incredibly easy. It also is fairly adaptable to indoor growing, potentially extending your harvest to year-round!

Salad greens are a cool-season crop, so you can plant them in very early spring or in late summer for a fall harvest. To grow lettuces, prepare beds as soon as the soil is workable with generous amounts of compost or well-rotted manure. You can sow seeds directly in the garden or begin them indoors in flats about six weeks before transplanting outdoors. Sow seeds one half inch deep and about one inch apart in rows one foot apart.

Harvest the leaves daily, so they don't get too big and crowded, which can encourage them to bolt (go to seed) sooner. If you expect you'll harvest somewhat less frequently, space rows $1^1/_2$ feet apart.

As the seeds sprout and reach two inches in height, thin them, adding the pickings to your salads. Continue to thin the lettuce sprouts as they grow to prevent overcrowding. As the greens get established, fertilize with a balanced organic fertilizer or a liquid fish fertilizer. Keep them watered regularly, particularly as the season gets warmer.

To grow indoors, use seed flats instead of individual pots. Fill the flats with well-aged compost to ensure good drainage and nitrogen to stimulate leaf production. Place them in a very sunny location or use supplemental lighting. Use seedling mats to speed germination if the location is a bit chilly.

Indoor lettuce is best harvested as young greens. Some varieties are cut-and-come-again; others are not, so sowing a second flat a couple of weeks after the first will ensure you always have a fresh supply of greens.

| planting and growing | **varieties** | produce selection and harvest | preparation methods |

There are four widely used types of lettuce, and hundreds of other types of salad greens, so depending on your needs, location, and preferences, select your seeds with this in mind.

Crisphead: 'Great Lakes', 'Summertime', 'Ithaca'

Butterhead: 'Bibb', 'Buttercrunch', 'Esmeralda'

Loose leaf: 'Lollo Rosso', 'Deer Tongue', 'Flashy Butter Oak'

Romaine: 'Cimarron Red', 'Winter Density', 'Parris Island', 'Forellenschluss'

Other Salad Greens: 'Wild Garden Chicory', 'White Russian Kale', 'Purple Osaka Mustard', 'Tres Fin Endive', 'Epazote', 'Blonde Escarole', 'Red Head Quinoa', 'Burgundy Amaranth'

| planting and growing | varieties | **produce selection and harvest** | preparation methods |

Look for well-hydrated greens with good color, no discoloration, and, needless to say, no gooey or rotten areas. The lettuce should smell fresh and not musty. To reduce the risk of bacterial contamination, always look at the expiration dates on salad greens packaged in bags.

Harvesting salad greens at home means identifying whether they are loose leaf, romaine (cos), or headed varieties. To harvest loose leaf greens, you can begin cutting the outer leaves as

pests and diseases

Cutworms; Aphids; Slugs; Leafhoppers; Mosaic virus

soon as the plant is just five inches high, not removing too much of the plant at any one time. Head-forming greens are not harvested until the head is established, and then the entire plant is harvested. Romaine and other lettuce hybrids can be harvested at either time.

All salad greens can be harvested as "micro-greens," or when they are very young and tender. When harvested this young, the plants may not reproduce, so be sure to succession sow every few days to ensure ongoing harvests.

ROBIN RIPLEY

Let Mother Nature help out with your gardening chores. I usually let lettuce in my garden go to seed when it stops producing in hot weather. Invariably, I have little lettuce volunteers that appear around the garden the next year that I can leave in place or transplant to a more suitable location.

planting and growing | varieties | produce selection and harvest | **preparation methods**

Lettuces are usually eaten raw, as a vehicle for a wide variety of dressings, and as a companion to a host of other delicious foods. But more substantial salad greens can be added to soups, grilled, or even braised.

- **Fresh:** Of course, all salad greens can be eaten fresh. It's the easiest way to prepare them!
- **Grilled:** Any salad green that has "body" can be grilled. Varieties like romaine and radicchio hold their shape and taste great when lightly grilled.
- **Braised:** The French often cook endive. Try braising it by cutting it in half and placing it into a pan (over medium heat) with a bit of olive oil. Let it cook about 5 minutes or so. When it's brown and crispy, turn and brown the other side. Add a cup or so of chicken stock. Simmer and cook until tender.

- **Stir-Fried:** In Chinese kitchens, iceberg lettuce is often stir-fried with a bit of garlic, soy sauce, rice wine, and vinegar.
- **Baked:** Italians bake radicchio. Simply cut heads in half, drizzle with olive oil, and salt and pepper to taste, and bake at 400° for 10 minutes. Turn and bake for 10 minutes or until the core is tender when pierced with a knife.

DID YOU KNOW?

People on diets almost always eat salads thinking they're doing their waistlines a favor. This would be true if they didn't add all that fatty salad dressing. To keep your calories and waistline in line, have your dressing on the side or experiment with olive oil sprays instead of the pour-on dressings.

preserving

Lettuce does not store particularly well. Hardier greens, such as kale, can be blanched and frozen.

Caesar Salad

There seems to be a Caesar salad recipe on every restaurant menu. Here's one you can make at home the traditional way with torn romaine lettuce, grated Parmesan cheese, and croutons. You can also make divine Caesar salads that include such items as corn, sprouts, capers, and zucchini. Simply toss your preferred ingredients with the dressing described here, and enjoy!

½ tsp. salt

½ tsp. white pepper

¼ tsp. dry mustard

½ tsp. Dijon mustard

1 tsp. lemon juice

1 clove garlic, minced

2 Tbsp. white wine vinegar

1 tsp. Worcestershire sauce

3 Tbsp. olive oil

½ cup vegetable oil

1 egg (1 Tbsp. mayonnaise can be
   used instead of the egg)

Pinch of sugar

- In the bottom of a large salad bowl, combine the salt, white pepper, mustard, Dijon mustard, lemon juice, garlic, vinegar, Worcestershire, olive oil, vegetable oil, egg, and sugar. Mix well. Toss in salad ingredients of your choice and mix well.

Never-Fail Vinaigrette

4 Tbsp. vegetable oil

2 Tbsp. olive oil

2 Tbsp. good quality vinegar

1 tsp. lemon juice

1 clove garlic, minced

½ tsp. dry mustard

1 tsp. Dijon mustard

Salt and fresh-ground black pepper

- In a small bowl, whisk the vegetable oil, olive oil, vinegar, lemon juice, garlic, mustard, Dijon mustard, and salt and pepper to taste. Toss with salad greens.

Baby Spinach Salad with Blueberries and Pecans

Fresh baby spinach leaves, rinsed and spun dry

1 pint fresh raspberries, cleaned

1 pint fresh blueberries, cleaned

$\frac{1}{2}$ cup chopped pecans, toasted

Feta cheese, crumbled

Blueberry Vinaigrette

$\frac{1}{2}$ cup fresh blueberries

$\frac{1}{3}$ cup white balsamic vinegar

1 tsp. honey

Salt and fresh-ground black pepper

$\frac{2}{3}$ cup extra-virgin olive oil

- Combine the spinach, raspberries, blueberries, pecans, and feta in a large bowl; toss. To prepare the vinaigrette, in a food processor add the blueberries, vinegar, honey, and salt and pepper to taste. Process to break down the blueberries. While the food processor is running, slowly add the olive oil. Taste the vinaigrette and adjust any of ingredients to suit your taste. Pour the vinaigrette over the spinach salad and toss well.

Baby Spinach with Blueberries and Pecans

Sunny Citrus Salad

6 oz. mixed greens
2 small golden beets, roasted and chopped
1/4 cup hazelnuts, chopped
4 oz. asparagus, blanched, cooled in cold water, and cut into 1-inch pieces
1 small red onion, chopped
4 oz. shelled peas
4 oz. Mandarin orange segments, drained

Citrus Vinaigrette
1 tsp. Dijon mustard
2 oranges, juice only*
1 lime, juice only
Salt and fresh-ground black pepper
Pinch of sugar, optional
1/2–3/4 cup extra–virgin olive oil

- In a large bowl, combine salad ingredients. Set aside. In a small bowl, whisk the Dijon mustard, orange juice, lime juice, and salt and pepper to taste. Continue whisking while slowly adding the olive oil. Taste and adjust seasonings according to your taste. Add the sugar, if desired. Mix well.

*A nice variation is to reduce a bit of the orange juice and substitute Champagne vinegar.

Salade Niçoise

This traditional French salad takes a few steps to make, but it is worth the effort!

2 fresh tuna steaks

Olive oil

Salt and fresh-ground black pepper

3–4 new potatoes, cut into wedges

2 handfuls of green beans, trimmed

2 heads crisp lettuce, rinsed, spun dry, and torn into bite-sized pieces

3 hard-boiled eggs, shelled and sliced

3 ripe tomatoes, quartered

1 red onion, thinly sliced

Niçoise olives

Vinaigrette

1 shallot, finely minced

1 lemon, zest and juice

2 Tbsp. Dijon mustard

1 tsp. fines herbes*

$1/4$ cup white wine vinegar

Salt and fresh-ground black pepper

$2/3$ cup olive oil

2 Tbsp. small capers

Fines herbes is a mainstay of French cooking. This combination of herbs is often found at a grocery store ready to buy. It generally consists of chervil, parsley, chives, and tarragon.

- To prepare the vinaigrette, in a small bowl add the shallot, lemon zest and juice, Dijon mustard, fines herbes, vinegar, and salt and pepper to taste. Whisk to combine. Whisk the mixture continuously while adding the olive oil. Add the capers and whisk briefly.

- Prepare your type of grill. Drizzle the tuna steaks with the olive oil, and salt and pepper both sides. In a small bowl, coat the potatoes with olive oil, and salt and pepper to taste. Place the tuna and potatoes on the grill. Grill the tuna until medium-rare. Grill the potatoes until brown on the outside and soft on the inside.

- Add the green beans to a large saucepan of boiling water; cook 2 to 3 minutes. Remove the green beans and place into an ice bath. Drain and dry.

- To compose the salad, spread the lettuce across the bottom of a salad platter. Cut the grilled tuna into bite-sized portions and arrange. Layer the grilled potatoes and green beans over the tuna. Layer the eggs and tomatoes. Scatter the onion and olives across the platter. Drizzle the vinaigrette over the salad. Serve with a crusty baguette.

Salade Niçoise

Strawberry and Stone Fruit Coulis

Fig and Arugula Composed Salad

6–8 oz. arugula, cleaned

4 fresh figs, stems removed and
quartered

1 Bosc pear, cored and sliced

1 medium red onion, sliced

3 oz. Gorgonzola, crumbled

2 oz. pine nuts, toasted

Dressing

¼ cup balsamic vinegar

1 tsp. fresh-ground black pepper

Pinch of salt

Pinch of sugar

½ cup olive oil

- To prepare the dressing, in a small bowl whisk the vinegar, pepper, salt, and sugar. Continue whisking while drizzling in the olive oil.

- A composed salad is formed in layers. Start with a bed of the arugula. Layer the figs, pear, onion, Gorgonzola, and pine nuts on top of the arugula. Drizzle the dressing over the salad and serve.

 information:// **Nutrition**

As a rule of thumb, the greens with the darkest leaves have the highest nutrient content. Romaine, for instance, is rich in vitamins A and K. One cup provides 82 percent of daily vitamin A needs and 60 percent of vitamin K requirements. There are decent amounts of vitamin C and folate too, as well as other minerals and vitamins.

With red leaf lettuce, you'll get half the vitamin A and much less vitamin C than with romaine. But red leaf does contain high levels of vitamin K and traces of other minerals and vitamins.

Butterhead lettuces—like Boston and bibb types— have high vitamin K levels. However, they have considerably less vitamin C than romaine and slightly less than half the vitamin A.

Don't forget to add other greens. Endive has iron, potassium, calcium and vitamin A. Watercress is healthy too. A cup of fresh watercress will provide nearly a quarter of your vitamin A and C daily needs for 4 calories.

vegetable:// **Peas**

planting and growing | varieties | produce selection and harvest | preparation methods

Peas have many endearing qualities. They are among the first vegetables you can harvest as you shake off winter. They enrich the soil with their nitrogen-fixing abilities. They will be harvested and gone early enough that you can use their garden space for a different crop. They freeze and dry amazingly well. And, of course, they are nutritious and taste sublime, whether eaten raw while still standing in the garden, in a salad, or cooked. Peas get our vote for the garden!

If you want to plant peas, you must start early. They dislike the heat and will slow growth and eventually stop producing altogether once temperatures reach about 70 degrees.

Some gardeners in warmer climates get a jump-start on spring by sowing peas in late fall. Other gardeners use St. Patrick's Day as their pea planting target date. You can calculate your own sowing date by counting back four to six weeks from your area's last average frost.

Choose a location that gets sun most of the day and has good drainage. Peas are deep rooted, so make sure the soil is loose and amended with compost. Don't bother starting peas indoors since they don't like to be transplanted. Instead, you can fast-track germination by soaking them overnight before directly sowing into the soil.

Although it isn't absolutely necessary, it's a good idea to a use a bacteria inoculant powder, available at your nursery or through mail order, before planting. University trials have shown that inoculated peas produce about three-quarters more than those not treated. Just mix the powder with the peas or directly into the soil.

Sow seeds an inch apart and thin to about two inches apart when the seedlings are two inches high, using the thinnings in salads or soups. Keep the soil moist, but make sure the peas aren't standing in water.

Peas grow up more than out, so except for dwarf varieties, you'll need to provide some support to keep them from sprawling on the ground. You can make trellises from stakes and string or even use found materials, such as pruned tree branches. Planting along the garden fence or even using old tomato cages can work in a pinch.

planting and growing | **varieties** | produce selection and harvest | preparation methods

planting and growing | varieties | **produce selection and harvest** | preparation methods

There are three types of peas: shelling peas, eaten without the shell; sugar snap peas, eaten whole when the peas inside are plump; and snow peas, eaten whole when the peas are still tiny and the shell is flat. If one of your goals in growing peas is to feed a crowd, choose a snap or snow pea so you can use the pods in salads and other dishes.

Shelling Peas: 'Wando', 'Green Arrow', 'Improved Laxton's Progress'

Snap Peas: 'Sugar Snap', 'Sugar Ann', 'Sugar Mel'

Snow Peas: 'Mammoth Melting Sugar', 'Dwarf Grey Sugar', 'Golden Sweet Edible Podded'

ROBIN RIPLEY

Pea picking is a two-handed operation. Hold the vine with one hand while gently pulling the pea with the other. Try it one-handed and you risk pulling up the whole vine.

pests and diseases

Aphids; Pea weevils; Slugs/snails; Thrips; Fusarium wilt; Mosaic virus; Root rot; Downy mildew; Powdery mildew

Although you can find fresh peas in the produce aisle, you'll probably discover they are considerably more expensive than in the freezer section. What's more, those peas have probably been sitting around for a while, making them less nutritious than peas that have been flash frozen after picking to lock in the nutrients. So for the best value and nutrition, choose freshly picked or frozen peas if you're not growing your own.

Harvesting peas at home is very easy. The most important thing to remember is to harvest when the peas are young, generally three weeks after blooming. Pick all peas when they're relatively young and tender and plan to eat them the day they are picked so the sugars don't turn into starch and the peas lose their flavor.

Shelling peas are ready to harvest when the pod is filled with big, beautiful peas. Snow peas should be picked when the pods are still flat. Snap peas can be picked when the pods are flat or harvested when pods are plump and tender. Any pea that has passed its prime can be shelled, dried, and stored for future use.

DID YOU KNOW?

If you're short on space, you can grow peas in containers. Just follow the same general planting instructions, making sure to provide support for the growing vines.

planting and growing | varieties | produce selection and harvest | **preparation methods**

- **Fresh:** Many a child has discovered a love of peas by standing next to the vine and popping the sweet, green peas right into their mouths. When fresh, they can be added directly to salads or used on a crudité platter with dip. Garden peas are a popular salad with onions and mayonnaise, but you can add radishes and shredded carrots to turn a traditional dish into a confetti salad.

- **Blanched:** All peas can be tossed into a pan of boiling water for a quick, 1 to 2 minutes, of cooking. Serve immediately, or immerse in an ice bath for use in cold dishes. Sugar snap peas, once blanched and chilled, make a fantastic accompaniment to a refreshing herb dip or as a last minute addition to a spring salad.

- **Sautéed/Stir-Fried:** Sugar snap and snow peas are often used in stir-fries or sautéed with olive oil or butter. Snow peas should be added at the end of a recipe, snap peas a bit earlier. For a twist, try adding mint, parsley, lemon, or curry powder.

- **Dried:** Peas that have matured beyond what is edible in a fresh state are perfect for drying. Use them as you would other dried beans, particularly when a touch of sweetness is needed.

preserving

Freezing; Dehydrating

Creamed Peas

2 Tbsp. butter
2 Tbsp. all-purpose flour
1 cup half and half
2 cups shelled peas

⅓ cup grated Parmesan cheese
Salt and fresh-ground black pepper
Grating of nutmeg

- Add the butter and flour to a saucepan over medium heat. Stir until the butter melts, then cook for 1 minute. Whisk in the half and half, watching for any lumps. Whisk continuously over heat until the mixture thickens. Reduce the heat to low. Add the peas, Parmesan cheese, salt and pepper to taste, and nutmeg. Stir to combine. Cook for 3 minutes. Remove from the heat and serve.

Be careful not to have the heat too high while making this recipe. It is easy to burn the solids in the milk and butter.

Creamed Peas

Sugar Snaps with Rotini and Goat Cheese

2 Tbsp. olive oil

1 large onion, chopped

2 cups sugar snaps, trimmed and cut into ½-inch pieces

1 8-oz. package rotini pasta, cooked according to package directions
  to al dente stage

8 oz. soft goat cheese

1½ cups chicken stock

½ cup chopped fresh herbs, such as basil, parsley, oregano, or marjoram
  (or a mix)

Salt and fresh-ground black pepper

- Heat the olive oil in a large, nonstick skillet over medium heat. Add the onion and sauté until golden brown, about 10 minutes. Add the sugar snaps. Sauté until the peas are barely tender and are bright green.

- Add the prepared pasta and goat cheese to the vegetable mixture in the skillet. Over the heat, mix until the goat cheese is well incorporated. Add the chicken stock and herbs. Cover and simmer 5 minutes before serving. Season to taste with salt and pepper.

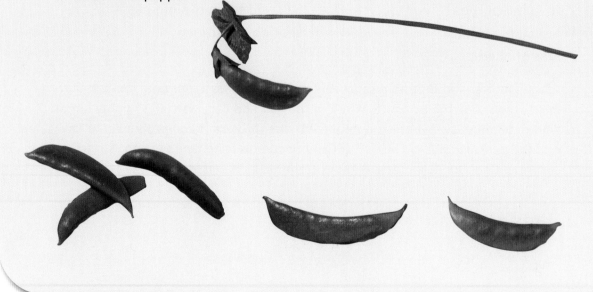

Indian Peas and Potatoes

Mashed potatoes take on a distinctive international flair—and a nutritional boost—with the addition of garden peas and Garam Masala, an Indian spice available at specialty food stores and some grocery stores.

1½ lbs. potatoes, peeled and diced
2 cups shelled garden peas
2 Tbsp. butter
1 Tbsp. canola oil
2 tsp. Garam Masala or other Indian spice powder
³/₄ cup cilantro, for garnish

- Over medium-high heat, bring the potatoes to a boil in a large saucepan with plenty of water. Cook until nearly tender. Add the peas. Cook until both the peas and potatoes are tender. Drain.

- In a large skillet, melt the butter and add the oil. Add the potatoes and peas and gently mash the vegetables with the back of a fork until they have a lumpy consistency. Add the Garam Masala and thoroughly mix. Heat the mixture through. Garnish with the cilantro before serving.

Indian Peas and Potatoes

Thai Summer Rolls (Shared by Laura Matthews)

These are best if they are assembled no more than two hours prior to serving.

Peanut Sauce

³/₄ cup unsweetened, natural creamy peanut butter	1 Tbsp. fish sauce
	2 Tbsp. rice wine or pear infused vinegar
½ cup sugar	3 Tbsp. red curry paste
1 13.5-oz. can coconut milk	Pinch of cayenne pepper

■ Prepare the peanut sauce (if you are using peanut butter containing sugar, do not add the ½ cup sugar listed in the ingredients). In a medium saucepan over medium heat, combine ½ cup water, the peanut butter, sugar, coconut milk, 1 tablespoon of the fish sauce, vinegar, and the remaining red curry paste and cayenne to taste. Whisk to blend as mixture simmers. Reduce the heat a bit. Cook for 3 minutes and set aside to cool. Stir occasionally as it cools.

Summer Rolls

2 Tbsp. sesame oil

Two boned skinless chicken breasts cut into 12 narrow strips

¼ cup Thai red curry paste, divided

3 Tbsp. fish sauce, divided

2 tiny pinches of cayenne pepper (or, for the truly daring, use slivers of Thai chili peppers to taste)

1 package rice paper (available in many markets or Asian food stores), soaked in warm water according to package directions or as described

1½ cups spring mix lettuce or any fresh garden lettuces

12 medium shrimp, steamed, tails off, peeled, and deveined (if you use precooked shrimp, remove the tails)

12 Thai basil leaves, washed, dried, and cut into ½-inch strips (can use any type but I like the pungency of Thai. Two leaves of basil are needed per roll.)

4 scallions, cut into 12 pieces (white and light-green parts only)

1 large green cucumber, cut into 12 narrow pieces

1 cup thinly sliced snow peas

- Heat the sesame oil in a large skillet over medium-high heat. Add the chicken and 1 tablespoon of the Thai red curry paste. Add 1 tablespoon of the fish sauce. Add the cayenne (use a good pinch if you're brave). Cook the chicken until just done, about 6 minutes, stirring frequently. Set aside to cool.

- Start assembling the rolls by filling a deep plate or wide bowl with warm water. Soak the rice paper in the water until it softens, about 1 minute. Once it's pliable, spread the rice paper on a cutting board. It helps to add another rice paper to the water to soften before assembling the roll so the wrapper is ready for the next roll.

- Sprinkle lettuce across the top half, to barely cover the top half of the circle about ½ inch in from the edge of the half circle. On top of lettuce, add 1 piece of chicken and 1 shrimp toward the center of the upper half. Cover with 2 pieces of basil, 2-3 slices of snowpeas, 1 piece of scallion, and 1 piece of cucumber. Drizzle the top half with 1 tablespoon peanut sauce per roll.

- Fold the top and bottom edges of the rice paper to meet in the center of the roll. Tightly pinch the left side of what now is nearly a rectangle, and roll toward the end. The roll will stay together as the rice paper meets and dries. Repeat until all rolls have been assembled.

Mockamole

Mockamole

Peas combine beautifully with avocados to make this a healthy twist on the Mexican food favorite. You can use this as a traditional chip dip or as a topping on grilled fish, chicken, or vegetables.

1 large clove garlic

½ tsp. salt

1 ripe avocado, pitted and mashed

1 cup garden peas, cooked and mashed

½ cup tomatoes, finely chopped

¼ cup onion, finely chopped

3 Tbsp. lemon juice

½ tsp. ground cumin

Fresh-ground black pepper

- Mash the garlic with the salt using a mortar and pestle or with the back of a fork in a small bowl. Add the avocado, peas, tomatoes, and onion. Mix thoroughly. Sprinkle with the lemon juice, cumin, and black pepper to taste. Blend well.

information:// Nutrition

Fresh peas are a real culinary treat, especially as only about 5 percent of all green peas come to the market fresh. Most are canned or frozen.

Low in calories, green peas are an excellent low-fat source of protein. A three-quarter cup serving of green peas provides more protein than an egg—with no cholesterol. Sugar snap peas contain less protein, but are still good sources of vitamins and minerals.

Both types of peas are rich in vitamin C. In fact, one cup of raw peas contains more than 90 percent of your daily needs. Peas also feature vitamin A, vitamin K, thiamin, folic acid, and iron, not to mention decent amounts of other nutrients.

Like all legumes, peas are high in fiber. A high-fiber diet helps reduce your risk of diabetes, heart disease, and stroke.

Eat your peas lightly steamed or raw to retain the nutrients.

vegetable:// **Peppers**

| planting and growing | varieties | produce selection and harvest | preparation methods |

Peppers are one of the easiest vegetables to grow in the grocery garden as long as you have enough heat and sun. They can be sown directly in the garden, but you'll start harvesting earlier if you start the seeds indoors about eight weeks before the last average frost date or buy seedlings from the local nursery.

To start your seeds indoors, plant seedlings into peat pots or larger soil block containers to avoid having to re-pot before setting out. While they are germinating, keep the seeds warm on a seed mat or near a heat source. Don't bother transplanting the peppers to the garden until the soil is quite warm—with nighttime temperatures above 55 degrees—or your pepper plants will sulk.

In the garden, prepare the soil with some compost, but avoid composted manure since too much nitrogen will give you big, hearty plants but few peppers. Plant peppers depending on their mature size, with bell peppers about two to three feet apart. Hot peppers can be planted more closely, but avoid crowding.

Peppers will need a steady supply of moisture to avoid blossom end rot. They will also benefit from an infusion of fish emulsion fertilizer during the growing season.

Most hot peppers grow on smaller plants that will not need staking. But bell peppers can grow to more than three feet tall and benefit from some support. Those small tomato cages or just a simple stake and twine combination will do the trick.

| planting and growing | varieties | produce selection and harvest | preparation methods |

There are two kinds of peppers: sweet peppers (the most common of which is the bell pepper) and hot peppers. All peppers come in a rainbow of shapes and sizes.

Sweet Bell Peppers: 'Ace', 'Big Bertha', 'Satsuma', 'Baby Bell', 'Purple Bell'

Other Sweet Peppers: 'Sweet Banana', 'Alama Paprika', 'Jimmy Nardello', 'Giant Marconi'

Hot Peppers: 'Black Hungarian', 'Chinese Five Color', 'Cayenne Long Thin', 'Tabasco', 'Habanero', 'Anaheim', 'Jalapeño'

planting and growing | varieties | produce selection and harvest | preparation methods

How do you pick a peck of peppers? Look for peppers that are firm and without any wrinkles, a sign of age or poor storage conditions. Just say "no" to peppers with sunken areas, slashes, or black spots. The best peppers should feel heavy for their size.

Harvesting peppers at home is super easy. They can be picked and eaten at any stage of development. Sweet peppers start life as a green pod and develop their final color as they mature. They are generally at their sweetest after the color change has occurred.

Hot peppers also come in a wide variety of colors. Some start green and change color as they mature; others start in a wide range of colors… sometimes on the same plant. Hot peppers are most flavorful when they're fully mature.

Be sure to harvest all peppers regularly to encourage continued production. If a pepper is left too long, it may signal the plant to stop new fruit development.

DID YOU KNOW?

If you have overindulged or accidentally ingested hot peppers that are making you miserable, milk will work better at putting out the fire than water. Milk contains a protein that will separate the burning capsaicin from the nerve receptors. Relief!

ROBIN RIPLEY

Be very careful when handling hot peppers, and consider using gloves. One year I processed a bunch of habanero peppers for drying. Although I washed my hands well, it wasn't enough to remove the capsaicin that burns—as I found out when I removed my contact lenses later that night. Oh, the pain!

pests and diseases

Aphids; Corn earworms; Cutworms; Flea beetles; Hornworms; Leaf miners; Pepper maggots; Pepper weevil; Whiteflies; Anthracnose; Bacterial spot; Early blight; Mosaic virus; Verticillium wilt

planting and growing

varieties

produce selection and harvest

preparation methods

There are many ways to prepare the huge variety of peppers. Beginning pepper eaters seem to find the red and yellow bell peppers better than the green bell peppers, which are somewhat less sweet. Remember that peppers can be eaten at any stage of growth…use the subtle flavor changes to vary favorite recipes.

- **Raw:** Bell peppers make lovely additions to raw salads or served with dip. Peppers cut into strips also make a handy and oddly satisfying snack. Take them along in a little baggie for munchie food.

- **Baked/Stuffed:** Everyone seems to like stuffed bell peppers, whether it is with beans and rice in a tomato sauce or a meat and nut combination.

- **Roasted/Grilled:** Peppers are perfect for roasting, either on the grill or right over the open flame of a gas stove. Place peppers on the grill and use a pair of tongs to turn regularly. Keep an eye on the peppers, as this is a quick process. Let the skin blacken and the pepper collapse. Pop into a paper bag or a covered bowl and let it continue to steam for 10 minutes. Use the bag or a towel to rub off the burned skin and they are ready for use. You can also roast them under the broiler in your oven. Just halve and seed the pepper, brush lightly with oil and roast. Allow the pepper to get black and try not to be alarmed. After you let it sit for a few minutes you can remove the blackened areas and reveal the beautifully roasted pepper.

- **Flavored:** Peppers make great additions to sauces, pestos, soups, or in concoctions such as bruschettas eaten on crusty bread.

preserving

Freezing; Canning; Dehydrating; Vacuum packing

Do you have an abundance of peppers? Just dry them in a dehydrator or in an oven set at 200° for several hours. Store them to use later either dried or reconstituted with hot water.

Dried and Smoked Peppers

You will need a charcoal grill and hardwood chips to smoke the peppers.

Large harvest of peppers, any kind, cleaned and dried

- Soak the hardwood chips in water. Build a fire on one side of the grill. The fire shouldn't be above 250º, so use a grill thermometer to check. Drain the hardwood chips and add to the hot coals. Lower the grill hood and place the peppers on the opposite side, away from direct heat. You will probably need to add more charcoal at least once. It is important to keep the vent mainly closed in order to control the temperature and capture the smoke. It will probably take 3 to 4 hours of smoking to infuse the peppers with smoke and dry them fairly well. If some of the larger peppers aren't dry, either add more coals or leave them in a sunny window to finish. If you want to vary the flavor, you can find a variety of hardwood chips that have unique characteristics. Another option is to harvest fresh, woody herbs, such as rosemary and thyme, soak them, and place them on the coals.

Roasted Red Pepper Cream Sauce

This sauce is a great topping for pasta and rice dishes. It also serves as a wonderful flavor element when drizzled over chicken or pork. Peppers can be roasted on a grill, under a broiler, or over a flame on a gas stovetop. Regardless of the heat source, the peppers should be blistered and blackened and starting to soften. Once the peppers have been roasted on all sides (which is in a matter of minutes), drop them into a bowl and cover with plastic wrap to steam. When the peppers are cooled, rub off blackened outer skin using a paper towel. Remove the stem and seeds and coarsely chop.

3 red peppers, roasted and chopped	Salt and fresh-ground black pepper
1 Tbsp. olive oil	2 cups half and half
2 garlic cloves, minced	½ cup Parmesan cheese

- In a saucepan over medium-low heat, combine the roasted peppers, olive oil, garlic, and salt and pepper to taste. Sauté for a few minutes to infuse the oil and allow the garlic to mellow. Transfer to a blender or use an immersion blender to create the sauce. Add the half and half and Parmesan cheese. Warm through. Serve.

Stuffed Bell Peppers

Make sure you do not cut through the skin and into the cavity of the bell pepper when you level the bottom. You just want to remove enough so that it will stand upright.

1 medium yellow onion, diced

1 lb. ground lamb (can substitute ground beef, chicken, or turkey)

Olive oil

1 Tbsp. fennel seeds

1 tsp. dried oregano

2 cups cooked brown rice

1 8-oz. can tomato sauce

3 garlic cloves, minced

2 bay leaves

Salt and fresh-ground black pepper

4–6 bell peppers, tops cut off, seeds and membrane removed, and bottoms cut off to level

Shredded Muenster cheese*

- Preheat the oven to 375°. In a medium skillet over medium heat, sauté the onion and lamb in a bit of olive oil. Add the fennel seeds and oregano. Cook until the lamb is browned. Add the rice, tomato sauce, garlic, bay leaves, and salt and pepper to taste. Cook 10 minutes.

- Fill the peppers with the mixture. Place in a deep baking dish. Bake 20 minutes or until the peppers are tender. Remove from oven and turn on the oven broiler. Top with the Muenster cheese. Finish by melting the cheese under the broiler.

*Soft cheeses can be a challenge to shred. Pop them into the freezer for 10 minutes so they're firm prior to shredding.

Nopales Salsa

Nopales are the round, succulent leaves of the prickly pear cactus. They are fresh and tangy, a great component to salsa. They can be purchased jarred as Nopalitos or Nopales. But they are great when fresh. If you are using fresh nopales (by mail order or store bought), you will need to wear gloves and use a vegetable peeler to remove the tiny spines left after the harvest. Once that is done, rinse, score the pads, and coat with olive oil, salt, and pepper. Pop these on the grill and let them grill 15 minutes or so. This will impart flavor and reduce the amount of mucilaginous liquid in the cacti. Once grilled, you are ready to start the recipe. Let the flavors develop by refrigerating for a couple of hours or so. Serve with chips or as an accompaniment to fish, chicken, or pork.

Olive oil

1½ lbs. nopales, cleaned, quartered, grilled, chopped

1 pineapple, cleaned, quartered, grilled, chopped

2 ears fresh corn, grilled, kernels removed from cob

3–4 limes, zest and juice only

Sea salt and fresh-ground black pepper

1 red onion, chopped

4–6 tomatoes, seeded and chopped

2 bell peppers (yellow, red, or orange), chopped

1 bunch fresh basil, chopped

1 jalapeño, chopped (seeded if you prefer less heat)

Dried chipotle pepper flakes to taste

- Coat the nopales, pineapple, and corn with olive oil and grill until carmelized. Remove corn from the cob; dice nopales and pineapple. In a fridge-friendly container, mix the lime zest and juice with a healthy dose of the salt and black pepper. Whisk in enough olive oil to create a nice dressing. Add the nopales and pineapple. Add the corn, onion, tomatoes, peppers, basil, and jalapeño. Add the chipotle pepper to taste.

(Shared by Shawna Coronado) Corn and Pepper Scallop

1 14-oz. can cream-style corn

1 11-oz. can whole kernel corn, undrained

½ cup butter, melted

1 cup sour cream or milk

2 Tbsp. sugar

2 tsp. baking powder

1 cup all-purpose flour

1 cup white or yellow cornmeal

2 eggs, slightly beaten

1 Tbsp. chili powder

1 poblano pepper, seeded and diced

1 serrano pepper, seeded and finely minced

■ Preheat the oven to 350º. In a medium bowl, combine the cream-style corn, whole kernel corn, butter, sour cream, sugar, baking powder, flour, cornmeal, eggs, chili powder, poblano pepper, and serrano pepper. Mix well. Pour into a greased 9-inch square dish. Bake 40 to 45 minutes.

Apple, Zucchini, and Red Pepper "Tortilla"

(Shared by Mike Lieberman, raw foodie)

2 large zucchini, peeled

2–4 apples, peeled

½ red bell pepper, seeded and chopped

½ lemon

1 Tbsp. olive oil

Fresh or marinated vegetables for serving

■ Place the zucchini, apples, and red pepper in a blender. Add a squeeze of the lemon, a splash of water, and the olive oil. Blend until smooth. Pour into circular shapes to form the "tortilla" on a nonstick dehydrator tray. You should be able to fit about one wrap per tray. Place in a dehydrator set to 110º about 6 to 8 hours. Turn and place back in the dehydrator for another 1 to 2 hours. Fill with fresh or marinated veggies. Wrap up and enjoy.

Corn and Pepper Scallop

Apple, Zucchini, and Red Pepper "Tortilla"

Pozole-Inspired Gazpacho

8 medium to large ripe, heirloom
  tomatoes, seeded and quartered
3 cloves garlic, coarsely chopped
1 red bell pepper, diced
1 poblano pepper, diced
2–3 chipotle peppers in adobo sauce,
  finely diced
1 15-oz. can white hominy, drained
2 medium cucumbers, peeled and diced

4 green onions, cleaned and sliced
  (white and light-green parts only)
2 cups good-quality vegetable stock
2 limes, zest and juice only
1 tsp. dried Mexican oregano or
  regular oregano
1 bunch flat leaf parsley, chopped
1 small bunch cilantro, chopped
Sea salt and fresh-ground black pepper

- Place the tomatoes and garlic in a blender; pulse several times to liquefy. Press through a food mill or through a cheesecloth-lined colander to strain into a large bowl. Add the bell pepper, poblano pepper, chipotle peppers, hominy, cucumbers, green onions, stock, lime zest and juice, oregano, parsley, cilantro, and salt and pepper to taste. Stir well to combine. Adjust seasonings, if needed. Chill at least 1 hour. Serve.

information:// Nutrition

Regardless of their various shapes and colors, all peppers are high in vitamin A and C. This is especially true of red bell peppers, which have significantly more vitamins A and C than green bell peppers, and much more vitamin A than yellow bell peppers.

One raw red pepper—sweet or hot—meets your daily needs for vitamin A and C. These nutrients are powerful antioxidants, which may reduce your risk of heart disease, stroke, cataracts, and cancer.

Peppers also contain salicylates, an active ingredient in aspirin. Recent research shows salicylic acid may help prevent heart attacks, strokes, and cancer.

Hot peppers, such as chili and cayenne, contain the component capsaicin. Often used in pain-relieving creams, capsaicin increases circulation and body temperature. As with other spicy foods, hot peppers act as natural decongestants by stimulating the free flow of mucus from congested chests and stuffed-up noses.

vegetable:// **Tomato**

planting and growing | varieties | produce selection and harvest | preparation methods

For many gardeners, tomatoes represent gardening nirvana. But homegrown tomato heaven can be difficult to reach because they are susceptible to a host of pests and diseases. Choosing disease-resistant varieties and growing in optimal conditions will boost your chances of success.

Start tomatoes indoors six to eight weeks before your area's last average frost date. You can begin seedlings in peat pots or in trays, but plan to repot them as they grow to give each tomato plant plenty of space. When potting up, plant the seedling deep in the soil, up to the first set of leaves, in order to create a strong root system. As with all seedlings, harden them off by setting them outdoors for increasing amounts of time each day.

Tomatoes need warm summer days and plenty of sunshine. Pick a very sunny location and enrich the soil with well-rotted manure, peat moss, and compost to create a bed that is nearly fluffy.

Transplant your tomatoes to the prepared bed when nighttime temperatures are consistently above 55 degrees. Plant tomatoes three feet apart, again placing them several inches deeper than the soil level.

Tomatoes need supports to keep them off the ground as they grow. To avoid injuring the tomatoes or addressing the support issue too late, plan your

structure before the tomatoes are planted. The small tomato cages sold in garden centers are woefully inadequate for most tomato plants, especially indeterminate varieties. Homemade cages, extra large tomato cages, or heavy duty staking works best.

Tomatoes need a steady source of moisture as they grow, particularly once the tomatoes set. Too little or too much water will impact the health of the fruit and could endanger your whole harvest with problems such as blossom end rot, cracking, or making them susceptible to other diseases and pests.

Feed tomatoes with fish emulsion or other organic fertilizer every couple of weeks. A sidedressing of compost will also help feed the plants.

217

There are two types of tomatoes: **determinate** and **indeterminate**. Determinate (D) tomatoes are short, bushy plants that set all their fruit at one time—handy timing if you plan on canning your tomatoes. Indeterminate (I) tomatoes can grow to as much as 15 feet on long, vining-type branches that will need sturdy support. Indeterminate production is spread over a longer period of time.

Canning/Sauce: 'La Roma' (D), 'Amish Paste' (I), 'Speckled Roman' (I), 'San Marzano' (I)

Fresh Eating: 'Big Beef' (I), 'Beefsteak' (I), 'Yellow Pear' (I), 'Currant Gold Rush' (I)

Early/Short Season: 'Oregon Spring V' (D), 'Early Girl' (I), 'Legend' (I), 'Jetsetter' (I)

Heirloom: 'Brandywine OTV' (I), 'Mr. Stripey' (I), 'Wapsipinicon Peach' (I), 'Pineapple' (I)

Green: 'Green Zebra' (I), 'Aunt Ruby's German Green' (I), 'Green Sausage' (D), 'Green Grape' (D)

Purple: 'Cherokee Purple' (I), 'Black Krim' (I), 'Paul Robeson' (I), 'Black Plum' (I)

Yellow/Gold: 'Golden Boy' (I), 'Gold Medal' (I), 'Golden Sunray' (I), 'Plum Lemon' (I)

Orange: 'Moonglow' (I), 'Orange Banana' (I), 'Sun Gold Cherry' (I)

White/Cream: 'Cream Sausage' (D), 'Little White Rabbit' (I), 'Snowball' (I)

ROBIN RIPLEY

I was once at a chic restaurant where the waiter snootily described the salad special as "heirloom tomatoes."

"What kind of heirloom tomatoes?" I asked, since I know different tomatoes have vastly different characteristics. Baffled at what he thought was an intensely stupid question, he repeated, "heirloom."

Tomatoes at the market should be heavy for their size. Choose tomatoes that are somewhat firm, but yield to gentle pressure. Avoid rock-hard tomatoes or those that have bruises, markings, or cracks.

Harvesting tomatoes at home is relatively easy. The first step is identifying the ripe color of the tomatoes you are harvesting. Most of these fruits undergo significant color changes, but some tomatoes stay green throughout the growing cycle. When picking, look for those whose color has developed and that have some give when pressed lightly.

It is not necessary to wait for a tomato to fully ripen to harvest. Leave those that are slightly unripe on the counter for a couple of days until they're ready. Finally, tomatoes can also be eaten when "green" or unripe. They have a lovely tart-tangy flavor!

pests and diseases

Flea beetles; Colorado potato beetle; Cutworms; Tomato hornworm; Aphids; Nematodes; Blossom end rot; Powdery mildew; Mosaic virus; Early blight; Blossom drop; Downy mildew; Verticillium wilt; Fusarium wilt; Late blight

planting and growing | varieties | produce selection and harvest | **preparation methods**

The nutritional value of tomatoes is fantastic! Using something as concentrated and nutrient dense as tomato paste or dried tomatoes is a great way to boost the value of your food. In addition, you will also get a big kick in the flavor department, too!

- **Fresh:** A fresh tomato brought in from the garden at the peak of ripeness is about as close to tasting summer as you can get. In fact, sliced tomato sandwiches on soft bread with nothing but mayonnaise, pepper, and salt are a summer ritual for many gardeners. Aside from tomatoes in salads, raw tomatoes are the base of cold soups such as spicy gazpacho, that summer mix of tomatoes, cucumbers, peppers, onions, and herbs. And we can't forget homemade salsa!

DID YOU KNOW?

Don't be afraid to prune the unruly vines of indeterminate tomatoes. Just leave enough leaves behind to shade the developing fruit.

- **Stuffed:** The biggest, firmest tomatoes from your garden can be scooped out and used to make a picture pretty presentation by stuffing them with salads or dips. They are also fantastic when stuffed with a savory mixture and baked.
- **Sauces/Pastes:** Tomatoes are, of course, used as the foundation of hundreds of sauces. They can either be the base of the sauce, or added in a concentrated paste form to deepen the flavor of a sauce.
- **Roasted/Dried:** Roasting tomatoes concentrates the flavor, even if they are just partially roasted. Try substituting tomatoes cut into chunks and roast at 300° for 1 hour for some or all of the fresh tomatoes in your salsas or other raw tomato dishes for a deeper, richer flavor. Drying tomatoes is accomplished similarly and can be done in the oven (at 175°–200°), in a dehydrator, or outside in the sun. Wash tomatoes and cut into similarly sized pieces. Let them dry until the liquid is drained, but the tomatoes are still flexible. Store in an airtight container.

preserving

Freezing; Dehydrating; Canning

Fresh from the Garden Tomato and Jalapeño Salsa

(Shared by Helena Wolkonowski)

This is great as a salsa, bruschetta, or in a veggie roll-up. It's a great way to use fresh produce either from the market or from your garden.

1 tomato, diced

1 red bell pepper, seeded and diced

2 Tbsp. fresh cilantro, chopped

½ lemon, juice only

½ lime, juice only

¼ cup red onion, chopped

1 Tbsp. garlic, minced

1 tsp. jalapeño, chopped

- Combine the tomato, bell pepper, and cilantro in a large bowl. Sprinkle with the lemon juice and lime juice. (These citrus juices are the acid that will help break down the tomato and pepper.) Add the onion, garlic, and jalapeño for a little extra kick. Mix well. Refrigerate about 1 hour to let all the flavors blend.

Herb-y Cherry Tomato Salad (Shared by Marcelle Layne)

This is a quick and useful recipe if you have loads of cherry tomatoes from your garden and you have to make a side dish in a hurry.

16 oz. cherry tomatoes, halved

1 large spring or green onion, finely sliced

2 Tbsp. olive oil

2 Tbsp. torn fresh basil leaves

2 Tbsp. fresh curly parsley, finely chopped

1 Tbsp. whole fresh oregano leaves

Lemon pepper

2 oz. toasted pine nuts

- In a medium bowl, combine the tomatoes, onion, olive oil, basil, parsley, oregano, and lemon pepper to taste. Stir well and chill at least 30 minutes. Just before serving, sprinkle the pine nuts over the salad.

Note: Do not cut or chop the basil leaves as this makes them turn brown and impairs the flavor. Just tear the leaves into small pieces.

(Shared by Judy Bennett) Calypso Mary

This drink goes great with a salty garnish such as pickled asparagus, okra, green beans, or olives.

2 large yellow heirloom tomatoes, sliced

1 clove garlic

1 Tbsp. lime juice

$3/4$-inch piece of fresh jalapeño

1 Tbsp. Jamaican Me Sweet Hot and Crazy marinade

Splash of liquid from jar of banana wax peppers

1 Tbsp. Bragg Liquid Aminos

1 Tbsp. balsamic vinegar

$1/2$ tsp. fresh-ground black pepper

1 tsp. sea salt, plus more for the tomatoes

Dark rum

Pickled asparagus, okra, green bean, or olives for garnish, if desired

- Prepare your type of grill or preheat the oven broiler. Salt the tomatoes and grill or broil 10 minutes. When they are lightly toasted and juicy, put the tomatoes, garlic, lime juice, jalapeño, Jamaican Me marinade, banana wax pepper juice, Bragg Liquid Aminos, vinegar, pepper, and salt in a blender. Purée until smooth. Strain to remove the fibers, then cool to room temperature. In individual glasses filled with ice, add 1 shot of the dark rum. Top off with the tomato mixture. Stir gently.

Verde Mary (Shared by Judy Bennett)

5–6 fresh tomatillos (or you can substitute 'Green Zebra' tomatoes), husked

1/4 medium onion

1/2 medium-sized jalapeño pepper

1 Tbsp. fresh or canned nopalitos

1/2 lime, juice only

1 Tbsp. sugar

1 Tbsp. olive brine (from a jar of olives)

Salt

Tequila

Cherry tomatoes and cocktail onions, for garnish

- Place the tomatillos, onion, jalapeño, nopalitos, lime juice, sugar, olive brine, and salt to taste in a blender or food processor. Purée until well combined, but still chunky rather than smooth. Spoon about 1/2 cup into a cocktail shaker with 1 shot of tequila. Shake well. Serve over ice. Garnish with a cherry tomato and a couple of white cocktail onions.

Tomato Cucumber Salad

This is a classic salad that can be eaten alone or as a topping on lentils and rice, fish, or even chicken. Using fresh herbs is a great way to create a variety of taste experiences. Try this salad with basil, parsley, oregano, thyme, rosemary—even mint... both tomatoes and cucumbers are very user-friendly vegetables.

1 small clove garlic

Salt

1/2 cup lemon juice

1/2 cup olive oil

3 large tomatoes, chopped

2 cucumbers, seeded and chopped

1 small red onion, chopped

- Mash the garlic with salt to taste in the bottom of a bowl or with a mortar and pestle. Add the lemon juice and olive oil and whisk. Add the tomatoes, cucumbers, and onion. Mix well. Season to taste.

Summer Tomato Tart

Tart Pastry

1½ cups pastry or all-purpose flour
½ tsp. salt
8 Tbsp. butter
4 Tbsp. ice water

- Combine the flour and salt. Cut in the butter and work with a pastry cutter or your fingers until the flour and butter mixture resembles coarse meal. Add the ice water to the mixture. Mix lightly. Form into a ball. Turn onto a lightly floured surface and knead a couple of times to ensure the water is evenly incorporated. Roll the dough into a tight ball and press into a flat square. Using a rolling pin, roll the dough into a 12-inch circle or large enough for your baking pan. Gently peel up the crust and fit it into a tart pan or pie pan, crimping the edges. Chill the pastry shell while preparing the filling.

Tart Filling

1 Tbsp. (or more) Dijon mustard
3 cups Gruyère cheese, grated
3 cups tomatoes, seeded and sliced
⅓ cup olive oil
½ cup combination of chopped basil, thyme, or parsley
Salt and fresh-ground black pepper

- Preheat the oven to 350°. Remove the pastry shell from the refrigerator. Spread the Dijon mustard on the bottom of the pastry shell. Add the Gruyère and top with the tomatoes in a visually pleasing arrangement. Whisk the olive oil with the herbs, and salt and pepper to taste. Drizzle the dressing over the tomatoes. Bake until the crust is golden brown. Let the tart sit 10 to 15 minutes before slicing or it will fall apart.

Summer Tomato Tart

Fried Green Tomatoes

Fried Green Tomatoes

This recipe comes in handy at the end of the season or if you are having a cool summer. They are tart and crisp and completely yummy! Try adding shredded Parmesan cheese to the cornmeal. Southwestern spices would be great, too: cayenne, cumin, chili powder, and garlic powder are natural companions for cornmeal.

Vegetable oil for frying

3–4 green tomatoes, sliced

½ cup cornmeal

Sea salt and fresh-ground black pepper

- In a large skillet over medium heat, add the vegetable oil until it is about a quarter of an inch deep. Let the oil heat until fully warmed. Dredge the tomato in the cornmeal, then pop it in a skillet with vegetable oil . . . keep your burner a bit above medium, and do not put the tomatoes in until the oil is hot!

- The tomatoes don't take long to fry. When they are browned on both sides, remove them to drain on a paper-towel-lined plate. Immediately sprinkle with the salt and pepper.

information:// Nutrition

Juicy homegrown tomatoes don't just taste delicious; they are also nutritious. Tomatoes are a great source of vitamin A, fiber, and vitamin C. They also contain potassium, folic acid, and other nutrients, all for about 25 calories a cup.

Orange tomatoes have more vitamin A and C than red ones. But a cup of raw red tomatoes will still supply about a third of your daily needs of both nutrients. Meanwhile, vine–ripened tomatoes have about twice the vitamin C content as those grown in hothouses.

Raw tomatoes taste terrific in salads and on sandwiches. But tomatoes cooked, especially with a little oil, are a rich source of the carotenoid lycopene. This antioxidant gives tomatoes its red color and has been shown to significantly reduce the risk of prostate cancer. Recent studies show lycopene may also reduce blood pressure as well as protect against heart attacks and other types of cancer.

PRESERVING YOUR HARVEST

Each edible has a season when it is produced in abundance, but if you want to eat fruits, vegetables, and herbs beyond that time, learning how to preserve is important.

There are many ways to store food for longer periods of time. We'll show you how to use techniques like canning, freezing, and dehydration to save your produce for future use. Though it is fun to do this with what you grow yourself, keep in mind that it is also great to find produce at U-pick farms or buy in bulk at the store or farmers' markets and preserve for future use, too.

Preserving Safety

Fresh foods contain a high percentage of water. Combine that with the activity of food enzymes and you have a perfect breeding ground for yeasts, molds, and bacteria to reproduce. You can't scrub away all these microorganisms, so you have to take other measures to ensure they don't spoil the food and create a safety hazard.

Take Clostridium botulinum, the infamous bacterium that causes the fatal food poisoning botulism. It is present on most fresh foods. It doesn't cause harm on fresh foods because it only grows in the absence of air. But, if you pack that fresh food into a sealed jar and leave it at room temperature for a while, voila—botulism! But heat that jar and its contents to a temperature of 240 degrees F. in a steam pressure canner or add some sort of acid, as in pickling, and the Clostridium botulinum bacterium can't survive.

Freezing foods doesn't kill harmful microorganisms, but it does stop them cold. That's why you should never re-freeze foods after they have thawed—those yeasts, molds, and bacteria have had a chance to be fruitful and multiply.

Drying removes the moisture that microorganisms need to thrive and slows down the actions of enzymes. Adding salt, vinegar, or other agents can also create a hostile environment for all those naturally occurring bacteria, helping to preserve food.

Preserving food isn't difficult, but it does take an appreciation for the harm all those yeasts, molds, and bacteria can do and some attention to specific safety practices to ensure microorganisms that spoil food don't create health hazards.

Canning

Because heat has the power to destroy harmful microorganisms it is one of the safest and most effective methods of preserving food. Unlike the old-fashioned method of just dipping canning jars into boiling water and then filling with produce, modern canning requires processing the jars at high temperatures for extended periods of time, usually specified in the recipe.

There are two types of equipment for canning food: water bath canning and steam pressure canning.

Water bath canning utilizes a large canning pot fitted with a bottom rack to insulate jars from the high heat on the bottom of the pot and to keep jars from tipping or leaning during processing. The canner is filled with enough water to allow a minimum of one inch of water above the jar and one inch of space between the water level and the lip of the pot when it's filled with jars. The size of a water bath canner is largely dependent on the size of the jars you plan to process. At the bare minimum the canning pot should be at least twelve inches tall, and preferably taller.

Steam pressure canners can achieve much higher temperatures than water bath canners. They are different from home pressure cookers because they can achieve the higher temperatures required for successful preserving. Never use a home pressure cooker for canning.

The pressure canner has a heavy bottom and a tight-fitting lid that locks into place. A dial gauge or weighted gauge measures the pressure inside the canner from heating two to three inches of water with the lid secured. The size of the canner depends largely on the extent of your canning ambitions. A 16-quart pressure canner is a good size for most home canning projects.

Whether you need to use a water bath canner or a pressure canner will depend on the acidity of the food you plan to preserve. Some fruits and vegetables, such as grapes and apples, are highly acidic. They can be successfully processed in a hot water bath. Other foods, such as beans and corn, are low acid, and require processing in a steam pressure canner to ensure that harmful micro-organisms are killed and the food is safely preserved. If you process high-acid foods in a pressure canner, it can destroy their taste and texture.

Successful canning isn't complicated as long as you pick the right equipment for the job and process according to the recipe directions. A great resource for canning information, recipes, and equipment, as well as finding pick-your-own farms, is http://www.pickyourown.org.

Canning Basics

- Select and review recipes and standard canning procedures. Ensure that you have all the ingredients and proper quantities needed.
- Inventory equipment and supplies prior to starting. If you're using a pressure canner, inspect it to ensure all parts are present and in working order. Refresh your memory on the proper use by reviewing the manufacturer's instructions.
- Inspect canning jars for cracks or chips that can prevent proper sealing or cause jars to break from the heat and pressure. Vintage containers, including those with wire clamp-on lids, are attractive, but may not be safe for preserving. Mason jars that use two-piece, self-sealing lids are recommended by the USDA. Screw bands are reusable if they are clean, rust free, and not dented. Always use new lids (the rimless disk that seals the top of the jar).

  Although the large 1½-quart and 2-quart canning jars are still available, they are not recommended because they require a very long processing time. As heat penetrates to the center of an oversized jar, the food in the outer part of the jar may be overprocessed, negatively impacting flavor and color. In addition, most modern water bath canners aren't tall enough to accommodate that size with adequate water coverage.
- Clean equipment thoroughly. Wash jars, rings, and lids thoroughly with hot, soapy water or in a dishwasher.
- Heat lids and screw rings. Prepare a pot with boiling water and immerse the lids and screw rings. Reduce the heat to a simmer and simmer for at least 10 minutes. Keep the water heated until ready for use.

- Prepare the water bath or pressure canner. Place a rack in the bottom of a canner and fill with water. Cover the water bath canner and bring to a boil and then a simmer. Fill a pressure canner with two to three inches of water and heat.

  If you're using a water bath canner, keep the jars hot until you're ready to use them by immersing them in a simmering water bath canner to an inch above the rims of the containers. Keep the containers immersed until you're ready to pack them with food.

- Organize and prepare ingredients. Measure spices, sugars, oils, and other ingredients into small bowls and have them ready for use. Wash fruits and vegetables thoroughly to remove debris, sand, and dirt. Prepare the produce according to the recipe's instructions.

- Follow the recipe for the food being preserved. Using the hot pack method, remove jars from the water bath; fill to within ½ inch of the top of the jar. Cover with a lid and screw a ring on lightly. Place the jars directly into water bath canner or pressure canner for the appropriate amount of time. Remove and let the jars stand to cool.

- Remove air bubbles. Using a spatula, chopstick, or other nonmetallic tool, release any air bubbles trapped inside the jars.

- Clean, cover, and seal jars. Wipe jars with a clean, damp cloth to remove any food or liquid that may have spilled during filling. Take care to wipe the screw threads, also.

  Remove lids and screw rings from the holding pot using tongs or a lid wand. Make sure the lids are properly centered and screw and snugly tighten the lids.

Useful Preserving Equipment

It's amazing how much of what you need can be scavenged from relatives' basements or at yard sales. Keep your eyes open for these useful kitchen tools and equipment for preserving.

Pots, Pans, & Equipment
8-quart and 4-quart stainless steel stockpots
Collapsible wire basket
Double boiler
Extra-large colander
Juicer
Mixing bowls, especially extra-large mixing bowls
Pressure canner
Saucepans
Water bath canner
Wire racks

Storage Containers
Canning basket
Plastic freezer bags
Plastic freezer containers
Preserving jars, dome lids, and screw bands

Other Supplies
Cheesecloth
Dish towels
Freezer tape
Heavy-duty gloves
Latex gloves

Tools & Gadgets
Apple corer
Candy thermometer
Cherry pitter
Food mill
Freezer thermometer
Jar lifter and tongs
Kitchen scale
Kitchen shears
Kitchen timer
Knives
Ladle
Lid wand
Long-handled spoons
Measuring cups
Measuring spoons
Melon baller
Slotted spoons
Spatulas
Strawberry huller
Tongs
Vegetable brush
Vegetable peeler
Wide-mouthed canning funnel
Zester

- Process jars in canner. Carefully process jars according to the recipe's instructions, making special note of time and temperature to ensure that all microorganisms that can spoil food are killed and that the lids seal properly.

  Carefully follow pressure canner instructions, making sure to wait for the pressure to drop to zero before opening the canner.

- Remove jars and cool. Take care when removing hot jars to avoid burns and avoid tipping them. Place the hot jars on towels or wire racks, allowing enough space between the jars for air circulation to cool them. Pat dry with paper towels. Allow jars to remain undisturbed 12 to 24 hours. The jars will make a distinctive popping sound as they cool.

- Check seals. Press the lids down in the center. Lids should stay down without popping back up. Any jars whose lid pops back when pressed should be placed in the refrigerator and its contents eaten within a couple of weeks.

- Wash, label, and store jars. Wash jars in warm, soapy water; rinse; and pat dry. Label jars with the canning date and ingredients. Store in a cool, dry, dark place.

Freezing

Freezing foods is fast, easy, and effective. It doesn't take heaps of special equipment, and in just a few minutes you can freeze small batches of produce at their peak of freshness.

The key to preserving freshness is quick freezing. To accomplish this, fruits and vegetables should be cut into uniform sizes, processed, and frozen as quickly as possible.

Freezing Basics

- **Make sure your freezer is in good working order.** Set the temperature control of minus 10 degrees to compensate for the addition of room temperature foods, which will raise the air temperature in the freezer. Check the manufacturer's instructions for freezing recommendations.

- **Gauge your freezer capacity.** As a rule of thumb, plan on two to three pounds of food per cubic foot of freezer space.

- **Inventory equipment and supplies prior to starting.** Make sure to have on-hand an adequate number of bags or containers, wax pencils or permanent markers, and freezer tape so you can label your finished foods.

- **Prepare the food.** Pick fruits and vegetables at their peak. Wash them in cold water and sort by size, discarding any that are bruised, damaged, or over- or underripe. Stem, peel, pit, or slice to prepare the fruits and vegetables, working in batches to avoid having cut foods exposed to the air for extended periods, which can cause browning. Prepare sugar syrups or other additives in advance so they are ready to go once the food is processed.

- **Blanch**. Blanching involves scalding vegetables in boiling water or steam to stop enzyme action that can degrade flavor, color, and texture. Blanched vegetables produce a higher quality product than ones packaged raw. Check your recipe for the correct blanching time for the food you are processing. Plunge blanched foods into cool water to stop them from continuing to cook. Drain completely.
- **Package and label.** If you're using plastic containers, make sure you leave enough head space for liquids to expand during freezing. Make sure you include the name of the food and packaging date on each package. Frozen foods keep for about 8 to 12 months, after which the food quality will begin to degrade.

- **Freeze.** Place packages in the freezer, leaving one inch of space between packages to ensure good air circulation and quick freezing that will reduce the formation of ice crystals and preserve texture and quality.
- **Check and repackage the freezer.** After 12 to 24 hours, examine packages to ensure they are evenly freezing, removing any that seem soft. Stack fully frozen foods to conserve space, putting older foods and those that will be used first within easy reach.
- **Adjust freezer temperature**. Reset the freezer temperature control to 0 degrees. Use a thermometer to ensure the freezer is at the proper temperature.

Why Preserve?

Canned and frozen goods seem like a great bargain at the grocery store. So why go to all the trouble of preserving your own food?

- **Lower your food costs.** If you have surplus produce from the garden or find good prices on produce in season, you can lower your food costs by preserving them.
- **Have food on hand.** A well-stocked freezer and pantry means you can reduce the number of emergency restaurant meals or last-minute dashes to the grocery store to forage for dinner ingredients.
- **Live sustainably.** By preserving your own produce, reusing canning supplies, and avoiding purchasing food that has been trucked thousands of miles to the market, you'll be living a more earth-friendly lifestyle.
- **Avoid additives.** Many frozen and canned foods contain added salt and other ingredients to preserve color and extend shelf life.
- **Creative expression.** The options for preserving food go way beyond just plain produce. The range of recipes for jams and jellies alone can make your head spin. Once you get really good at it, you can enter your preserved goods into competitions at the county and state fairs!

Freezing Fresh Herbs

Most people immediately think drying is the way to preserve fresh herbs. But freezing wins the taste contest hands down.

To freeze herbs, pick them at their peak in the morning, before they wilt in the hot sun. Wash in cold water to remove grit and any buggy hitchhikers. Blanch the herbs quickly in a pot of boiling water by holding stems with tongs and dipping them for a few seconds per stalk. Immediately plunge the blanched herbs into an ice bath to stop them from cooking. Layer onto cloth or paper towels to dry.

Depending on the herb, chop the entire herb or remove the leaves. Place prepared herbs in a single layer on waxed paper, roll up, and store in a plastic bag.

Alternatively, herbs can be mixed with water and frozen in ice cube trays. Once the cubes are frozen, pop them out of the trays and into a freezer bag. To use, just take out a cube and drop it into soups, sauces, or other foods as you're cooking.

When the Power Fails

The safety of your frozen bounty can be jeopardized if you lose power due to storms, fire, or other disaster. Fortunately, modern refrigerators and freezers are well insulated and can keep foods cold or safely frozen for several hours. Avoid opening refrigerator and freezer doors to seal in cold air until the power returns, and follow these safety tips.

- Have canned or dried goods on hand in the event of a power failure to prevent having to open refrigerator and freezer doors.
- Keep freezers fully stocked. Frozen foods in a fully loaded freezer will stay safely frozen for 48 hours in hot weather. In a half-full freezer, they should keep for 24 hours.
- To test for food safety when the power returns, check the internal temperature of foods with a food thermometer. Frozen foods at 40 degrees or cooler and frozen meats at 32 degrees or cooler may be refrozen.
- Never eat food that has come into contact with floodwaters.
- Do not move frozen foods into the snow for storage in power outages. Fluctuating temperatures, the sun's rays, foraging animals, and exposure to bacteria outdoors make outdoor storage unsafe.

Dehydrating Fruits, Herbs, and Vegetables

One of the easiest ways to store produce is to dehydrate (or dry) it. It is far easier than canning, uses less energy to store than freezing, takes up less storage space, and concentrates flavors. When dried food is ready for use, it is reconstituted by adding warm water.

It is important to control food temperature when dehydrating. If it is too low, mold, mildew, and bacteria will start growing. If it is too high, temperatures will cook rather than dry food, resulting in a crusty exterior. If you are using a dehydrator, choose the setting that fits the type of produce you are drying. If you're using an oven, set it as low as possible. If you're drying produce outside, use a thermometer inside the container.

Ascorbic acid is sometimes used in drying as a way to prevent browning and to create an acidic environment that will help prevent bacterial growth. Vegetables should be dried completely until they're hard and crisp.

There are four types of drying

- **Sun drying**—Produce is dried on screens, on cotton sheets, or on cheesecloth stretched tightly on a frame. To prevent birds and insects from making off with your food, cover it with another screen layer. Leave the food in the sun, turning regularly during the drying process. Bring all food in at night to protect it from the damp night air. Once the food has dried, freeze it two to four days to ensure any pest eggs have been destroyed. Bring the produce to room temperature and store it in airtight containers for up to six months.

- **Air drying**—Produce is strung on strings and hung to dry in a hot location, such as under the eaves of a house or in an attic. After drying, bake the produce in the oven at 175 degrees for 30 minutes to ensure any pest eggs have been destroyed. This is probably one of the easiest ways to dry herbs.

- **Oven drying**—Preheat the oven to 145 degrees and lay produce directly on the oven racks or on muslin or cheesecloth. Check regularly and turn once.

- **Dehydrator drying**—A dehydrator is an electric device that heats and circulates air. Just fill the trays with prepared produce and follow the manufacturer's instructions.

Drying Basics

- **Prepare the food.** Food should be blemish-free and at their peak of ripeness. Chop or slice food into uniform pieces for even drying. The smaller the food, the faster it will dry.
- **Blanch.** Blanch as described in the freezing section.
- **Dry.** Follow the instructions for the type of drying you're doing. Allow plenty of room around each piece of produce for air to circulate.
- **Package and label.** Make sure you include the name of the food and packaging date on each package. Initially, store fruit in a loosely sealed container to ensure all pieces have thoroughly dehydrated. After 5 to 10 days, if there is no moisture or condensation in the container, you are ready to move to a longer-term storage option. Storing dehydrated produce in vacuum-sealed bags creates the longest shelf life. Dried produce can also be frozen or stored in an airtight container.

Cold Storage or Root Cellar

Root cellars have long been used to store the harvest for upcoming winter months. But unless you have an old home that happens to have a root cellar, chances are good that you won't be outside digging a pit for your edibles anytime soon. That doesn't mean that there aren't many opportunities to take advantage of this storage method.

Instead of thinking of a root cellar as a location, think of it as a storage method. The chances are good that there are nooks and crannies around your house or property where you can store food without too much effort. This becomes particularly important when you start running out of freezer space, when the produce doesn't freeze well, or when you have a big harvest.

The temperature and humidity of a root cellar are two main reasons that it is so effective in storing fruits and vegetables. However, different types of produce require different conditions. It is important to know the differences in order to ensure proper storage. By understanding and mimicking root cellar-like conditions, you can benefit from this storage method without breaking out the backhoe.

Some vegetables will benefit from a traditional root cellar environment. This means 90 to 95 percent humidity, 32 to 40°F, and darkness. There are a couple of ways that home gardener can create storage "microclimates" in the house, attic, garage, or basement.

1) Start by looking for unheated spaces that don't drop below freezing. Depending on your zone, this could be a portion of the garage, under the stairs in the basement, or a container in the attic. Finding a space with the right temperature is primary, as light and humidity can be more easily altered.

2) Once you have found a space, assess the lighting. Block any incoming light by taping black plastic over sources of sunlight, or use containers with opaque sides and lids.

3) Check humidity levels. If you live in a part of the country that has low winter humidity or if you are living in a house that uses central heat,

it is likely you will need to take a couple of extra steps. If it is a large storage area, you can use a pan of water to increase humidity. Change the water regularly to reduce any potential for mold growth.

4) Air ventilation and/or circulation is a bonus. If your storage area has air exchange, the harvest will last longer…if not, storage time will be a bit shorter, but still worth the effort.

5) Don't clean produce before storage. Don't store any produce that has cuts, nicks, bruises, or is otherwise damaged. Potatoes need to be cured in the ground for a few days to prepare for storage.

If you are storing in containers, layering with damp sand is a good way to surround the vegetables with the right moisture levels. This works particularly well for root crops such as carrots, beets, and turnips. Just add a layer of lightly dampened sand between each layer of the vegetables.

Apples and some pears can be stored this way, as well. However, apples emit a gas that can cause other vegetables and fruits to spoil, so separating them in an area or wrapping them with newspaper before storage is an important step for controlling spoilage.

Vegetables that are naturally well suited for this type of storage are biennials. These plants are already programmed for the roots to survive a winter underground in order to produce seed the following year. Here's a list of some of the crops that work well with this method:

Potato	Sunchoke
Carrot	Winter Radish
Rutabaga	Turnip
Parsnip	Horseradish
Beet	Apple
Kohlrabi	Pear
Celeriac	

Another alternative to harvesting and storing these vegetables (with the exception of potatoes and kohlrabi) is to store them in the ground where they are growing. In parts of the country where the soil doesn't freeze, this means adding a layer of straw and calling it good. If you live in an area where winter rain is an issue, you may need to add a layer of plastic to prevent rotting from standing water.

If your ground freezes, you can still keep these crops outside for the winter. Start by adding straw, up to 12 to 18 inches, depending upon temperatures. Then, drape the site with plastic and secure with landscape staples. When you're ready to harvest, move the straw and plastic to the side and dig the vegetables out of the ground, then replace the straw and plastic. The biggest

challenge for some of you will be brushing all of the snow off of the plastic in order to get down to ground level.

Not all fruits and vegetables can tolerate high humidity. For those crops, finding dry, cool storage space is critical in preventing spoilage.

1) In this type of storage, finding a space that is both cool and dry is the first priority. It is challenging to remove humidity without the use of a dehumidifier, which may mean that finding a site will take a bit more work.

2) Fortunately, these crops don't need temperatures that are as low as a traditional cellar environment. Look for a site that hovers around 45 to 50 degrees. This can often be found in unheated corners of home basements.

3) Darkness is critical to prevent spoilage. Whether it means using large containers or covering windows, the darker the better.

4) Many of these crops will need to be cured prior to storage. If you skip that step you risk losing the whole lot.

5) Circulation is critical for most of these veggies. Boost storage time by hanging, using shelves, adding pallets, and using containers with built-in ventilation.

6) Don't clean the produce before storage. Don't store any produce that has cuts, nicks, bruises, or is otherwise damaged.

Vegetables that store well in this environment include:

Onion
Garlic
Winter Squash
Sweet Potato
Tomato

Onions are cured over the course of a few weeks in a process that starts with the harvest. When most of the onion tops have started to dry back, bend them over to one side and leave them in the ground for ten days. Pull them from the ground on a sunny day, letting them dry for 24 hours. Tops can be removed at this time, if you choose. Be sure not to cut the stem any closer than an inch or so. Gather the onions and spread them out in an area that is dry and warm, but out of the sun. Spread them on screens or turn onions as they cure, making sure all sides stay dry. This process can last two to three weeks; when it's complete, store onions in a mesh bag or in a nylon stocking, knotting between bulbs to separate.

Garlic is a bit different in the harvesting and curing process. Instead of waiting until most of the leaves are dead, harvest the garlic when there are four to five leaves that are still green. Spread the garlic on screens, or tie the tops together in small bundles. Store the screens and hang bundles in a warm, dry location that has good ventilation.

Cure garlic for three weeks. Store in a mesh bag or nylon, as described for onions.

Winter squash are amazing keepers. Start by harvesting hard-shelled squash before the first freeze. Leave three inches or so of stem on them. Let them cure in a warm, dry space for a few days until any cuts or abrasions have calloused. Store in a location that stays around 50 degrees and has a relatively high humidity. Squash preserve best when elevated off the ground, sitting on straw. Do not stack in layers. Check frequently and remove any that have spoiled.

Though many choose to can tomatoes for storage, you may want to try your hand at harvesting and storing green tomatoes. The easiest way to do this is to pull the entire plant from the ground before freezing temperatures arrive. Hang it upside-down, over a soft mat, and eat the fruits as they ripen and drop from the vine. Green tomatoes can also be stored individually, wrapped in paper or in a container. Keep a close eye on

235

these fruits as they can spoil quickly if they're not taken out of the wrapping or box when ripened. Note that tomatoes also emit a gas that can cause other vegetables and fruits to spoil. It's best to keep them separated from other crops that might be affected.

Storing Vegetables and Herbs in Oil

Extending the use of your harvest is one reason to use oil in the storage of herbs and vegetables. An added bonus is that the oil will absorb the flavors of the produce, resulting in a terrific ingredient for salad dressings, marinades, and pasta dishes.

Using oil to store herbs and vegetables creates a potential risk for botulism poisoning, as any canning does. It is important to take steps to control conditions that contribute to the growth of bacteria.

Flavored oils are a great way to experience the flavors of your herb garden. There are three primary ways of doing this:

1) Dried herbs and tomatoes in oil: Adding dried herbs and dried, unseasoned tomatoes to oil creates a condiment that can be stored at room temperature. To reduce any potential for rancidity, this can also be stored in the refrigerator.

2) Hot oil infusion: Herbs and vegetables such as garlic, onions, and peppers can be used to infuse an oil. Pour hot oil over clean produce and let it stand for a few minutes to infuse. Strain the oil to remove all vegetable matter. Store in the refrigerator.

3) Fresh vegetables and herbs in oil: A wide variety of edibles can be stored this way. Ideas include: garlic, citrus zest, mushrooms, peppers, and a range of herbs. Thoroughly

clean and dry fresh vegetables and herbs; cover with oil. Experiment with the wide variety of flavor combinations. Store in the refrigerator for two to three weeks. Freeze mixtures for longer storage times.

Vacuum Packaging

Many foods can be stored with a method called vacuum packaging. Though fresh fruits, herbs, and vegetables need additional conditions in order for this method to work, it is an excellent accompaniment to freezing and drying. Storing your harvest in a vacuum-sealed bag reduces freezer burn and prevents moisture from spoiling dried produce. There are a number of vacuum sealers on the market today, many of which are affordable.

Tips for getting the most from vacuum sealing:

- Choose a sturdy vacuum sealer, particularly if you have a lot of produce to store. Though it may seem like a bargain in the beginning, cheap vacuum storage systems may burn out or be less effective in the long run.

- Freeze items you don't want "squished" by the sealer. Remember, the vacuum sealers are sucking all of the air out of the bag. If you have fragile produce, such as berries, they will be a runny mess in the end. Freezing them first provides a sturdier structure and reduces breakage.
- Liquids and sauces should be frozen prior to using the vacuum. Again, this is a vacuum and it will suck the liquid and sauce right out of the package. This results in an unbelievable mess and a poor seal.
- Clean your sealer according to manufacture's directions regularly to prevent bacterial build up.

Food Preserving Tips

- Did you know water boils at lower temperatures in high altitudes? Because of this, you will need to adjust processing times to compensate for lower boiling temperatures. If you're not sure, consult your local county extension agent about the proper conversion formula.

- If you're using purchased vegetables or fruits, make sure they have not been treated with waxes or resins to preserve freshness. Apples, cucumbers, eggplants, squash, tomatoes—even beans and asparagus—are sometimes treated. When in doubt, ask.

- Sunlight and air can degrade herbs and spices. Always store them in opaque, well-sealed containers in a cool place.

- If you're using freezer bags for freezing your produce, don't put them directly on the wire racks of your freezer. They will conform to the racks as they freeze and create odd shapes. Removing them can cause small holes that can allow air to enter the bag and cause freezer burn.

- Dried herbs have more concentrated flavor than fresh herbs. When using dried rather than fresh herbs in canning, reduce quantities by one-third to one-half.

- Canning, freezing, or other preserving does not improve damaged or over- or underripe fruits and vegetables. Always use undamaged fruits and vegetables at the peak of quality for preserving.

- Do not use artificial sweeteners, including Splenda, instead of sugar unless the recipe specifically calls for it. Sweeteners may affect shelf life stability and leave an aftertaste.

- Use a wide-mouthed canning funnel to transfer foods into canning jars without spilling and splattering.

- Never repurpose containers such as milk boxes or yogurt containers for freezing. They are not adequate to preserve food quality.

- To ensure you don't accidentally waste all your preserved food, keep a list of your stored canned and frozen foods taped inside a cabinet door along with their expiration dates.

- Freezer burn isn't harmful, but it makes most food inedible. Avoid freezer burn by ensuring foods are frozen in moisture- and air-proof wrapping.

- Since freezing does not destroy bacteria, the best way to thaw frozen foods is slowly and at cold temperatures. Place frozen food in the refrigerator several hours before you need it.

- Do you collect old cookbooks? Good for you. But pass on using them for instructions on safe food preservation. Modern understanding of food contamination and contemporary methods are your best bets at keeping your preserved food from contamination.

information:// Nutrition

FROZEN: As soon as possible after harvest, freeze foods to retain nutrients and preserve freshness. Preservatives aren't required for freezing, making this one of the healthiest ways to preserve foods when done properly.

CANNED: Nutrients can be retained in canned foods if the produce is picked at peak quality and canned quickly after harvest. Depending on the crop, however, large amounts of vitamin C, thiamine, and riboflavin may be lost during the high processing temperatures used during canning. Canned vegetables also can be high in sodium. Reduce your salt intake by rinsing canned produce with water for a minute or two before cooking.

DRIED: You can actually get more vitamins and minerals from some dried foods than canned or frozen produce. That's because the drying process concentrates large amounts of vitamin A and other nutrients. The nutritional value of 100 grams of dried peaches, for instance, is much higher in vitamins A and C, riboflavin, iron, and calcium than the same amount of frozen or canned peaches. For green vegetables, you're better off with canned or frozen produce. When dried peas are reconstituted for stews or soups, their nutritional levels drop below that of canned or frozen peas. Store dried foods in airtight containers, preferably made of glass, to retain freshness. Keep away from heat and direct sunlight.

COOKED OR RAW?

Raw vegetables aren't always more nutritious. Several studies have shown that gently cooking certain vegetables allows more healthy plant chemicals to be released and absorbed.

Green beans, celery, and carrots were found to have higher antioxidant levels after cooking, according to a report in the "Journal of Food Science." Certain cooking methods were better than others, however.

Researchers at the University of Murcia in Spain analyzed how well twenty different kinds of vegetables retained antioxidants after being cooked in six different ways. Boiling and pressure cooking led to the greatest losses of antioxidants, while griddle- and microwave-cooking retained the highest antioxidant levels.

Steaming broccoli actually increases cancer-fighting plant compounds called glucosinolates, according to an Italian study. And cooked tomatoes, especially prepared with a little olive oil, provide more of the powerful antioxidant lycopene than when they were served raw.

Raspberry Rhubarb Jam

8¼ plus ¼ cups sugar, divided

1 package pectin

4 cups raspberries, cleaned and drained

2 cups cooked rhubarb, (generally, 6–8 stalks will yield 2 cups cooked rhubarb)

You will also need:

4 12-oz. jelly jars, lids, and rings (I prefer the wide-mouth jars, which are easier to fill)

a nonstick saucepan

a large canning pot or stockpot for the canning process

jar tongs

regular tongs or magnetic canning stick

a funnel

- Wash the jars in a dishwasher to sterilize. Leave them in the dishwasher in the heated dry cycle to keep warm. Add water and the lids (but not the rings) to a small saucepan and heat over medium heat, keeping below a boil, 5 minutes. Add enough water to the stockpot to cover the jars by one inch. Bring the water to a boil while making the jam.
- In a small bowl, combine ¼ cup of the sugar with the pectin. Mix thoroughly to reduce any lumps of pectin.
- Add the raspberries, rhubarb, and sugar-pectin mixture to a medium saucepan; bring to a boil. Stir occasionally to avoid burning the jam. When the jam is boiling, add the remaining 8¼ cups sugar. Stir well and bring back to a rolling boil for 1 minute.
- Remove the jam from heat and strain to remove any seeds. Let the strained jam stand 5 minutes.
- Fill the prepared jars with the jam. (If you have any excess jam, fill a fridge container and use relatively quickly.) Seal with the lids and rings. Put the jars into the canning pot or stockpot. Add boiling water and process 10 minutes. Remove the jars and cool to room temperature.
- During the first 15 to 30 minutes of cooling, check the jam to ensure it has sealed properly by pushing on the top of the lid with your finger. If the lid moves up and down, the seal did not form. Pop it in the fridge and use as freezer jam.

All-Day Apple Butter Preserves

8 lbs. cooking apples (such as Golden Delicious, Gravenstein, Granny Smith),
  cleaned and quartered (leave the peel and the cores)

2 cups apple cider vinegar

2 cups apple cider

½ cup unsulfured molasses

¾ cup honey

2–3 cups brown sugar (depending upon sweetness of apples)

1 orange, zest and juice

1 Tbsp. cinnamon

1 tsp. ground cloves

1-inch piece of fresh ginger, peeled and grated

1 tsp. salt

■ Put the apples into a large saucepan. Add a splash of water and cook over low-medium heat until the apples disintegrate. Press the apples through a food mill and return them to the pan. Add the vinegar, cider, molasses, honey, brown sugar, orange zest and juice, cinnamon, cloves, ginger, and salt.

■ Cook the apple mixture over low heat for several hours, stirring occasionally to prevent burning. This can also be cooked overnight in a slow cooker on its lowest setting. The sauce should be reduced in volume and have a spreadable consistency. Follow the sterilizing and canning methods for hot water bath canning.

Basic Tomato Sauce

One of the challenges of making homemade sauce is seeding and peeling the tomatoes. Rather than go through all of that blanching, squeezing, and peeling business, we will just press the final product through a food mill.

There are tomato varieties that make better sauce. Plum tomatoes, for example, are great. They have more flesh and less water, which makes for a very tasty sauce. When canning different types of tomatoes, it is important to know the ones that have lower acidity. These fruits are best canned via the pressure canning method.

The challenge is that it can be difficult to know which tomatoes have a higher pH, therefore making them less acidic and more susceptible to bacterial growth. The USDA recommends using either a pressure canner to can low-acid tomatoes or adding 1/4 tsp. citric acid per each quart of finished product.

2 Tbsp. olive oil

1 shallot, minced

2 Tbsp. dried basil

1 Tbsp. dried oregano

1 tsp. dried rosemary

1 tsp. dried thyme

1 Tbsp. fennel seeds

2 Tbsp. sugar

8 medium tomatoes, quartered

Salt and fresh-ground black pepper to taste

¼ tsp. citric acid per each quart of sauce (add after cooking, if needed)

- In a large stockpot, warm the olive oil over medium heat. Add the shallot, basil, oregano, rosemary, thyme, fennel seeds, and sugar. Sauté for a couple of minutes. Add the tomatoes, salt, and pepper.

- Cook down until the tomatoes form a sauce and have reduced by half. Taste and adjust seasonings for flavor. When you are satisfied, press the tomatoes through a food mill to remove the skins and seeds.

PEST & DISEASE CHART

Even professional gardeners discover diseases and pests in their gardens with alarming regularity. But using sound horticultural practices and taking prompt action, when needed, can reduce the chances that your garden will suffer from disease and pests and increases the chances that you will still be able to save your crop.

General Guidelines

- Make a habit of carefully and regularly inspecting plants for early signs of pests and disease. When you're unsure of the problem, take a sample to a local nursery or your local agricultural extension agent to diagnose the problem and develop a management plan.
- Avoid overcrowding plants and promote good airflow by pruning and staking.
- Carefully wash soil off hoes, shovels, and other tools after each use.
- Clean and disinfect tools and plant pots at the end of the season.
- Wash hands and garden gloves after handling diseased plants.
- Rotate crops from season to season.
- Avoid watering the garden late in the day so foliage is dry by nightfall or irrigate at the soil level to avoid wetting foliage.
- Don't work in the garden when it's wet, as you can more easily spread spores or bacteria that are already present.
- Avoid mechanical injury to plants by mowers, weed eaters, or other garden tools.

- Destroy diseased plant material by putting it in the trash. Never compost disease or pest-ridden plants, as the compost may not reach temperatures high enough to destroy the pathogens.
- Choose certified disease-free plants and plant varieties that are disease resistant. Many seed companies and nurseries provide this information on tags and labels, which indicate the diseases to which the specific plants are resistant. This is indicated by letters after the name of the variety. The determinate tomato 'Rutgers VFA', for example, is resistant to Verticillium (V), fusarium (F) and alternaria (A).
- Don't automatically reach for fungicides or pesticides to solve the problem. Many problems can be managed through improved hygiene and cultural controls.

Diseases	Plants Affected	Signs	Prevention & Management
Anthracnose	Bean Blueberry Brambleberries Cucumber Pepper Squash Strawberry Tomato	• Sunken brown spots on bean pods, lower berry canes, or on leaves • Water-soaked, circular lesions under ripening fruit that turns brown as the fruit ripens	• Practice crop rotation with non-host crops • Avoid excess moisture • Irrigate from overhead early in the day to allow plants to dry before nightfall • Choose certified pathogen-free seeds or plants and disease-resistant varieties • Prune to increase air circulation • Remove and destroy affected leaves and plants after harvest • Apply sulfur sprays to prevent spread
Bacterial wilt & Verticillium wilt	Cucumber Melon Pepper Squash Tomato	• Initial dulling of leaf color and wilting of terminal leaves followed by overall permanent wilting	• Choose certified pathogen-free seeds or plants and disease-resistant varieties • Ensure soil pH is 5.5 or higher • Promptly eliminate cucumber beetles, which carry the bacteria • Remove and destroy infected plants
Black rot	Apple Broccoli Cantaloupe Cucumber Winter squash	• Dwarf or one-sided plants with yellow to brown leaves • Discoloration in the vascular rings of stems • Fruit/Vegetable symptoms vary widely. Vegetables may develop yellowish, irregularly shaped spots that turn brown/black. Pale dots or oozing may develop on the spots and crust over.	• Practice a long rotation between similar crops • Choose certified pathogen-free seeds or plants and disease-resistant varieties • Plant in well-drained soil • Avoid injury to plants when harvesting • Control powdery mildew, aphids and cucumber beetles
Black leg	Broccoli Brussels sprouts Cabbage Cauliflower Collards Kale Kohlrabi Mustard greens	• Pale spots on leaves that turn gray with black specks • Spots on stems, dark, sunken, circular to irregular with purple borders • Decaying roots • Plants may wilt and die	• Practice a long rotation between similar crops • Choose certified pathogen-free seeds or plants and disease-resistant varieties
Blossom drop	Bean Pepper Squash Tomato	• Plants set flower but then dry up and fall off without setting fruit	• Grow vegetable varieties suited to the climate • Ensure pollination by avoiding the use of pesticides that kill beneficial insects • Attract beneficial insects with flowers or hand-pollinate with a small brush • Water deeply in dry weather

PEST & DISEASE CHART

Diseases	Plants Affected	Signs	Prevention & Management
Blossom end rot	Pepper Squash Tomato Watermelon	• Sunken, leathery brown or black patches develop at the bottom of the fruit, usually during the early stages of development • Secondary diseases or pests may infest fruits	• Maintain soil pH of 6.5, applying lime to increase the absorption of needed calcium • Avoid overfertilizing during fruit development • Plant in well-drained, aerated soil • Avoid wide fluctuations in soil moisture by mulching and watering during dry periods • Avoid injury to plants and roots when cultivating or weeding around roots
Downy mildew	Bean Cantaloupe Cucumber Grape Lettuce Melon Peas Squash Tomato Watermelon	• Discoloration of upper sides of leaves, which may wilt and die • White, grey, bluish, or violet downy patches form on undersides of leaves	• Avoid excess moisture • Irrigate from overhead early in the day to allow plants to dry before nightfall • Choose certified pathogen-free seeds or plants and disease-resistant varieties • Prune to increase air circulation • Remove and destroy affected leaves and plants after harvest • Spray potassium bicarbonate sprays or Neem • As a last resort, use copper-based fungicides
Fusarium wilt	Asparagus Peas Tomato	• Leaves begin to yellow, starting with lower leaves, then turning brown and brittle, curling under • Vascular tissues in stem become yellow to dark brown	• Practice a long rotation between similar crops • Choose certified pathogen-free seeds or plants and disease-resistant varieties
Mosaic virus	Bean Carrot Cucumber Dill Fennel Lettuce Melon Parsley Peas Pepper Squash Tomato	• Symptoms are variable by plant • Mottled or distorted leaves that curl upward and are stunted • Fruits are pale and may have a mottled appearance	• Choose certified pathogen-free seeds or plants and disease-resistant varieties, when available • Remove and destroy affected leaves and plants • Remove perennial weeds adjacent to growing areas

chart:// Pest & Disease

Diseases	Plants Affected	Signs	Prevention & Management
Powdery mildew	Apple Brambleberries Cucumber Grape Melon Peas Squash Strawberry Tomato	• White, powdery coating on leaves	• Plant in a sunny location with well-drained, aerated soil • Remove affected leaves • Avoid excess moisture • Irrigate from overhead early in the day to allow plants to dry before nightfall • Avoid overcrowding • Prune to increase air circulation • Apply sulfur-based sprays or a spray or crushed garlic and water at the first sign of disease. (Test a small area for sensitivity before spraying the whole plant.) • Apply a baking soda spray (1 teaspoon baking soda, 1 quart water, a few drops of dishwashing liquid)
Rust	Bean	• Orange-red, reddish-brown, or black pustules on leaves and stems	• Irrigate from overhead early in the day to allow plants to dry before nightfall • Choose certified pathogen-free seeds or plants and disease-resistant varieties • Prune to increase air circulation • Remove and destroy affected leaves and plants after harvest

Pests	Plants Affected	Signs	Prevention & Management
Aphid	Apple Bean Brambleberries Broccoli Lettuce Melon Peas Pepper Squash Tomato	• Usually found on undersides of leaves • Small pests, usually smaller than $1/8$", with pear-shaped bodies • Colors are highly variable, but are usually green, yellow, or black • Two short tubes extend from the back of the pest	• Spray plants with a strong stream of water or prune away large clusters • Apply insecticidal soap
Cabbage maggot	Beet Broccoli Brussels sprouts Cabbage Cauliflower Kale Radish Rutabaga Turnip	• Plant growth appears stunted • Wilting leaves • White, legless maggots in the soil around roots	• Remove contaminated plants • Prevent infestation by covering plants with floating row covers or planting transplants through soil barriers • Remove roots and plants in the fall to destroy host area

Pests	Plants Affected	Signs	Prevention & Management
Colorado potato beetle	Eggplant Pepper Potato Tomato	• Beetle is ½ inch long and has yellow/orange body with 5 brown stripes • Small yellow/orange eggs on undersides of leaves • Large holes in plant leaves	• Prevent infestation by rotating crops, mulching with straw, and use floating row covers • Hand-pick adults, larvae, and eggs and destroy • Apply Beauveria bassiana or Spinosad
Cutworm	Lettuce Tomato	• Stems are severed at soil level by soil-colored caterpillars	• Control weeds around plants and in the vicinity • Prevent cutworms by surrounding the base of plants with a cardboard collar or aluminum can with tops and bottoms removed and pushed 1" into the soil • Spread bran moistened with Bacillus thuringiensis kurstaki when planting
Flea beetle	Broccoli Cool-season greens Pepper Tomato	• Young leaves have tiny holes • Small brown/black, often shiny, beetle	• Use floating row covers or sticky traps • Use garlic sprays or kaolin clay • Plant trap crops, such as giant mustard or radish
Japanese beetle	Numerous plants, flowers, and fruits	• Metallic green and copper-brown beetles • Skeletal holes in leaves	• Hand-pick and destroy the beetles • Do not use traps, which attract more beetles than they trap • Prevent infestation by covering plants with floating row covers • Apply Neem, insecticidal soap, or pyrethrins • Control grubs with milky spore or beneficial nematodes
Scale	Apple Peach Pear Plum	• Scale insects vary widely in appearance, but most are flat or rounded and appear permanently attached, like scales, to the leaves, stem,s and fruit • Sticky substance on leaves and stems • Poor growth • Secondary infection of sooty mold	• In late winter, apply dormant oil • In late spring, apply Neem or summer oil

Pests	Plants Affected	Signs	Prevention & Management
Slugs/snails	Lettuce Peas Strawberry	• Irregular holes in leaves • Slime trails	• Remove weeds and dispose of decayed plant material • If practical, prune lower branches • Avoid heavy mulching • Hand-pick and destroy • Place beer in shallow pans as traps • Use iron phosphate baits
Squash vine borer	Cucumber Melon Squash	• Sudden wilting • Small holes at base of stems with greenish excrement • Larva is fat, white, grublike caterpillar • Adult borers may be visible—black moths with metallic green front wings and reddish-black markings	• Remove vines at the end of harvest to prevent harboring larva • Cover vines at leaf joints with soil to promote secondary roots • Cover stems with a barrier, such as a nylon stocking • Catch and destroy moths; hand-pick eggs • Slit vine to remove borer
Tarnished plant bug	Apple Bean Beet Brambleberries Cabbage Cauliflower Celery Cucumber Grape Pear Potato Strawberry Turnip	• Stunted fruit growth and scarring • Dwarfed and misshapen plants • Fruit bud drop • Flat, ¼-inch greenish-brown insect with piercing mouth parts	• Remove weeds and dispose of decayed plant material • Use floating row covers • Apply dormant oil in dormant periods

apple

Almost Applesauce, 96

Apple, Fennel, and Goat Cheese
Dressing, 93

Applejack Chicken, 94

Blue Cheese Baked Apples, 92

Easy Applesauce Bundt Cake, 95

nutrition, 96

pests and diseases, 90

planting and growing, 89

preparation methods,91

preserving, 91

selection and harvest, 90

varieties, 89

asparagus

Asparagus and Goat Cheese
Tart, 150-51

Asparagus Salad with Chervil
Pesto, 149

Creamy Asparagus and
Pea Soup, 148

nutrition, 152

pests and diseases, 147

planting and growing, 145

preparation methods, 147

preserving, 146

Roasted Asparagus in Olive Oil, 152

selection and harvest, 146

varieties, 146

basil

Basil Sorbet, 43

Lazy Margherita Pizza, 44

Not Just Another Pesto, 46

nutrition, 46

pests and diseases, 42

planting and growing, 41

preserving, 42

selection and harvest, 42

Thai Basil Fried Rice, 45

varieties, 41

bean

Baby Lima Bean Salad, 156

nutrition, 160

pests and diseases, 154

planting and growing, 153

preparation methods, 155

preserving, 154

Roasted Potato and Green Bean
Salad, 159

selection and harvest, 154

Spanish-Inspired Hummus, 160

Stir-Fried Green Beans, 158

Three Sisters Salad, 158

varieties, 154

White Bean and Turkey Chili, 157

blueberry

Blueberries and Barley, 104

Blueberry-Basted Grilled Pork, 101

Blueberry Chicken Salad, 100

Blueberry Ginger Muffins, 99

Blueberry Ice Cream, 103

Blueberry Mascarpone Pancakes, 102

nutrition, 104

pests and diseases, 98

planting and growing, 97

preparation methods,98-99

preserving, 99

selection and harvest, 98

varieties, 97

brambleberry

Berry Crumble, 108

Berry Delight, 109

Blackberry Apple Compote, 112

Bramble Refrigerator Jam, 110

nutrition, 112

planting and growing, 105

preparation methods, 107

preserving, 107

Raspberry Ripple Ice Cream, 111

selection and harvest, 106

varieties, 106

broccoli

3 B's Salad, 166

Best Broccoli Quiche in the World,
165

Bodacious Tomato, Broccoli, and
Cheese Tart, 167

Broccoli Cheddar Soup, 164

nutrition, 168

pests and diseases, 162

planting and growing, 161

preparation methods, 163

preserving, 162

Raw Apple-Sage Stuffing, 168

Roasted Broccoli and Cauliflower
Salad, 163

selection and harvest, 162

varieties, 161

carrot

Beet, Carrot, and Cabbage Stew, 173

Curried Carrot Soup, 176

Maple-Glazed Carrots, 173

Italian Ragu Sauce, 174

nutrition, 176

pests and diseases, 170

planting and growing, 169

preparation methods, 171

preserving, 171

selection and harvest, 170

Shepherd's Pie with Carrot and
Sweet Potato Topping, 172

Thai Noodle Salad with Zucchini
and Carrots, 175

varieties, 170

chives

(Almost) Mashed Potato Salad, 50

Chive Dip, 49

Chive Oil, 52

nutrition, 52

pests and diseases, 48

planting and growing, 47

preserving, 48

Index

Roasted Sweet Corn and Chive Scones, 51

selection and harvest, 48

varieties, 47

cilantro/coriander

Cilantro Pesto, 58

Coriander Pork Chops with Hot Stuff Sauce, 56

Cucumber Tomato Salad, 56

nutrition, 58

pests and diseases, 54

planting and growing, 53

preserving, 54

Ramen at the Ritz, 55

Red Quinoa Salad with Cilantro, 57

Rock Star Salsa, 55

selection and harvest, 54

varieties, 53

compost, 14

controls, pests & disease

biological, 28

chemical, 28

cultural, 24-26

physical, 26

cucumber

Asian Cucumber Salad, 180

Cucumber Yogurt Salad, 183

nutrition, 184

pests and diseases, 178

planting and growing, 177

preparation methods, 179, 184

preserving, 179

selection and harvest, 178

varieties, 178

dill and fennel

Braised Fennel, 62

Chicken and Fennel Salad Sandwiches, 62

Fennel-Flavored Hollandaise Sauce, 64

Herbed Cucumber Salad, 63

Lemon-Dill Tartar Sauce, 61

nutrition, 64

pests and diseases, 60

planting and growing, 59

preserving, 60

selection and harvest, 60

Tuna Pasta Salad with Dill and Capers, 61

varieties, 59

disease, 30-32, 243-48

fertilizer, 13–14

fruit

apple, 89-96

blueberry, 97-104

brambleberry, 105-112

grape, 113-120

melon, 121-128

rhubarb, 129-136

strawberry, 137-144

gardening

containers, 16, 19-21

planning, 11

vertical, 21

grape

Asian Pear and Raisin Chutney, 119

Champagne Grape and Tomatillo Salsa, 119

Concord Grape Crumble, 120

Curried Chicken Salad, 116

Grape Juice, 118

nutrition, 120

Panettone Bread Pudding, 116

pests and diseases, 114

planting and growing, 113-114

preparation methods, 115

preserving, 115

selection and harvest, 114

Stuffed Grape Leaves, 117

varieties, 114

Vegetarian Stuffed Grape Leaves, 118

greens

cool-season

Brazilian Collard Greens, 189

Crispy Kale, 192

Grandma's Stuffed Cabbage, 190

nutrition, 192

pests and diseases, 186

planting and growing, 185

preparation methods, 187

preserving, 187

selection and harvest, 186-87

Spinach and Tomato Frittata, 191

Swiss Chard and Spaghetti, 188

varieties, 186

Wilted Spinach Salad, 189

lettuces and salad greens

Baby Spinach Salad with Blueberries and Pecans, 197

Caesar Salad, 196

Fig and Arugula Composed Salad, 200

nutrition, 200

pests and diseases, 194

planting and growing, 193

preparation methods, 195

preserving, 195

Salade Niçoise, 199

selection and harvest, 194

Sunny Citrus Salad, 198

varieties, 194

herbs

basil, 41-46

chives, 47-52

cilantro/coriander, 53-58

dill and fennel, 59-64

mint, 65-70

oregano, 65-70

parsley, 71-76

rosemary, 77-82

sage and thyme, 83-88

melon
  Angel Food Cake with Cantaloupe Glaze, 126
  Cantaloupe Blackberry Smoothie, 128
  Casaba Melon Salad, 125
  Honeydew Mint Fizz, 124
  Lobster and Honeydew Salad, 127
  Melon Sorbet, 127
  nutrition, 128
  pests and diseases, 122
  planting and growing, 121
  preparation methods, 123
  preserving, 123
  selection and harvest, 122
  varieties, 122
  Watermelon Popsicles, 125
  Watermelon, Red Onion, and Feta Salad, 124

mint
  Blender Tabouleh, 70
  Fresh Mint Chocolate Chip Ice Cream, 67
  nutrition, 70
  pests and diseases, 66
  planting and growing, 65
  preserving, 66
  selection and harvest, 66
  varieties, 65

mulch, 18-19

oregano
  New Potatoes and Green Beans in Herb Garlic Béchamel, 69
  nutrition, 70
  pests and diseases, 66
  planting and growing, 65
  preserving, 66
  selection and harvest, 66
  Slow and Low Pot Roast, 68
  varieties, 65

parsley
  Chicken Kiev, 74
  Chimichurri, 76
  nutrition, 76
  pests and diseases, 72
  planting and growing, 71
  Pork Churrasco and Chimichurri, 75
  preserving, 72
  selection and harvest, 72
  Turkey Noodle Soup, 73
  varieties, 71

pea
  Creamed Peas, 203
  Indian Peas and Potatoes, 205
  Mockamole, 208
  nutrition, 208
  pests and diseases, 202
  planting and growing, 201
  preparation methods, 203
  preserving, 203
  selection and harvest, 202
  Sugar Snaps with Rotini and Goat Cheese, 204
  Thai Summer Rolls, 206-7
  varieties, 202

pepper
  Apple, Zucchini, and Red Pepper "Tortilla", 215
  Corn and Pepper Scallop, 215
  Dried and Smoked Peppers, 212
  Nopales Salsa, 214
  nutrition, 216
  pests and diseases, 210
  planting and growing, 209
  Pozole-Inspired Gazpacho, 216
  preparation methods, 211
  preserving, 211
  Roasted Red Pepper Cream Sauce, 212
  selection and harvest, 210
  Stuffed Bell Peppers, 213
  varieties, 209

pests, 29, 243-48

planting
  companion, 22
  succession, 22

preserving, 225-26, 230, 238
  canning, 226-29
  dehydrating, 231-32
  freezing, 229-31
  nutrition, 239
  storage, 232-36
  vacuum packaging, 236-37

produce
  organic, 36, 38
  purchasing, 34-36
  selection, 37-38

rhubarb
  Brined Turkey Breast with Rhubarb-Orange Compote, 133
  nutrition, 136
  pests and diseases, 130
  planting and growing, 129
  preparation methods, 130
  preserving, 130
  Rhubarb Bread, 136
  Rhubarb Cake with Citrus Glaze, 135
  Rhubarb-Cherry Ice Cream, 131
  Rhubarb-Orange Compote, 134
  Rhubarb Pie, 132
  Rhubarb, Strawberry, and Thyme Sorbet, 134
  selection and harvest, 130
  varieties, 129

rosemary
  nutrition, 82
  pests and diseases, 78
  planting and growing, 77
  preserving, 78
  Rosemary Bread, 80-81
  Rosemary-Infused Vinegar, 82
  Rosemary Refried Black Beans, 79

Index

selection and harvest, 78

varieties, 77

sage

nutrition, 88

Pesto, Meatballs and Pasta, 2.0, 86-87

pests and diseases, 84

planting and growing, 83

preserving, 84

selection and harvest, 84

Tempura Sage Leaves, 88

varieties, 83

seeds, 15-17

transplanting, 17

soil, 12

squash

Butternut Squash and Brown Rice Risotto, 181

nutrition, 184

pests and diseases, 178

planting and growing, 177

preparation methods, 179

preserving, 179

Roasted Summer Squash Dip, 182

selection and harvest, 178

varieties, 178

strawberry

Mascarpone Crostata with Strawberries and Apples, 140-41

nutrition, 144

planting and growing, 137

preparation methods, 139

preserving, 139

selection and harvest, 138

Strawberry and Stone Fruit Coulis, 144

Strawberry-Topped Cheesecake with Cinnamon Graham Cracker Crust, 142-43

varieties, 138

thyme

nutrition, 88

Pesto, Meatballs and Pasta, 2.0, 86-87

pests and diseases, 84

planting and growing, 83

preserving, 84

selection and harvest, 84

Squash Sausage Soup, 85

varieties, 83

tomato

Basic Tomato Sauce, 242

Calypso Mary, 221

Fresh from the Garden Tomato and Jalapeño Salsa, 220

Fried Green Tomatoes, 224

Herb-y Cherry Tomato Salad, 220

nutrition,

pests and diseases, 219

planting and growing, 217

preparation methods, 219

preserving, 219

selection and harvest, 218

Summer Tomato Tart, 223

Tomato Cucumber Salad, 222

varieties, 218

Verde Mary, 222

vegetable

asparagus, 145-52

beans, 153-60

broccoli, 161-68

carrot, 169-176

cucumber and squash, 177-84

greens, cool-season, 185-92

lettuces and salad greens, 193-200

peas, 201-8

pepper, 209-16

tomato, 217-24

RECIPE INDEX

(Almost) Mashed Potato Salad, 50

3 B's Salad, 166

All-Day Apple Butter Preserves, 241

Almost Applesauce, 96

Angel Food Cake with Cantaloupe Glaze, 126

Apple, Fennel, and Goat Cheese Dressing, 93

Apple, Zucchini, and Red Pepper "Tortilla", 215

Applejack Chicken, 94

Asian Cucumber Salad, 180

Asian Pear and Raisin Chutney, 119

Asparagus and Goat Cheese Tart, 150-51

Asparagus Salad with Chervil Pesto, 149

Baby Lima Bean Salad, 156

Baby Spinach Salad with Blueberries and Pecans, 197

Basic Tomato Sauce, 242

Basil Sorbet, 43

Beet, Carrot, and Cabbage Stew, 173

Berry Crumble, 108

Berry Delight, 109

Best Broccoli Quiche in the World, 165

Blackberry Apple Compote, 112

Blender Tabouleh, 70

Blue Cheese Baked Apples, 92

Blueberries and Barley, 104

Blueberry Chicken Salad, 100

Blueberry Ginger Muffins, 99

Blueberry Ice Cream, 103

Blueberry Mascarpone Pancakes, 102

Blueberry-Basted Grilled Pork, 101

Bodacious Tomato, Broccoli, and Cheese Tart, 167

Braised Fennel, 62

Bramble Refrigerator Jam, 110

Brazilian Collard Greens, 189

Brined Turkey Breast with Rhubarb-Orange Compote, 133

Broccoli Cheddar Soup, 164

Butternut Squash and Brown Rice Risotto, 181

Caesar Salad, 196

Calypso Mary, 221

Cantaloupe Blackberry Smoothie, 128

Casaba Melon Salad, 125

Champagne Grape and Tomatillo Salsa, 119

Chicken and Fennel Salad Sandwiches, 62

Chicken Kiev, 74

Chimichurri, 76

Chive Dip, 49

Chive Oil, 52

Cilantro Pesto, 58

Concord Grape Crumble, 120

Coriander Pork Chops with Hot Stuff Sauce, 56

Corn and Pepper Scallop, 215

Creamed Peas, 203

Creamy Asparagus and Pea Soup, 148

Crispy Kale, 192

Cucumber Tomato Salad, 56

Cucumber Yogurt Salad, 183

Curried Carrot Soup, 176

Curried Chicken Salad, 116

Dried and Smoked Peppers, 212

Easy Applesauce Bundt Cake, 95

Fennel-Flavored Hollandaise Sauce, 64

Fig and Arugula Composed Salad, 200

Fresh from the Garden Tomato and Jalapeño Salsa, 220

Fresh Mint Chocolate Chip Ice Cream, 67

Fried Green Tomatoes, 224

Grandma's Stuffed Cabbage, 190

Grape Juice, 118

Herbed Cucumber Salad, 63

Herb-y Cherry Tomato Salad, 220

Honeydew Mint Fizz, 124

Indian Peas and Potatoes, 205

Italian Ragu Sauce, 174

Lazy Margherita Pizza, 44

Lemon-Dill Tartar Sauce, 61

Lobster and Honeydew Salad, 127

Maple-Glazed Carrots, 173

Mascarpone Crostata with Strawberries and Apples, 140-41

Melon Sorbet, 127

Mockamole, 208

New Potatoes and Green Beans in Herb Garlic Béchamel, 69

Nopales Salsa, 214

Not Just Another Pesto, 46

Panettone Bread Pudding, 116

Pesto, Meatballs and Pasta, 2.0, 86-87

Pork Churrasco and Chimichurri, 75

Pozole-Inspired Gazpacho, 216

Ramen at the Ritz, 55

Raspberry Rhubarb Jam, 240

Raspberry Ripple Ice Cream, 111

Raw Apple-Sage Stuffing, 168

Red Quinoa Salad with Cilantro, 57

Rhubarb Bread, 136

Rhubarb Cake with Citrus Glaze, 135

Rhubarb, Strawberry, and Thyme Sorbet, 134

Rhubarb-Cherry Ice Cream, 131

Rhubarb-Orange Compote, 134

Rhubarb Pie, 132

Roasted Asparagus in Olive Oil, 152

Roasted Broccoli and Cauliflower Salad, 163

Roasted Potato and Green Bean Salad, 159

Roasted Red Pepper Cream Sauce, 212

Roasted Summer Squash Dip, 182

Roasted Sweet Corn and Chive Scones, 51

Rock Star Salsa, 55

Rosemary Bread, 80-81

Rosemary Refried Black Beans, 79

Rosemary-Infused Vinegar, 82

Salade Niçoise, 199

Shepherd's Pie with Carrot and Sweet Potato Topping, 172

Slow and Low Pot Roast, 68

Spanish-Inspired Hummus, 160

Spinach and Tomato Frittata, 191

Squash Sausage Soup, 85

Stir-Fried Green Beans, 158

Strawberry and Stone Fruit Coulis, 144

Strawberry-Topped Cheesecake with Cinnamon Graham Cracker Crust, 142-43

Stuffed Bell Peppers, 213

Stuffed Grape Leaves, 117

Sugar Snaps with Rotini and Goat Cheese, 204

Summer Tomato Tart, 22

Sunny Citrus Salad, 198

Swiss Chard and Spaghetti, 188

Tempura Sage Leaves, 88

Thai Basil Fried Rice, 45

Thai Noodle Salad with Zucchini and Carrots, 175

Thai Summer Rolls, 206-7

Three Sisters Salad, 158

Tomato Cucumber Salad, 222

Tuna Pasta Salad with Dill and Capers, 61

Turkey Noodle Soup, 73

Vegetarian Stuffed Grape Leaves, 118

Verde Mary, 222

Watermelon Popsicles, 125

Watermelon, Red Onion, and Feta Salad, 124

White Bean and Turkey Chili, 157

Wilted Spinach Salad, 189

JEAN ANN VAN KREVELEN

Jean Ann Van Krevelen is one of the most influential gardening communicators in the country. She hosts various blogs, Facebook groups and pages, websites, and Twitter profiles. Through all of these channels, Jean Ann inspires, educates, and challenges tens of thousands of gardeners each month. Her blog is nationally syndicated on a variety of popular websites such as *Chicago Sun Times, The Wall Street Journal*, and *USA Today*. Jean Ann has been named to the 2009 Top 20 Green, Raw Organic Tweeters; 2009 Top 50 Tweeters in Portland; 2009 Top 100 Entrepreneurs on Twitter; 2008 Top 50 People to Follow on Twitter; Top 30 Most Powerful and Influential Women in Social Media; and 30 Entrepreneurs to Follow on Twitter. She can be reached on Twitter through her username @JeanAnnVK or on her blog **www.gardenertofarmer.net**.

AMANDA THOMSEN

Amanda Thomsen is a garden designer, Master Gardener, and plantswoman who communicates her somewhat sassy garden theory to gardeners across the country as a contributing editor and writer for *Horticulture* magazine's website and blogs. She is one of the most powerful communicators in garden-related social media where she tirelessly educates her followers on Twitter, blogs, and on various Facebook pages and groups. She is the co-host of the gardening podcast "Good Enough Gardening," where she uses humor and real life experience to make gardening approachable and enjoyable. Thomsen can be reached on Twitter under her user name @kissmyaster or on her blog **www.hortmag.com/kissmyaster**.

ROBIN RIPLEY

Robin Ripley is a writer, prolific cook, and a garden speaker in great demand who educates gardeners on how best to create a productive garden that is also pleasing to the eye. She is the national garden columnist for Examiner.com and an influential blogger and communicator on sites such as Facebook and Twitter where she inspires thousands of readers to grow their own food, cook it, and enjoy it. Robin can be found on Twitter under her username @robinripley or on her blog **www.bumblebeeblog.com.**

TERESA O'CONNOR

Teresa O'Connor is a Master Gardener and garden writer who reaches thousands of gardeners through her articles for publications such as *Gardening How-To Magazine* and the National Home Gardening Club website. She has written for U.C. Cooperative Extension Service and reports about seasonal folklore, gardening, and eating nutritionally on her blog, Twitter, and Facebook profiles. Teresa can be reached on Twitter under her username @seasonalwisdom or her blog **www.seasonalwisdom.com.**